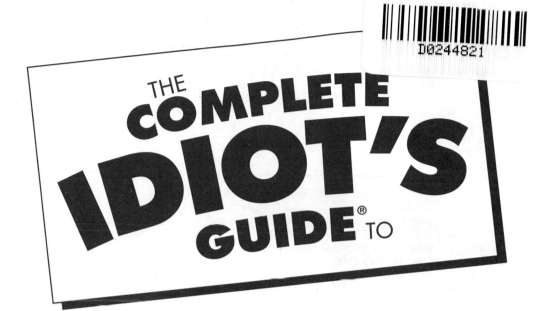

THE COMPLETE IDIOT'S GUIDE® TO

e-Commerce UK

by
Brian Salter &
Naomi Langford-Wood
with
Rob Smith, Mark Speaker
and Mark Thompson

A Division of Macmillan Publishing
201 W. 103rd St., Indianapolis, IN 46290 USA

PEARSON EDUCATION LIMITED

Head Office:
Edinburgh Gate
Harlow CM20 2JE
Tel: +44 (0)1279 623623
Fax: +44 (0)1279 431059

London Office:
128 Long Acre
London WC2E 9AN
Tel: +44 (0)20 7447 2000
Fax: +44 (0)20 7204 5571

First published in Great Britain in 2000 by Pearson Education Limited

Authorised adaptation from the English language edition
published by Que Corporation Copyright © 2000
Adaptation published by Pearson Education Limited
© Pearson Education Limited 2000

The rights of Brian Salter, Naomi Langford-Wood, Rob Smith, Mark Speaker and Mark Thompson
to be identified as Authors of this Work have been asserted by them in accordance with the
Copyright, Designs and Patents Act 1988.

ISBN 0-13-090402-3

British Library Cataloguing in Publication Data
A CIP catalogue record for this book can be obtained from the British Library.

10 9 8 7 6 5 4 3 2 1

Typeset by Pantek Arts Ltd.

Printed and bound in Great Britain by Redwood Books Ltd, Trowbridge.

The Publishers' policy is to use paper manufactured from sustainable forests.

Contents At A Glance

Contents

About The Authors

Brian Salter and **Naomi Langford-Wood** are 21st-century business experts. Having come from very different backgrounds, they are specialists in all aspects of communication and business usage of internet technologies and e-commerce and the building of powerful online communities, as well as being leading international speakers in this arena.

Because of these core skills, they have increasingly found themselves in demand for advice on the use of emerging technologies within business and, in the process, recognised that the cornerstone requirement for all of this commenced with conducting client internet and communications audits, as a prerequisite to creating effective market positioning and customer-focused internet strategies for these clients. This approach has led to commissions by companies worldwide – both 'blue chip' and SMEs – to undertake internet audits and consultations for them.

Together, Brian and Naomi help companies realise their full potential by incorporating the new technologies into their business processes as painlessly and profitably as possible while looking after each company's core assets – its people.

Rob Smith is founder of Exordium Technology Corp, a technology think-tank and consulting firm, and is a graduate of the University of Calgary.

Mark Thompson has written dozens of manuals on personal computing and networking, and has delivered hundreds of lectures and seminars on networking technology. He is a founding partner of Learnlots.com.

Mark Speaker is the president of 2MN8 Inc., a company focused on delivering home networking education, and is a founding partner of Learnlots.com.

Dear Reader,

e-Commerce is not just a modern-day paradigm. It is a very real thing – a new way to do business, a new way to use technology, and a new way to build companies. It is complex and constantly changing and is causing people to alter the way they do business, from ordering supplies and communicating with employees to reaching customers and shipping products. Nothing is untouched by this wave sweeping over the world. In fact, some experts argue that we are even changing the very foundation of communication itself.

Emails, websites and automated supply chains are just the start of e-commerce. Online businesses are starting to change the way entire industries function by building their companies specifically to take advantage of these modern technologies. This includes such drastic actions as destroying their own distribution networks, eliminating long-standing supply relationships, and partnering with competitors. Just how successful can a company be by doing these things?

Very, very successful. In fact, investors think these companies will be so successful that they have driven up the value of some of these companies to unheard-of IPO levels, even though few of these organisations have track records or profits. What all these investors see is the future of all businesses.

To be a successful e-commerce company, start with a blend of technical expertise in areas such as websites, networking and communications. Add knowledge in building and running businesses by using these technologies. Mix in some skills in design, information content, programming, innovation, strategy, and marketing. Then update all these skills daily as new advancements occur. Now, you're ready to create or run a successful e-commerce company.

Need a fast jump up the e-commerce learning curve? Read the book.

Introduction

What an incredible journey we are all embarking on. This thing called the Internet which only began towards the very end of the last century has formed the foundation of entirely new ways to build, conduct, run, manage and operate a company. We call it a foundation because we are standing at the base of a volcano of opportunities that is about to explode. While this is based on technological advances, what it really needs is a new business mind-set. Forget all those old business school models that extolled the virtues of various types of organisational charts. They no longer apply. They have gone. Dead.

Welcome to the new world of business, and the dawning of the era of advanced corporate technology, virtual companies, and virtual employees.

Here's a worrying thought. The greatest risk to any traditional business today is the fact that it conducts business as usual and maintains the status quo. We don't think you should take our word for it. Walk into any major traditional retailer and ask whether they feel threatened by the Internet. The honest ones will tell you that they take the threat very seriously and are doing something about it if they haven't already done so.

What about the rest of the business world?

If you think that because someone makes steel or runs a coffee shop the Internet won't affect them, think again. Remember your competition? Yes, the guys down the street. Well, they can now buy, process, and sell both coffee and steel for a fraction of the price that those places can – and they don't even have to open an office.

You don't have to concern yourself with this, though, because maybe you don't make steel or sell coffee and because you're the one holding this book.

So get ready because this is the definitive book on e-commerce. From secure socket layers to holding your own IPO streaming web conference, we are going to tell you what all the hype is about, and why it's a lot more than hype. Plain and simple, it's business survival.

Who should buy this book?

Entrepreneurs and directors who want to understand how to move their business onto the Internet, how to redesign their companies to take advantage of e-commerce, or how to build a brand new e-business should buy this book. These people should also buy it:

- ➤ Individuals who are considering starting an Internet-based (or enabled) business.
- ➤ Anyone who wants to know where the world of e-commerce is going.
- ➤ Shareholders who want to know what their company is doing in response to the Internet risk.
- ➤ Investors who want to know where the best e-commerce investment will be.

➤ Information technology professionals who want to know how the Internet will impact the way their businesses operate.

➤ Anyone who is looking for a new business opportunity.

How to use this book

The Complete Idiot's Guide to e-Commerce is broken into five sections. Earlier sections feed into later sections, and there are useful hints, tips, and website locations that you can surf to. If you own a business and are thinking of conducting or have already started to conduct business online, this book is full of helpful information in the first chapters that can bring you up to speed on some of the latest developments and pitfalls of the world of e-commerce. If you are starting an entirely new online business, these first chapters fit very well with the later chapters that look at some of the new e-commerce business models and new ways of doing business. If you work for a large organisation, the entire book will give you enough high-level understanding of this new e-world and enough detail to make those mission-critical information decisions.

We don't think that every business will use all of the concepts in this book, but as a business owner, the more information that you have, the better your decisions will be and the more successful your organisation will become. Our goal is to give you some new concepts to consider and a better understanding of what the new e-businesses of tomorrow are thinking today. So, we suggest starting at Chapter 1 and going straight through to the final chapter that brings everything together in what we call the 'definitive e-commerce business model'. We think you will find something useful in every chapter.

Part 1: What Is e-Commerce?

Part 1 covers a general view of what e-commerce is and what has led to this new buzzword. It also looks at why Internet companies are worth so much, how to build virtual organisations, and how you can make your own company or idea the next great e-commerce 'killer app'.

Part 2: Opportunities In e-Commerce

This part describes some of the newest opportunities in the e-commerce world and how to build an e-business, including automated supply chains and real-time back-office systems. It also looks at electronic funds transfers, data mining, virtual workers, and customer service using the Internet.

Part 3: e–Marketing

In this part, we take some of the concepts from the first part and the e-business building tools in the second part and tell you how to market your business both on and off the Internet. This will include discussions of Internet advertising, promotion, public relations, and how data mining will help all of these. We will also give you details about some of the newest Internet marketing models.

Part 4: e-Strategies: Managing The e-Company

In Part 4, we go beyond the Internet to give you the tools you need to run an e-business. We will discuss resource planning and knowledge management and help you to understand where the land mines are on the Internet and how to avoid them.

Part 5: Pulling It All Together

In this part, we bring it all together with the definitive e-commerce model that will apply to an e-business. Whether you are changing your existing traditional business or building a new virtual corporation beside the Information Superhighway, this section will show you how to do it step by step.

Glossary

Just so you know how to 'out buzz' the techie down the corridor, we've compiled a comprehensive glossary of e-commerce. Now you can buzz with the best of them. But remember, this is a business book – it just happens to use some technological terms along the way.

Conventions Used in This Book

The book contains a number of sidebars that provide additional information to help you create a great e-commerce company.

This sidebar provides some pertinent statistical quotes, as well as definitions of some of the newer and more exotic technologies.

This sidebar contains hyperlinks to relevant websites that contain examples of the concepts discussed or additional information about the topic.

In the Success Stories sidebar, we discuss and sometimes hyperlink to the websites of companies that have successfully implemented the concepts we are discussing.

Part 1
What Is e-Commerce?

In this first part of the book, we will cover what e-commerce actually is and what is driving the e-commerce revolution. We'll study the factors that caused internet shares to go through the roof (and then make what the stock market quaintly calls 'adjustments') and what you might be able to do with your own company to move onto the e-commerce bandwagon to the Internet.

We will go into what is considered e-commerce and what pieces of e-commerce relate to the internet. However, there is a lot more to e-commerce than the Internet, and we'll explain what that is.

Later in this section, you'll find out what a virtual company is (if you don't already know!) and how you can build one or make your existing company virtual. We'll also discuss the concept of the 'killer app' and what it means to your new e-commerce business, including some pitfalls lurking in the killer app world.

In the last chapter, we'll provide you with some of the laws of the e-commerce jungle as well as some of the land mines and how to avoid them.

So fasten your seat belt and get ready to ramp up your e-commerce learning curve.

Chapter 1

What Is Driving The e-Commerce Revolution?

In This Chapter

➤ Faster computers

➤ Faster connections

➤ Critical mass

➤ Global access

➤ Lower transaction costs

Faster Computers

We are all increasingly under pressure and nowadays we have come to expect that our computers will move fast. So fast, in fact, that we get upset if we have to wait more than two seconds for the thing to react. Manufacturers of computers have responded to our angst. Intel is well into 750 MHz chips, with 1GHz chips due to be shipping in 2001. Moore's law predicted that the speed of processing power would double every 18 months while the price of chips would stay the same, and so far it seems to be holding true.

But why would computers need to be faster? The answer is that technology is changing rapidly in a vicious circle with computer speed. As the computers get faster, the current technology runs more efficiently, and changes are incorporated in the design of software that requires even more power. First, it was graphical user interfaces, then networking, then the Internet, and now high-definition TV and high-quality streaming video content. If we doubled the speed of the Internet and the computers attached to it, it still wouldn't be enough to satisfy demand which won't be satisfied until we are working in real-time interaction.

We feel the need for, and in fact demand, more speed from vendors with each new technology that hits the Internet. The success of increasing chip speed has led to innovations that are changing the very fundamentals of the way we do business. Businesses are now thinking about how they can serve their customers from inside their own systems by using the Internet as the communications tool of choice and backing it up with real-time automated systems inside the company. The acceptance of e-commerce is only a symptom of our ability to successfully process transactions for a relatively low cost.

The concept of the paperless office was always out there, but it seemed like an unattainable ideal for many years. This was simply because to achieve this goal, we would have required a significant change in the foundation of the way business works. The Internet was merely the catalyst that companies realised would gain them the benefits of moving to the paperless world without the high cost of massively integrated systems. Remember that in 1990, to achieve today's computing power would have cost many thousands of pounds per computer, but today those computers cost well under £1000 each.

The Fall Of The Mainframe

Another piece of the speed puzzle was what the software actually did for a company. Early in the history of computing, mainframes were the only means by which people could use the power of computers; but one decade later they became almost extinct as the asteroid called the personal computer (PC) hit their world. Suddenly, users had the power to process information and the rise of personal software took hold. Mainframe programs that had to be run at night and took a room full of staff were replaced with small, custom-built software that managed many of the same tasks faster and more efficiently. As chip power grew and the costs stayed static, the mainframes were the realm of the large corporations that just couldn't shake off their legacy systems.

Eventually, these new PCs started networking and users were able to share data without printing reports. The result was an incredible jump in the level of productivity as distributed software applications became the status quo. Now, users had computing power at their fingertips and specialised programs for centralised processing. The smaller and less costly server had replaced the mainframe. This information model is still the most prevalent in the business world, although some have moved on to a 'thin' client architecture that sounds very much like the old days of the mainframe.

Now with increasing power, thanks to Moore's law and software that was starting to be specifically designed to run in a distributed environment, companies could finally see light at the end of the tunnel. The holy grail of the paperless office was within reach. Of course, there were still problems, such as a wide range of software and proprietary standards in hardware, and operating systems that didn't communicate with each other. Building on the goal of getting a transaction such as a sale to go from order to nominal or general ledger without human intervention was the last step in the process to achieve the paperless goal. This was the point of enterprise resource planning software or ERP. Its goal was to make the management of resources throughout the organisation a complete and integrated process, usually with a single company's software.

Thin Client

A thin client is a computer with very minimal hardware devices. It still contains processing power, but the bulk of the storage and processing is run on a networked server. In these types of businesses all the applications and storage are performed centrally. This reduces the overall cost of the network clients and allows for greater centralised control of data processing. The thin client can be thought of as a dumb terminal that took some extra classes.

The Internet's Need For Speed

When the Internet finally caught fire, the concept of speed was an issue. 14.4 Kbps modems were slow and painful when graphics were being loaded, and if too many colours, animation or large text files were loaded, the computer ground to a halt while the transfer occurred. Once again, chip speed accelerated along with modem speed, and the Internet became a useful tool instead of a hard-to-use curiosity. Large graphic files, animation, and even programming functionality in applets could be loaded and run efficiently over regular telephone lines or fast cable modems. Companies that were already progressing towards integrated systems and distributed architecture were now starting to connect their internal networks to the Internet.

It didn't take long for someone to think about the possibilities of all those people connected together using standards and browser software that could process code. It was as though a crowd of a million people had all gathered together in one location to share and exchange ideas, but no one had bothered to open a really good food and drink kiosk. That is until the likes of Jeff Bezos (Amazon.com) rode up in their virtual bookmobiles.

Imagine the concept of the world's population shopping online anywhere in the world, using progressively faster technology. You could easily show a picture of a product and price list and get people to place an order. But what if the system then transferred the information to your ERP system? Or better yet, what if your ERP software supplier retooled his entire integrated package so that it would work with the standards of the Internet? That way, since it had to communicate using Internet standards, you would not only be able to process transactions, but you could communicate with your suppliers, given that their software vendors were also compatible with the standards of the Internet.

All of a sudden your system could integrate with your suppliers' system without requiring an interpreter, and instead of you carrying an inventory, you could look at your suppliers' on-hand stock in their system and have them ship the product directly to your customers. Or even better, have them show your customer their stock or inventory, made to look like your stock or inventory, and let the customer order directly from the supplier while making it look as though they were ordering from you. In that way, you could essentially become an information pipeline manager between the supplier and your customer. This whole ability to communicate with anyone and the ability to build an online business became known as e-commerce.

Changing The Way We Bank

Of the 11.5 million adult internet users (in 2000) in the UK about 1.5 million are using online banking. This number is expected to rise to more than 9 million users by 2004. Germany is the largest European market for online banking. More than 60% of German net users are expected to have online bank accounts by 2003.

The whole key to any of these systems succeeding was the speed of the personal computer. Without it, only a handful of people would surf the Internet, and its appeal would be limited. Luckily, computer speed and pricing did follow Moore's law, and the popularity of the Internet grew. Today, companies big and small are building on the net and starting the long task of establishing brand awareness among these new global users. The outcome has been a dramatic change in the business world. Not only are computers getting faster, but many organisations are finding the process of becoming an e-commerce business akin to making a jump to hyperspace in a spaceship or exchanging their old car for a jet. Battle the evil empire that is your competition while retooling your corporate engine; then hit the hyperspeed button by building an Internet site, and pray that the course you have charted doesn't have an asteroid lying in the middle of it. That asteroid can be any one of the dozens of land mines that lie waiting on the Information Superhighway.

Faster Connections

Of course, the Internet would just be a fancy email system if it were not for the changes to its infrastructure that have occurred over the past few years. Today, everyone can connect together simply because of the work done so early on by ARPA Advanced Research Projects Agency for the US military and companies such as 3Com. It pushed the relatively simple concept of sending small electronic packets of data from one computer through a wire to a second computer. Protocol defined the way this data was transmitted, and with companies such as Microsoft adding the concept to their new operating systems, the ability to communicate grew easier with each passing year.

Internet service providers (ISPs) flourished as a natural progression from their days as bulletin board operators. Bulletin boards were simple servers that everyone could dial into and get free software or send messages. They were notoriously easy to set up but generated almost no revenue because it was difficult to show advertisements and users were rarely willing to pay for access. When the concept of the Internet was rolled beyond the universities and research facilities, the natural progression for bulletin board operators was to add a bank of modems to their computers and get a leased, high-capacity phone line to the Internet from the phone company. Although costly, the newly created ISPs could purchase bandwidth in bulk from the phone company and resell it to its users. Thus started the birth of thousands of ISPs worldwide, of which many would succumb to the advance of the phone companies into the world of Internet service provision.

As the years progressed, some ISPs became more adept at providing better access to fast Internet connections while many of the firms that did not attain critical mass failed. Consolidations occurred, and the shakeout of the ISP world began. During this period, there were advances to make better use of the copper lines entering most people's homes and to increase the speed of modem technology to permit much faster access. Today, the old copper infrastructure is gradually being replaced with fibre.

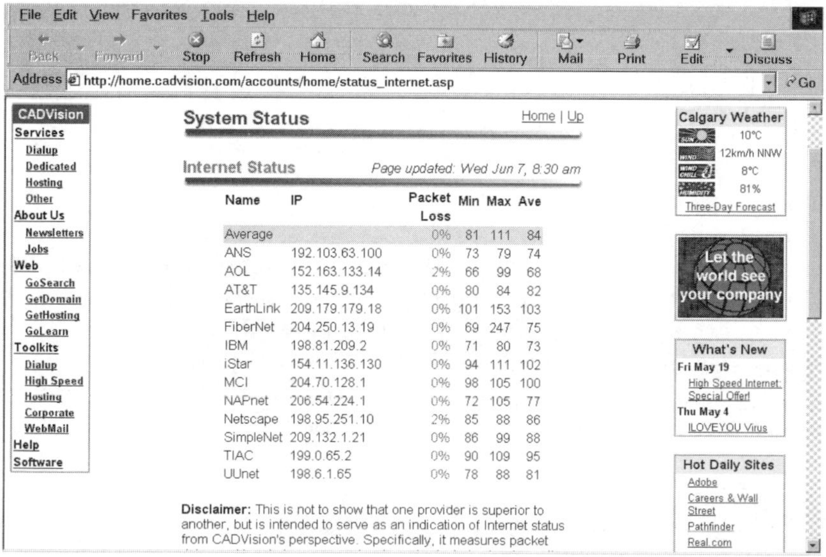

Figure 1.1 *The networks that make up the internet backbone, and status information such as the percentage of packets lost*

Backbone

The backbone of the internet are the cables that link all the main connection points – each one called a point of presence, or POP – to the Internet. The vast majority of internet traffic is carried on fibre optic cables that can route billions of packets each day.

More Speed . . .

The next great speed advancement for the Internet was the use of cable modems distributed by the cable TV companies to users who were already wired with coax cable, as well as the use of satellites such as Easat. This super-fast access capability came with a higher price tag, but file loads were delivered many times faster than the traditional phone modem.

Factors that impact the overall access speed of the Internet include:

➤   The size of the files that are being loaded.

➤   The speed of the web servers that are delivering the content.

➤   The speed of the connection between the server and the Internet.

➤   The capacity and speed of the Internet backbone.

➤   The speed and capacity of the connection between the Internet and the ISP.

➤   The connection between the ISP and the user.

➤   The speed of the user's modem.

If there are delays at any point, the user will see a slowdown in response times. All of these factors have led to the growing use of the Internet for a variety of purposes. People conduct research, exchange information, search for entertainment and shopping as well as buy and sell. None of this would have occurred if the speed of computers and the speed of access had not grown to the point that using the Internet was as simple and convenient as using your networked computer at work.

And Yet More Speed . . .

We are once again standing at the edge of more dramatic increases in computing and access power and once again it's not a moment too soon. E-businesses are pushing full steam ahead to bring even more spectacular content and applications to the net, such as video-on-demand, digital-quality music, advanced graphics and animation, and complete software applications that will operate entirely over the net.

Finance, banking, connecting to your home area network, delivery of entertainment, shopping, education, and virtual employment are greatly adding to the volume of traffic and the ongoing requirement for greater speed and capacity over the next few years. Innovations that are already taking advantage of these impending changes, such as web TV, MP3 music format, special graphic animation systems like flash and shockwave technology, and the use of Java servlets (server side) functionality will be the areas of the greatest growth over the next few years, not to mention the increasing use of Internet access through smaller devices which will see the human voice replace the keyboard or keypad. The opportunities for e-businesses to capitalise on the power of the Internet to conduct business have never been greater and the barriers to entry never lower.

Before everything gets pulled back together again into one form of electronic commerce, we now have divisions into e-commerce (i.e. commerce using Internet technologies), m- (or w-) commerce, being commerce utilising mobile (WAP) phones, and voice-enabled commerce known as v-commerce, which can be conducted on fixed-line telephones connected to a website as well as mobile phones. For the purpose of this book we will stick to e-commerce as a generic term, as the game plan in business terms is the same.

The Value Of Critical Mass

Metcalf's law that the utility of a network increases exponentially as each new user joins is a relatively simple concept that has been known since the first humans joined together into a community. Some of the greatest benefits of belonging to a group arise as a direct result of just belonging to that group.

Now is the time to anchor your business thoughts firmly in the annals of network history. For instance, the value of a telephone in the late 19th century was small unless you knew other people who also had one. Many people on being given their first fax machine in the early 1970s thought they had been given a very expensive paper weight.

So it is if you have a computer network. If there are no other machines on that network, the benefit of being on that network is zero. If, however, you add another machine and email software, the value of being on the network increases.

Now imagine if you added millions of computers onto that network. All of a sudden we have created a utility that is so essential that we cannot live without it. It establishes a standard simply because of the volume of users. This concept is known as critical mass, and it is what all e-businesses try to achieve when they start an online business or migrate their existing business over to the world of e-commerce.

Critical mass doesn't just apply to networks, it also applies to all types of groupings, including the grouping of cells that make up your body. Just as there is a point where having enough of the right cells makes a human being viable, technological innovations and e-businesses also have a point where the volume of users makes them viable. Of course, if you don't manage the critical mass well, it can disappear and take the entire network, business, or body with it. In humans, nature handles the management of the critical mass of cells very well during the 'start-up' phase, but in businesses the entrepreneurs take the place of nature, and the decisions that are made can either make the e-business viable or not.

Nature has a definite advantage in this regard because it has had millions of years to perfect the start-up of life, but the downside is that it has no way to leverage this ability. Humans, on the other hand, have a magical learning curve that they can jump upon by learning about the task of starting up an organisation from others. As a business leader, studying what successful companies have done will get you far up the e-commerce learning curve and partnering with other like-minded start-ups will accelerate this process. It's all a game of leveraging your knowledge assets.

The Role Of PR In Critical Mass

Gathering critical mass is the world of public relations, promotion, and advertising. Partnering suppliers provides the opportunity to create a product offering that will encourage the creation of critical mass. Using advertising and promotion to attract visitors generates 'traffic', and traffic can be leveraged into capital and even more traffic.

Having a phone line was a great time saver and an essential part of everyone's life, but now, thanks to a killer app called the Internet, having a single phone line is not enough. This is especially true when you start adding on functionalities such as telecommuting, online banking, and shopping. The addition of these services onto an existing phone network has driven up the demand and volume traffic on that network without changing its basic functionality. So, critical mass for a new phone network can be generated through advertising that encourages people to make calls or by creating new uses for the network.

Sun StarOffice

You can download Sun Microsystem's free software 'StarOffice', which provides similar functionality to Microsoft Office from www.sun.com.

The same is true for e-businesses. You can advertise to your customers to encourage them to visit your site, or you can add new functionality that everyone wants to use. This second method, if it creates critical mass, is becoming the standard.

Java is a standard; Windows is a standard; Microsoft Office is a standard; and HTML is a standard. They are standards because so many use them to the exclusion of other similar products. But being a standard does not guarantee longevity. Sun has released for free a competing software to Microsoft Office; Linux is a free operating system – an offshoot of UNIX – that rivals Windows; and HTML will soon be replaced with XML, by its own creators.

Standards do change, and usually the market will opt for the best marketed standard most of the time. In most cases, two competing applications or products that are considered competitive but different will compete head to head to gain acceptance. In the old days the products competed on the basis of price and options. Pricing has now been removed from the equation thanks to the concept of creating critical mass by distributing the product free – known as the open source model. This means that two similar products that are distributed on the Internet will have to compete on the basis of what functions the application offers to the user.

Creating A Standard

You can, of course, tip the scales in your favour by partnering with other organisations to promote your product as the new standard. Another thing you can do is promote or advertise your product or distribute the product for free with other offerings. Microsoft Windows is the standard operating system primarily because it is distributed with new computers in agreements that Microsoft has made with vendors. Microsoft has also used this association to bundle other types of software with Windows, such as Internet Explorer, which has been, and is likely to be, an ongoing legal wrangle.

However, the 'product' that is offered doesn't have to be software. Providing content on your website or building a community online can be the 'product', with the same principles about partnering and advertising to gain critical mass still applicable. You can distribute content, cross-promote, or advertise with a partner for the benefit of both parties. MSNBC is an example of cross-promotion through partnering, where two large organisations, NBC and Microsoft, have joined to form a website where traffic is generated both from Microsoft's website and through NBC's television broadcasts. More common partnerships include the using of one site's content on another site.

The benefit of critical mass to an online website is that if you can get millions of visitors, you can earn money through the sale of advertising, click-through micropayments, or through sales commissions on products purchased by your visitors on a click-through. Critical mass also tends to add longevity as long as you continue to supply the base product for free and continue to provide repetitive value to your customers. However, where benefits accrue to one organisation, another will be waiting around the corner to try to steal those benefits through competition.

Partnering Your Way To Critical Mass

One of the easiest ways to obtain critical mass is to partner. Partnering other organisations extends the reach of your product beyond the traditional markets in which you operate. Everyone partners to gain critical mass – car companies use privately owned distributorships; Microsoft uses the computer retailers; McDonald's uses franchises; and authors use a publisher (as well as publishing on the web). In some cases, the payment will flow from one party to the other, but in other situations, no money will exchange hands. Instead, the deal will be for the mutual exchange of something valuable like identifiable traffic.

Global Access

The Internet did not just provide extensive benefits simply because of its ability to communicate across the world. It provided significant benefits (or critical mass) because of its global nature. Countries, governments, businesses, and people all over the world are becoming wired to something that used to be exclusively American. The little Internet has become a global network capable of communicating with more than 100 million people, and this global reach has not only made the Internet more valuable as a utility, it has also made it more valuable as an informational tool. Now, anyone in almost any country can use this universal mechanism to communicate for personal reasons or to conduct business. This ability to communicate immediately, complemented by the worldwide courier services that are available to ship products, makes the concept of being a global company much easier to achieve. In fact, just about any company that is on the Internet is already a global company.

The continuing growth of worldwide technology means that geographic barriers to trade must fall to keep pace with the economic growth unleashed by the Internet. Our ability to use technology to turn our businesses into e-businesses means that the whole world will have to embrace the growth in technological development in order to compete.

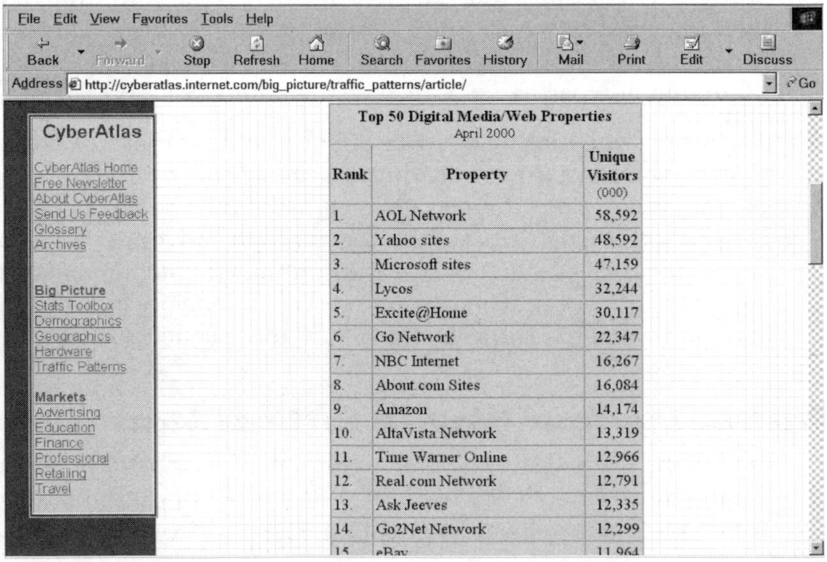

Figure 1.2
A survey showing some of the websites with the heaviest traffic

Rank	Property	Unique Visitors (000)
	Top 50 Digital Media/Web Properties April 2000	
1.	AOL Network	58,592
2.	Yahoo sites	48,592
3.	Microsoft sites	47,159
4.	Lycos	32,244
5.	Excite@Home	30,117
6.	Go Network	22,347
7.	NBC Internet	16,267
8.	About.com Sites	16,084
9.	Amazon	14,174
10.	AltaVista Network	13,319
11.	Time Warner Online	12,966
12.	Real.com Network	12,791
13.	Ask Jeeves	12,335
14.	Go2Net Network	12,299
15.	eBay	11,964

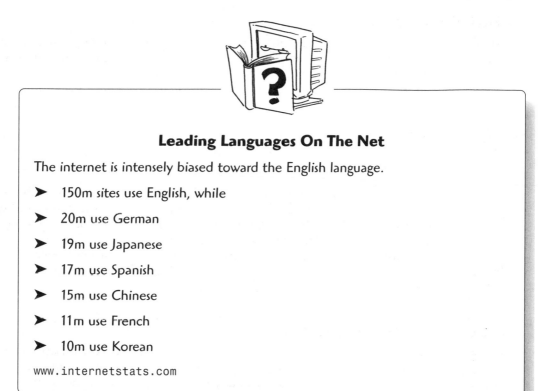

Leading Languages On The Net

The internet is intensely biased toward the English language.

➤ 150m sites use English, while

➤ 20m use German

➤ 19m use Japanese

➤ 17m use Spanish

➤ 15m use Chinese

➤ 11m use French

➤ 10m use Korean

www.internetstats.com

Traffic

When you visit a website, you are traffic, and when you visit certain types of websites you become 'lots' of traffic. Traffic is defined as the number of people who visit a website; however, when you visit some websites, you are counted as traffic at the site you are visiting as well as at the website that loads the banner ad, push content, etc. Traffic gives the world an indication of the number of visitors to a website, and this information can then be used by the site to charge for advertising, by investors to predict the company's value, or by advertisers to choose the best site to place their ads.

Global Partners

Another advantage that global access provides is for two businesses on opposite sides of the world to partner. This is advantageous for organisations that can now communicate directly with suppliers in another part of the world to obtain better pricing or to track supply. For instance, a clothing manufacturer can now order cloth direct from the supplier instead of from a distributor and expect to pay a lower price. Companies that stick to the old distribution channels will eventually supply product at costs significantly higher than their techno-savvy competitors. Proprietary advantage will also disappear in a stampede of products that perform identically to the originals. Although branding will be the key to differentiation, it will not guarantee corporate survival.

The opportunities – and threats – are endless. Global shopping, worldwide distribution, cross-border partnering, and distributed production are just some of the opportunities available to e-businesses. The ability to communicate with their Singapore, London, and San Francisco offices simultaneously in a variety of ways will give global corporations advantages unavailable to traditional companies. These advantages include lower cost of remote management, lower travelling expenses, and faster collaboration on projects managed from a central location.

Lower Transaction Costs

e-Commerce provides the opportunity for both traditional and new organisations to build structures that significantly lower the standard transaction costs for anything that they might sell. Electronic processing of any data is not free; however, some businesses are willing to bear this burden to provide other businesses with online applications that help them perform some of their day-to-day functions.

Figure 1.3
Freeserve is an online company which offers free web space to anyone who cares to sign up

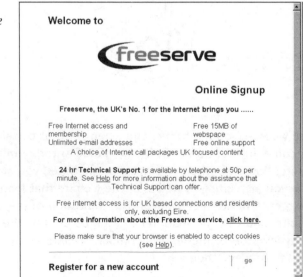

Welcome to

freeserve

Online Signup

Freeserve, the UK's No. 1 for the Internet brings you ......

Free Internet access and membership
Unlimited e-mail addresses
A choice of Internet call packages

Free 15MB of webspace
Free online support
UK focused content

24 hr Technical Support is available by telephone at 50p per minute. See Help for more information about the assistance that Technical Support can offer.

Free internet access is for UK based connections and residents only, excluding Eire.
For more information about the Freeserve service, click here.

Please make sure that your browser is enabled to accept cookies (see Help).

go

Register for a new account

Lowering the cost of the way you do business is just one of the many advantages of technology – from simple tasks such as accepting orders online to complex tasks such as automating the entire back office of a large multinational organisation along with its supply chain. Computers allow businesses to perform operational tasks more quickly and efficiently than humans. The staff can be directed to those tasks that computers are less capable of handling efficiently, such as development, sales, and management. The use of computers in this way lowers the transactional costs significantly by reducing either total overhead expenses or the per unit transaction costs.

The Internet also provides companies and individuals with the opportunity to completely change the way they conduct business. It allows them to disseminate information and applications online and link with widely dispersed partners to add functionality and value for their customers. This allows them to build a 'community of value' that provides discernible value to the membership of that community. The size of the community can then be used to attract advertising, link to online shopping sites in exchange for commission, or place direct links to other websites in exchange for micropayments or return traffic.

Of course, the ultimate business model is to be the first on the net with a new application and to capture the status of a technological standard.

Killer Apps

A killer app is some form of technological breakthrough that as a result of certain characteristics becomes the standard that everyone uses, such as Windows. Other examples include the telephone, the car, the personal computer, and the Internet. You can build the next killer app if you follow some basic rules and avoid some basic land mines lurking on the Internet. If you succeed in owning the next big technological change, such as the flying car for under £20 000, you will probably capture the business success that goes with owning a market.

The key to the success of a killer app such as the PC has always been affordability for the masses and reliability. (In 1943 the chairman of IBM predicted that there would only ever be a worldwide demand for eight computers – but then the cost was prohibitive, even for most companies.)

Even difficult products, such as the technology of today, can be accepted by the masses if the basic functionality of the product is easy to use, affordable, and reliable. It doesn't matter whether you can fix a PC or install a network, as long as you know what makes a killer app a killer app, and as long as you make it accessible to your customers, whether they are children or rocket scientists.

Killer Apps

Visit the killer app website at www.killer-apps.com to 'speak your mind' in killer app forums or check out the 'digital strategies centre'.

The Benefits Of e-Commerce

The benefits of successfully retooling your company or building a new one are phenomenal. These benefits include:

➤   Access to a rapidly expanding market that reaches more than 100 million people.

➤   State-of-the-art technology that provides you with new ways to deliver your message and brand your image.

➤   Instantaneous worldwide communications without long-distance charges.

➤   The massive potential of the ability to interact with users in their own homes at a transaction cost of almost zero.

Companies at the forefront of this revolution, regardless of their industries, will succeed well into the new millennium, and their shareholders will be amply rewarded. The task, however, is not as easy as upgrading your computers to the next generation of faster machines. Instead, it will be a series of gut-wrenching decisions that may make or break your organisation. The one thing that is clear is that waiting to be run over by Tesco Direct or Amazon is never a healthy, long-term strategy. Either run and hide by repositioning your company, or turn on your e-competitors with your virtual sword held high.

The Least You Need To Know

➤   How faster computers are driving the e-commerce revolution.

➤   How faster connections are driving the e-commerce revolution.

➤   Why critical mass is important to e-commerce.

➤   What opportunities are presented by Internet globalisation.

➤   How e-commerce leads to lower costs.

➤   What is a killer app?

Chapter 2

The Sky Is The Limit: Internet Market Valuations

In This Chapter

➤ What you need to know about Internet stock

➤ Why Internet stock prices are so high

➤ Raising money for your e-commerce company

➤ Building a prospectus

Big Money, No Return

In 1999, Amazon.com released its annual report for the 1998 operating year. The aggregate market value noted in the report was in excess of $11 billion; however, estimates in 2000 put the market capitalisation at $22 billion. For a company that started from scratch in 1995, this growth rate is phenomenal. Amazon was the leader of the new wave of 'e-tailers' (online retailers are often called e-tailers) exploding onto the market in 1997. Although Amazon initially started as a distributor of books through the Internet, it now sells electronics, conducts online auctions, and sells books, videos, and music (*see* Figure 2.1).

So to have a massive market value of $11 billion, according to traditional business models, Amazon should be earning a great deal of money, right? Wrong. According to Amazon's financial statements for the year ending December 1998, Amazon.com lost in excess of $124 million. That's a great deal of money to lose, and yet the market value of the organisation is still astronomical. It is not alone.

Figure 2.1
The Amazon.com website provides extensive financial information about the company

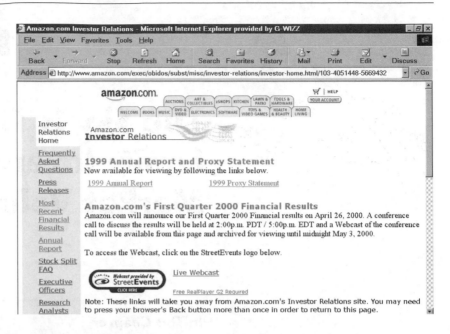

Ask Jeeves is a search engine that uses proprietary software to analyse grammatically correct English questions, such as 'What is a dog?', in order to conduct Internet searches. Ask Jeeves listed on the stock market in July 1999 and within one day created a market net worth of just less than $1.6 billion. Its net income reported in its prospectus and disclosure documents on June 30,1999 was not actually an 'income' at all; rather, it was a loss of $10 million for the previous three months.

These are only two of a long list of 'money-losing' Internet companies that are posting record market valuations and stratospheric stock price increases. Compare this performance to the stock performances of the big blue chip organisations whose share prices are staying level or are falling, even though their profitability is stable. To understand why this is occurring, we have to understand how these stocks are issued and valued by the market.

In the first quarter of 2000 we saw the first mega-merger of 20th-century technology with 21st-century technology as AOL and Time Warner merged. Share valuations in strictly dot coms also took a beating, with Lastminute.com floating on choppy waters as people queried the business model.

Amazon Customers

According to the Amazon website, its cumulative customer accounts are more than 20 million as of first quarter, 2000.

www.amazon.com

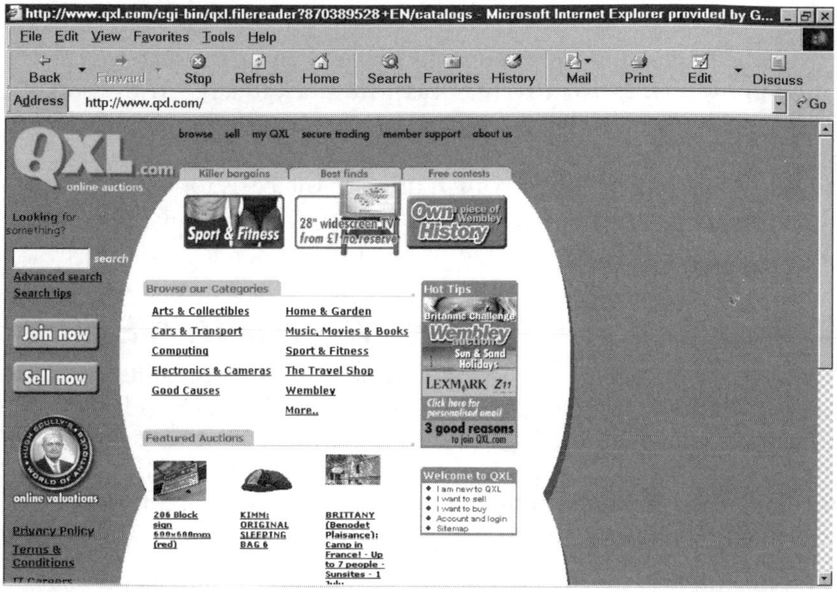

Figure 2.2
QXL, the online auction house, is an example of an internet company that had a very successful IPO

Shares

Shares are, as we know, the piece of paper we receive when we buy a piece of a company. When a company decides that it wants to raise some money to fund its growth through the building of new plants, warehouses, or websites, it can borrow from the bank or it can issue shares. Investors buy shares based on the anticipation of a return that is greater than leaving the money in the bank.

When a company is ready to issue shares, it goes through a relatively complex operation and series of requirements to do an initial public offering – often referred to as an IPO. (Prospective investors should also be aware of the old alternative: it's probably overpriced!) The Internet has changed everything here too. Whereas the normal length of time for traditional bricks and mortar companies to go for a full listing was between 7 and 10 years from start-up, since the dot com revolution there has been a tendency to concertina that timescale down to three years, which is the minimum. Funding prior to this stage, after seed corn or family start-up, is usually done through OFEX (off-exchange share matching and trading market), angels, venture capitalists or AIM (alternative investment market) – and is a minefield that every entrepreneur needs to tread through carefully.

At this point, the company receives a listing on a stock market (it gets a symbol and the right to sell its shares) and then issues a specific quantity of stock to the market at a certain price per share. Investors buy the shares, and depending on the demand, cause the price of the stock to rise or fall from its original issue price.

Full Listing

Underwriters are the large brokerage firms and banks that manage the process of issuing the stock, and in most cases exclusively release the stock to large institutional investors first. The ultimate price or value of a share is dependent upon many factors, but in theory, it should reflect the net worth of the company's assets, its current net income level and forecast net income levels (which provide the basis for a return on investment calculation), and its potential growth as measured by both the potential net worth of the company and its potential revenue stream.

How To Lose Money And Still Possibly Be Worth A Billion

You may be curious as to what then drives the share value of these companies through the roof, even though they are losing money. The answer is traffic. Traffic is Internet terminology for visitors to your website. Visitors, if they are managed correctly, will ultimately generate revenue. Initially, for most websites, this revenue is in the form of advertising, but it soon grows into sales commissions from affiliates and ultimately actual physical sales margins on products.

A comparable parallel example is advertising rates for newspapers. A newspaper that has a circulation of 200 000 people can charge hundreds of pounds per day for the ad revenue. The cost of producing the paper, of which the bulk is the actual newsprint, is covered by the cover price. But the overhead cost of gathering the content, such as reporters' wages, is covered by the advertising. If the circulation of that paper rises, so will the advertising rates because more readers will see the ads. What the newspaper is actually selling to the advertiser is traffic, or people reading the newspaper and potentially seeing the advertisement. With hundreds of ads in the paper, a revenue stream can produce significant profits.

How To Make Money The Internet Way

Let's say that you start a website on the Internet and, after promoting it, start to generate traffic. Remember the newspaper numbers? Well, in general, a simple linking site can often generate thousands of hits within the first few months of operation.

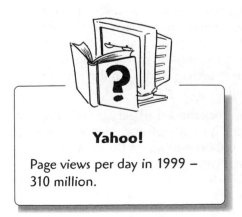

Yahoo!

Page views per day in 1999 – 310 million.

Now, imagine the revenue from advertising for repeated exposure to traffic levels in the millions. Amazon receives in excess of 12 million visits or 'hits' per month, and Yahoo! boasts 65 million users. That's a lot of exposure for a company looking to advertise. Yet the cost to Amazon of producing and displaying an ad is minimal compared with the cost of producing a newspaper. If you were an investor and you had the opportunity to invest in a newspaper or Amazon before it went public, which would you choose and how much would you value

Figure 2.3
*There are many
places online to find
information about
investing*

the stock? The original Internet IPOs, such as Yahoo! and Amazon, started a stock market feeding frenzy that has not ceased, although it has taken a bit of a beating.

However, it is becoming more difficult to achieve these record gains as investors start to question the value applied to these stocks. Can a company that is losing millions of pounds per year actually ever generate enough cash to grow?

What Good Is A Traffic Jam?

Advertising revenue is only the tip of the iceberg. The real value of online exposure is the potential to tie that market into online retailing, or e-tailing. Millions of visitors can generate a great deal of advertising revenue, but just a fraction of those people buying products can generate a huge revenue volume that can easily dwarf ad revenues at the busiest traffic sites. For example, Lycos, the information search engine, had in excess of 30 million 'unique visitors' according to statistics from Media Metrix for the month of July 1999 (*see* Figure 2.4).

Amazon was further down the list at just slightly more than 12 million visits. Yet the market capitalisation of Amazon was approximately $22 billion in September 1999 while Lycos's market capitalisation was approximately

Statistics

A great site for various web statistics is
www.cyberatlas.com

Figure 2.4
*Lycos UK is one of
the most successful
search engines*

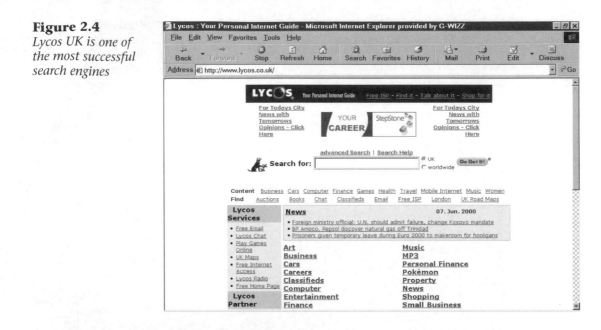

$3 billion. These figures reflect Amazon's potential to generate significant online revenue from its investments in distribution and e-tailing infrastructure.

Amazon has consistently reinvested the money it has raised in equity markets into systems and infrastructure, such as highly automated warehouses and e-commerce software. The result has been the turning of a community of book buyers into a community of shoppers, which has caused the investment community to sit up and take notice. Stock and market capitalisation values are based on the potential growth of a company's net worth or the potential growth in revenue. An extremely efficient retail distribution network that does not have the overheads of expensive retail stores (yet has millions of visitors a year) should be worth a great deal. This is what drives the stock value of companies like Yahoo! and Amazon so high. But it is not the only thing that inflates prices.

Puffing Up The Market By Inflated Share Prices

When a company issues shares, the brokers and the company's nominated advisers (often known as nomads) attempt to place a per share value on the offering when it is released into the market. This pricing is based on values that the brokers think will generate enough interest to sell out the issue. When the issue is released to the market, the brokers will take their share of the stock and sell it first to their best institutional investors who, in turn, may release the shares into the open market. This is usually why some IPOs hit the open market at significantly higher levels than the initial pricing.

The second reason that a stock takes off after issue is due to pent-up demand driven by past successes. The IPOs of Yahoo! and Amazon, for example, have underscored the

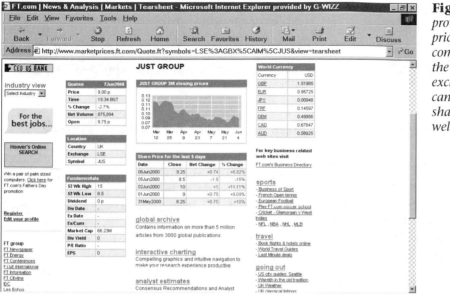

Figure 2.5 *FT.com provides online share prices for all companies listed on the various stock exchanges – here we can see clearly that shares go down as well as up*

potential profit that can be made from the initial rise in price. When Ask Jeeves went public in the USA, the stock skyrocketed from a $14 per share issue price to more than $77 in a single day, although it later fell back. Stock price increases like that can lead traders to make exceptional profits over a short period of time. This potential profit attracts seasoned investors and investing neophytes alike, which creates upward pressure on the stock price and adds value to the pressure already created by the concept of traffic.

Everyone's Jumping On The Bandwagon

Even established companies can benefit from the high Internet valuations. Existing retail organisations that are leveraging their expertise in procurement and distribution can easily move to the Internet and benefit from the move with increasing shareholder value. However, not all companies that move to the Internet will experience the same benefit. Sometimes it can be difficult for companies to move past their entrenched market image to capture the heart and imagination of the market, which is a critical factor for new Internet IPOs. The key appears to be the willingness of the organisation to develop more than just a virtual retail space. Building communities of value is one key to the process, as is the addition of new e-commerce initiatives, such as the redesign of distribution systems or the implementation of real-time back-office systems.

So, How Do You Issue Shares?

There are a number of steps related to the issuance of shares that e-commerce companies must carefully consider. Two critical steps in the process are the eventual

Business Plans

To download a free business plan template to fill in yourself, go to www.docta.com; for expert advice on everything you need to think about for a business plan, go to www.e-biz-pro.com

creation of audited financial statements and the creation of a business plan, complete with the admission of potential risks. The business plan should also include the identification of key staff and a clear definition of your 'killer app' (*see* Chapter 6, 'Killer Apps').

But We Don't Have a Track Record!

Investors seek information about an organisation to help them define the potential success that the company will have. This information helps to establish a potential risk level in the investor's mind and a forecast level of return that he or she can anticipate. New Internet companies usually have no track record for either the organisation or the application. How can an investor evaluate a start-up company with a new killer app if no one else has ever done the same thing?

The answer is that they use a mix of evaluating what history is available, traffic patterns, and what the business plan says. If an online retailer has built a website that attracts a consistent traffic flow, the investor can use this as the basis for evaluating the success of the organisation, but only with reference to what the company plans to do with the traffic, what competition is out there, etc. Just because a company has a limited history does not mean that it will be unable to raise money. In fact, the pressure is on the investor not to miss the next Amazon.

Develop A Good Story And Start Writing It Down

A 'story' in start-up investing language is the business plan of the organisation. Internet business plans usually cannot rely on an industry comparison or a track record of the company simply because neither exists. Half of the battle of raising capital or completing a successful IPO is to have a good clear story that usually includes a 'killer app' (discussed in Chapter 6). The more clear and precise the plan is, the greater the demand that will be created for the stock. A plan that has limited financial information can include other types of information to help the investor evaluate the company or the idea.

A Good Outline Is Essential

After you have created an outline of the information that you are going to include in the business plan, start filling in the details immediately. Make sure that your document is in a format similar to those used by successful start-ups in their IPO

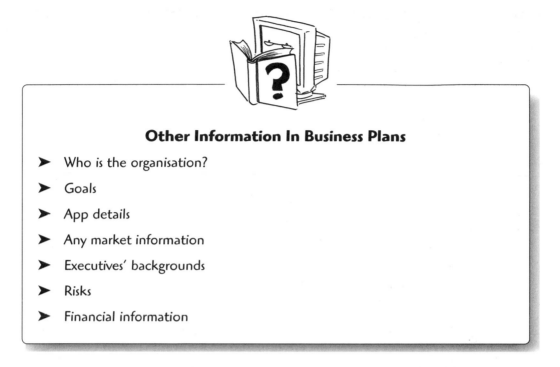

Other Information In Business Plans

➤ Who is the organisation?

➤ Goals

➤ App details

➤ Any market information

➤ Executives' backgrounds

➤ Risks

➤ Financial information

prospectus. Start this process when the business is still in the development stage. The benefit from starting early is that by the time you are ready to raise second-level capital or do an IPO, you essentially have a prospectus that you can provide to potential investors. If you have a rough prospectus already created, you can save yourself an incredible amount of effort and expense. The document should look professional and should be delivered to investors with a 'road show' or executive presentation.

A good source of easily customisable documents can be found at www.docta.com, which was set up by a British lawyer (who incidentally, used to be head of law at London's Stock Exchange) and a successful entrepreneur, so the pedigree of the documents is excellent.

Putting On The Ritz

Testing a road show involves writing, directing and producing presentations of varying length from five minutes to three hours and trying to pre-answer as many potential investor questions as possible. Testing also involves choosing key staff to make the presentation, ensuring that they are equipped with all the market information that is available, that they clearly understand the plan, that they know how to close a deal, and that they have practised the presentation numerous times in front of video cameras and test groups.

Just before your road team leaves, ensure that your website is running. It doesn't have to be completed, but it does have to have some information and functionality that investors and

Figure 2.6
Lastminute.com may have over-hyped itself at launch, but on the Internet its brand is very powerful

other parties can look at. The first stop for your team should be personal visits to affiliated companies that you would like to have as partners, such as search engines.

Personally visiting your partner sites makes a more favourable impression, as opposed to phone calls, and this favourable impression can start a momentum – what is called a 'buzz'. Industry buzz about a new company is a very powerful ally when your road team has to approach second-level investors. As you create a buzz, people should be able to surf to your website to get more information about your company or to see your Internet application. The goal is to create that buzz just prior to approaching the investment community for second-level financing. If the lag time is too great between creating the buzz and raising second-level financing, the buzz may die out, and the job of selling the organisation will be more difficult. If the buzz is growing, the likely reception from the investment community will be at least one of interest.

Beware, though – it is possible to over-buzz your company, as witnessed with Lastminute.com when the initial hype far out-reached reality and after initially being vastly oversubscribed, the share price plummeted as investors took fright. (Having said that, the result was a brand name that far exceeded what any of its founders could possibly have forecast – *see* Figure 2.6. Who was it who said there is no such thing as bad publicity?)

Locating Seed Capital For Your Business

Seed capital is the first financing that you will require to assist your company to construct the basic pieces to move to second-level financing. In an Internet company, there are a number of tasks that need to be funded at the start.

A Corporate Shopping List – Fundamental Requirements To Attract Investors

- ➤ Computer equipment
- ➤ Answering service
- ➤ Development software
- ➤ Communication to the Internet
- ➤ Low-traffic web hosting
- ➤ Domain name registration
- ➤ Trademarking
- ➤ Patent registration
- ➤ Application development staff
- ➤ Web development staff
- ➤ Web content and graphics
- ➤ Phones, travel, supplies
- ➤ Administration staff
- ➤ Executive staff

The seed capital will have to be enough to carry the organisation through to the second-level financing. A timetable for implementation must be developed to ensure that the cash doesn't disappear before the second level financing is obtained. Often, the seed capital is raised from family or friends, and sometimes it is raised from business angels or venture capital firms. Seed capital raised is usually exchanged for shares, and often a member of the board of directors is also appointed from the investors. The board should be chosen for their experience and expertise because they will help to define the business plan and may provide valuable contacts and support. It is now becoming the norm that executives may provide some of their work in exchange for an equity position (share options) in the organisation. This will greatly aid the growth and liquidity of the company by reducing the largest expense.

Building A Presence In The Marketplace

Creating a buzz is effective only if you have a presence. This means that the organisation must build an actual operation, whether it's a physical operation with an office, phones, development lab, and so on, or a virtual operation with only a website. The point is that interested people need a place to go to get more information. Often, the most cost-effective presence is an informational website. These low-traffic websites are placed primarily to highlight an application, product, service, or company. The website will disseminate information to interested users and help to spread the buzz by making it easy for people to find the information and pass on the location of this information to others. You should also ensure that the site is registered with all major search engines.

Hiring The Right Executive Staff Will Save Headaches Later

Any company needs staff. Depending on the ultimate size of your organisation, your key individuals or executive team will be an important piece of the overall team that will be an integral part of the business plan. Their background is essential to the success of the IPO because their experience or fit for the organisation will be reviewed very closely by investors to reduce any perceived risk. If the risks to the organisation are too great, the investors will not provide the financial backing that you require.

The Right Staff

17% of people responsible for adopting e-business in the UK are board-level executives.

Softworld

Your executive team should be experienced in their field with a proven and familiar track record. They should also have the correct blend of experience. If your killer app is highly technical, your executive team's experience should reflect technical backgrounds, such as electrical engineering degrees, application development management, and so on. If your website depends on promotion and marketing, the executive staff should reflect this value with their experience in marketing and business development. Many organisations recruit top-level executives only for their reputation and experience. Some of these chief executive officers (CEOs) and chairmen don't even become involved in the day-to-day operations of the organisation, but are simply paid for their presence at board meetings.

Approaching The Market – Private Placement

After you have obtained some seed financing, created a presence, collected information on the business plan and the company, and started the process of building your killer app, the next step will be to start approaching the financial community to raise second-level financing. Venture capital firms or wealthy investors usually supply second-level financing, also called interim or bridge financing, venture capital, or private placement financing. Many retired CEOs are involved in this type of financing through their investment companies, as are many large technical organisations such as Microsoft or Intel. The role of these individuals varies from company to company, with some people demanding controlling ownership (the right to make decisions) and other people investing as silent partners. Some investors require voting stock, while others invest with non-voting stock.

The decision of which type of investor to bring into the organisation depends on a number of factors. If you have created a significant buzz about your product or service, or you have developed a significant traffic level, you will have more options about which type of investor will provide funding. If you do not have a widely known application, your choices will be limited. This is the fundamental reason why it is important to create a buzz and traffic to your website prior to attempting to raise capital.

Standard Prospectus Table Of Contents

➤ Introduction

➤ Business strategy

➤ Development (what has been built or owned)

➤ Market or industry (if it is available)

➤ Areas of growth

➤ Risk factors

➤ Executive officers and directors

➤ Legal proceedings

➤ Shares

➤ Financial statements

➤ Notes to the financial statements

➤ Report from the auditors

➤ Management discussion of financial statements

When going for a fundraising exercise you should plan what would be the maximum you, and your founding shareholders, would be willing to give to an investor group in exchange for the funds you need to get yourselves launched into hyperspace in the business market. It should be remembered that Yahoo!, which is one of the best known and most profitable dot coms, retains only 15% of its original shares. The exchange of control and ownership of shares has, however, given it the market share and global branding that it has achieved today, and which it is very unlikely to have attained in any other manner. In its subsequent roll-outs across other countries it has been able to negotiate larger percentage share retention, partially because of its brand building and 'clout' but also probably due to its improved negotiating skills.

The primary purpose of second-level investors is to provide the funding necessary to take the organisation to the next level of funding, which is the IPO. The funding obtained at the second level will be used to grow the organisation by hiring the staff necessary to fill out operations such as marketing, investor relations, back-office and development, and to build traffic levels to the website through promotion and advertising. The company will incur very large expenses related to preparing for a share issue. The business plan will have to be turned into a prospectus and printed, often at a cost of many thousands of pounds. The road show team will run up significant hotel and travel expenses as it generates investment interest. Advertising, such as banner ads, and the development and execution of promotional programmes, including travel expenses, press releases, displays, and development, will all require additional capital.

Completing The Story

After your second-level financing is in place and you have the staff necessary to complete development on the website, you can start the process of taking the business public. There are a number of things that must be completed prior to issuance of shares on any market.

One of these is the prospectus, based on the business plan that you have gathered to date. You also need a set of audited financial statements inclusive of balance sheet, income statement, and a statement of changes in financial position and notes – this is known as due diligence. The prospectus and the audited financial statements provide the basis of the documentation necessary to go to the market with an IPO. Of course, each stock exchange has a complex series of rules and requirements, and some of the money raised in the second-level financing should be used to hire the lawyers and brokerage professionals to take on the task of issuing a successful IPO. These professionals are a great asset in the battle to issue shares, but strictly speaking they are not entirely necessary. There are organisations and incubators that will assist you in issuing shares on major markets without the exceptionally high fees extracted by traditional brokers.

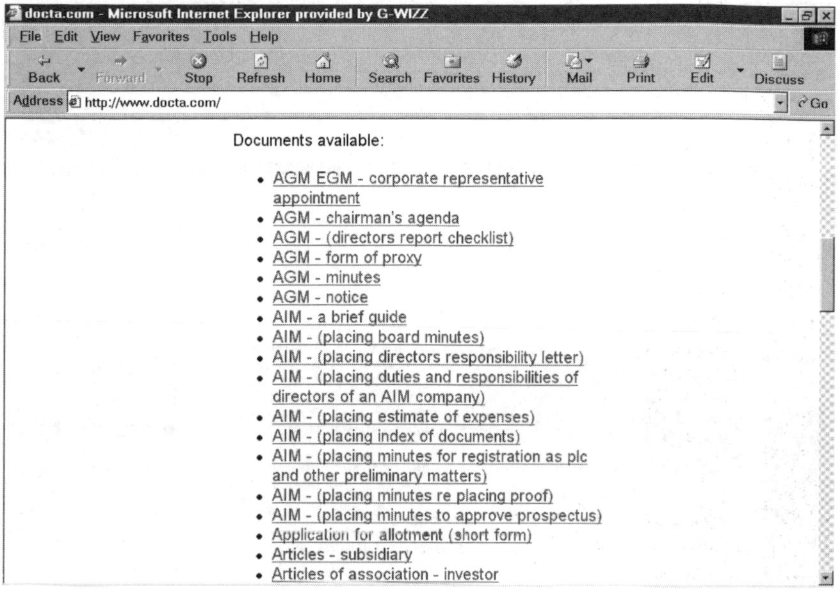

Figure 2.7
A number of websites are ready to offer free advice and downloads

Letting The Pros Take Over Or Getting Help

Once you are ready to issue your initial public offering of shares, you can involve an investment banker or a brokerage firm. They will take your preliminary prospectus, financial statements, and other information and determine whether the concept can be sold to the market. If they decide that the stock is marketable, they will provide one of two types of agreements. They will agree to guarantee the sale of the shares by purchasing it all or they will agree to distribute the shares on a 'best efforts' basis. The City of London is full of companies that specialise in taking companies to the market in IPOs. They have the contact with stock market analysts and the expertise to complete the formalities of the issue, such as the printing and distribution of both a final prospectus brokers, and notes.

These companies will also assist in the completion of the process by setting up a series of analyst meetings so that your road team can make presentations (often called a 'dog and pony show', 'mortician and oily rag show' and 'monkey and organ grinder show'), managing filing with the correct authorities, combining with other brokerages in a syndicate to distribute the shares, and releasing information and analysis after the shares have been issued. They will be compensated by a spread between the issue and sale price or set fees that are deducted from the money raised in the issue – or a mix of the two. The entire process of issuing shares is complex and costly; however, if the story or business plan is solid, the task will be made easier with the assistance of investment bankers or brokerages.

Figure 2.8 *There are plenty of professional firms ready to offer advice and assistance to the right people – at the right price*

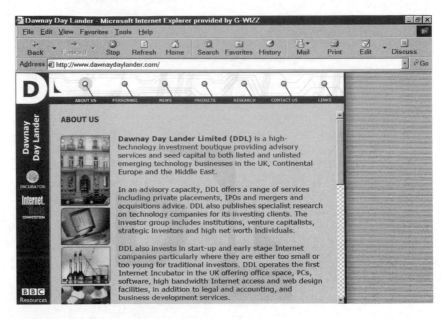

Nasdaq Market Value

1995 $1.1 trillion

1999 $5.2 trillion (as at year end)

Final figures demonstrate that share volume for the year reached 272.6 billion, up 35% from 202 billion in 1998. In 1999, Nasdaq® had 136 trading days with more than 1 billion shares trading hands. 1999 also saw 484 initial public offerings.

We're Looking At The Highest Level Of Investment – Ever

Another thing that is driving up the value of the stock market is the greatest volume of total investment capital ever in our history. This massive volume of money that is searching for a home is the result of increasing retirement savings in all age groups and the ease of investing provided by online services such as E-trade.com, Schwab and the like.

Another record that has been set is the number of individual investors in the stock market. This is a result of the large proportion of the population in the 30–50 age range who are involved in investing in the stock market. They also have the highest per capita disposable income ever. In this the UK and Europe are following the USA and the regulations are nearly in place for the floodgates to open with the recent amendments to the Finance and Markets Bill.

The combination of the highest level of disposable income in the largest number of middle-aged individuals has led to an excess of capital searching for investments in the market. This is one of the factors that has contributed to astronomical Internet valuations, in addition to the other factors outlined throughout this chapter.

The Least You Need To Know

➤ Why Internet share prices have been so high.

➤ How to determine the value of traffic.

➤ How to develop a good story or business plan.

➤ How to approach the market.

➤ What is creating a buzz?

➤ What is seed capital?

➤ What to consider when hiring staff.

➤ How to build a presence.

➤ The pitfalls of fundraising.

Chapter 3

The Next Great e-Commerce Company – Yours

In This Chapter

➤ Implications of e-commerce

➤ e-Commerce enabled operations

➤ The future direction of technology

➤ Technology strategy

Internet Audit

A term coined by the authors which does for the internet what audits do for financial management and valuation.

Any Company Can Capitalise On e-Commerce Today

Just how difficult is e-commerce? It can be as simple as building a website or as complex as re-engineering your entire company – and given that e-commerce technology changes at breakneck speed, just keeping pace with the changing world will be a full-time task. Since it is impossible for any individual to keep pace with all the changes in technology that are occurring today, you may require the assistance of staff, consultants, outsourced services, and suppliers. An Internet audit is a firm foundation for future decision making.

Just one aspect of e-commerce, such as the Internet, requires extensive knowledge of web languages like HTML, XML, or Java. Then there are the thousands of applications you might need to know, such as search engines, web servers, communications, and networking – all of which are significantly different from the internal technology structure of most organisations.

Understanding Technology – The Key To Your New e-Business

The task of restructuring your organisation requires that you clearly understand the business implications of e-commerce and technology. Since it is unlikely that you have the time to do it alone, you will need to hire technically competent people – outsourced or in-house. However, if you have tried to hire technical people before, you know that in this environment the best e-commerce experts are difficult to find, difficult to hire, and difficult to keep. This is doubly true of individuals who have crossover expertise between e-commerce and operations such as logistics.

One thing that will be a great help in this task of managing your technical resources is for the people at the top of the organisation to understand e-commerce, which is the goal of this book. You will need to understand concepts, such as building a community of value, that may be lost on the most technically competent web designer. However, for one single person to understand everything – from how to issue an IPO to how to code a servlet in Java – is asking far too much.

XML, HTML, and the World Wide Consortium

To understand the future of the internet, surf to the W3 consortium web page at www.w3.org.

Web Casts

A web cast is a streaming of bits of data between a server and a client computer. The data bits can be sound, video or text, and they are often used by technology companies to promote new products.

Any organisation can benefit from e-commerce, including those organisations that already have an existing web presence; perhaps they can benefit from a review of their old operations. Corporations expend a great deal of resources in servicing their customers through retail locations, service departments, and call centres. But this old style of operating structure is predicated on the notion that communications and distribution will never be efficient enough to operate centrally, and that there is not newer technology waiting round the corner which would enhance customer satisfaction and loyalty.

The Role of Communications In The e-Business

In fact, during the 1980s, a movement away from the centralised strategies of the prior decades was well under way with the move to satellite offices, complete with stand-alone accounting departments. Actually, some large companies had entity charts that had hundreds of legal entities. However, organisations rapidly realised that they could again capture significant savings by recentralising their operations to gain advantage in areas such as data storage, call centres, hub distribution, and centralised management. The results were a more efficient use of resources and stronger overall profitability.

However, a problem existed with communications and delivery. Without decentralised sales and distribution outlets, there was no way to effectively market or communicate with the end customers. When the Internet became a tool used by the average household, the opportunity for manufacturers to talk directly to the customer opened a world of opportunity. Shops and other retail outlets could be made redundant or at least more efficient since the customers could get information about the products sold and have them shipped directly to their home or office. Service returns could be reduced, thereby increasing customer satisfaction by providing better information to the customers. Distribution could be outsourced to courier companies that delivered products faster and cheaper than the manufacturers' own distribution network.

Online Services

To see an online brokerage, surf to www.stocktrade.com.

Service organisations have also learned to capitalise on the new age of communications by providing online products, such as virtual brokerages for selling shares, information and news services, and integrated help services such as the major search engines. Essentially, we have moved from the industrial age where we learned to turn raw material into finished products with a high level of efficiency, through the technological age where we learned to store and manage information, and into the age of rapid, global communications.

The Age Of Communication

So how will this new age of communication affect your organisation? It will depend on what type of business you operate and how good your understanding of this new world of e-commerce is. Manufacturers that have an extensive network of distributors and sales staff may find that direct selling to customers through the Internet is more profitable and provides a greater growth potential than capital spent on distributor network expansion. However, if manufacturers rush to set up a sales website and do not clearly understand concepts such as 'communities of value', it may result in those manufacturers being relegated to act only as suppliers to their competitor's website (*see* Chapter 6 for more extensive coverage of communities of value).

Local information providers who can successfully extend their reach on the Internet may find themselves out of business if they attempt to hoard or make proprietary any information that is currently freely distributed. Software companies that build applications but refuse to distribute them as freeware over the Internet in order to capture critical mass will find themselves without the ability to attract enough users to be profitable. So it is vital not only to understand the technology but also to understand the concepts of e-commerce in order to remain competitive and strong in the next century.

e-Commerce Enabled Operations

Structuring your current operations so that they are e-commerce enabled is a task that is made far easier if the operations are brand new. Companies that start with a blank sheet of paper have the best chance of building operations that take full advantage of the e-commerce environment. This doesn't imply that companies that want to re-engineer their current operations will fail. In fact, you could argue that experience and existing company efficiency reduce the potential of failure, as opposed to the blank page theory.

Anyone who has ever custom-built a house knows that after the first few months of building, you will start to see things that could be done better. The same concept applies to building or re-engineering e-commerce applications. Often, the most successful new organisations are those that are designed, using a blank sheet of paper, by individuals with a variety of talent and experience.

However, to encourage innovative thinking, some ground rules should be required, such as never allow anyone to say 'it can't be done' or 'that's not the way it's currently done'. The response to these statements should be that you will choose the best ideas, regardless of their origin or history, and that every problem has a solution. It should be the ultimate benefit to the company that will drive whether or not the solution is feasible.

Tesco Successfully Makes The Leap Into e-Commerce

One company that has successfully moved to internet retailing is the supermarket giant Tesco which, as market leader, turns over £125 million p.a. You can find it at www.tesco.co.uk (see Figure 3.1).

Understanding e-Commerce Can Save You Money And Headaches

Enabling your existing operations requires an extensive understanding of e-commerce applications that may directly impact your company. You need to understand the functionality of any new technology and how

Figure 3.1 *Tesco online is beating the other supermarkets, hands down*

these functions will impact your corporate procedures. For example, many organisations installed proxy servers on their networks that allowed multiple users to share modem pools or a router connection to the Internet. The executives clearly understood that access to the information contained on the web was vital to creating innovative operations. What they didn't expect was that their employees would spend an excessive amount of time surfing the web at the expense of company productivity.

Figure 3.2 *Microsoft's NetMeeting is one of a handful of free software programs allowing anyone to communicate in sound and vision across the world*

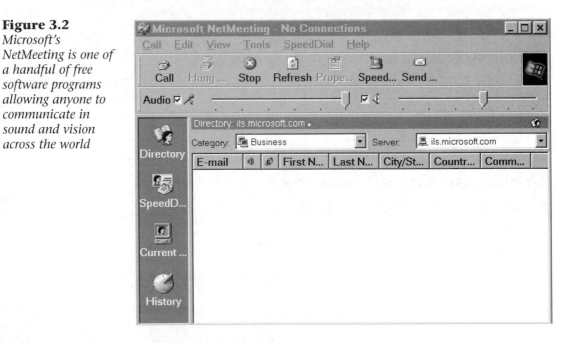

A second example of the application of technology is the use of Internet video to conduct online meetings. Companies decided that video technology would promote communication between employees. The capability to use software such as NetMeeting (*see* Figure 3.2) to conduct 'video phone' meetings does encourage communication. The problem is that it also uses most of the bandwidth on the corporate networks and causes them to grind to a halt. You have to estimate the impact of a new technology on your resources and decide whether this impact is going to provide a benefit greater than the expense of the technology.

NetMeeting – Not Your Regular Online Boardroom

To obtain a copy of the NetMeeting software, surf to www.microsoft.com, search for netmeeting, and follow the download link.

The Future Direction Of Technology

Another thing you have to decide is the future direction of the technology. In order to foresee the future of a particular technology, you need to understand clearly its implications on the market and assess its level of future user acceptance.

An awareness of what the technology means to the current market is an excellent starting point, and the best source of information on new technologies is the Internet. Even though it is fundamental to stay abreast of new technology, it should not become the sole focus of your executive team. Their familiarity with the direction of technology is important, but others can more efficiently compile and report on this type of change, and a number of companies offer such services.

One area of the Internet economy in which Europe is ahead of the Unites States – in fact, is expected to lead the world – is wireless access to the Internet. This leadership comes from the high penetration of cellular phones among consumers in Europe, the near universal adoption of the wireless application protocol (WAP) among suppliers, and the fact that Europe will soon have more Internet users than any other region. However, exciting as WAP phone Internet access is, we won't enter the era of true e-services until third-generation (3G) phones are available in 2002.

After you have studied changes in technology and the applicability of these changes to your company's operations, the next step will be to decide whether you are capable of integrating these new technologies into your operations. Resources have to be made available, including staff, equipment, and outsourcing. You will have to decide whether you need to raise funds to implement the technology, then raise these funds if required. Next you will have to map out the internal processes affected and the changes to those processes. You will also have to implement the technology and review the success of the implementation. Finally, you will have to continuously study

Figure 3.3 *The first internet-enabled mobile phones will soon look very dated*

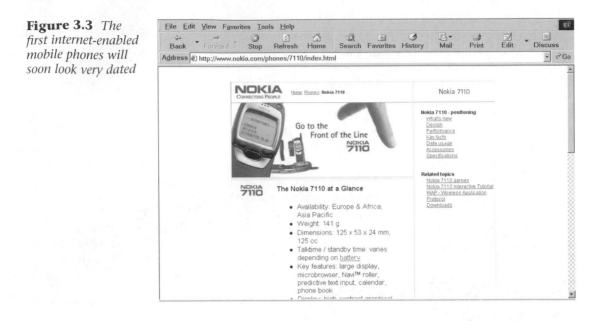

WAP (Wireless Application Protocol)

By 2003 Europe is likely to see more than 6.5 million subscribers to third-generation mobile phones as opposed to less than half that amount in the United States. Once 3G phones are in place, truly unique mobile-only services will appear, including customer support, phone-based billing for commerce, and location-dependent information services.

changes to the technology and other associated technologies. You should always have a contingency plan ready to help bail you out and implement a replacement application if necessary.

A perfect example is network technology. Whether a company installs Linux or NT is a decision that must be made today by many organisations. There are pros and cons of both systems; however, a decision to use one of these systems while completely ignoring the other may prove to be a very costly decision. If Linux replaces NT as the dominant standard (and it does have strong support), investment in NT may be an expensive decision. However, if Linux is chosen as the corporate technology of choice, the risk is that its critical mass will not be attained, and you will have invested in the wrong technology. A more likely scenario is that you will invest in one technology or the other, only to have an application on the Internet change the entire way that networking works.

What has become an existing standard (Windows) is now being threatened by a product from a different base (Linux) which is free, less processor hungry and more secure.

European Mobility – La donna e mobile?

Figures for Forrester Research suggest that net phone penetration throughout Europe will be

➤ 10% by 2001

➤ 28% by 2002

➤ 45% by 2003 – equivalent to 173 000 000 phones for a population of 389 million

Germany will be the dominant mobile phone user with Italy close on its heels and the UK coming in a sporting third.

New e-Commerce Applications

There are a variety of new programming applications ready to be released onto the market. However, an application in the language of e-commerce doesn't just refer to programs or programming languages, but to the entire way that a type of business is conducted electronically. For example, search engine software is a relatively simple application program, but a search engine website includes a number of programmed applications, such as free email and messaging software all combined in one location.

This combination of regular applications is itself an e-commerce application. It is an important distinction because if you consider e-commerce only as the programming of or implementation of a programmed application, you are missing a significant piece of the e-commerce puzzle. e-Commerce applications do include actual programs, such as shopping cart software used to create online orders at retail websites, but they also include concepts such as real-time systems, virtual corporations, and critical mass. There are free help sites that have thousands of step-by-step instructions on thousands of topics, low-cost, direct-to-home Internet connections that bypass the Internet service providers such as NTL, or web TV that requires only a keyboard, TV, and small processor hub.

Evaluating New Technologies

Each of these new applications may or may not have a direct impact on your business. Accepting a new technology may put you way in front of your competitors, or it may simply allow you to keep pace with them. Other applications may be very interesting but will provide limited or no benefit to your organisation. There is even the threat that a new technology may not be accepted at all, and if a company has invested heavily in that particular technology, the company may even go bankrupt.

Each new application that enters the marketplace must be carefully evaluated for its applicability to your company. Sometimes it is best to let your young, technically competent staff play with the applications first and then report to you on their functionality and usefulness. In fact, some organisations have employees who do nothing but this type of evaluation. Your staff's ability to understand the connection between these new technologies and such concepts as resource efficiency and impact on business strategy will be limited. However, you should encourage them to give their insight and opinions, and you should carefully review this input before you or your board of directors make any decision about technology.

Internet Technology Strategy

Every organisation regardless, of its size, should have an Internet technology strategy in place reviewed and approved by the board of directors. The implications of the tech strategy are so important that they should never be left exclusively to a chief information officer or technical leader. If you are uncertain of the technology, you can mitigate the risks by obtaining a second opinion from an outside consultant.

An Internet technology strategy is nothing more than a goal for the entire organisation and a map of how to get the company from where it is currently to that goal. Along the way are benchmarks and milestones with scheduled times attached. The strategy should be reviewed periodically to measure how close you are to the smaller goals.

It is important to remember that since technology changes so rapidly, these strategies should be developed and approved quickly and changed or updated frequently. Technology companies sometimes use a running strategy or one that is never fixed, and most sophisticated organisations employ a strategy technique that places a set time frame on the use of a new technology. Then, once the application is installed or implemented, it stays in use for a set period of time, such as two years, before any upgrades or changes are made, in order to maximise the return on the investment on that technology – with companies always looking over their shoulders in case there is a newer technology that could wipe them out if they don't change.

Another more costly way to reduce the risk to the company from changes in technology is to outsource to organisations that specialise in leasing technological solutions (*see* Figure 3.4). It is important to understand that not all new technology implemented by the company will be successful, but if you test a group of technologies carefully and clearly understand the implication of each technology on your company's operations, the likelihood of failure will be significantly reduced.

The Technology Template

The technology template is a series of standards that the business has decided will be the long-term technological environment of the organisation. For example, I may want to develop applications for my employees, and therefore I may set as a long-term standard that the corporate intranet will be the primary delivery mechanism for these applications. This establishes a way for the company to analyse new technology. If it doesn't work on the intranet, it has failed an important hurdle in the analysis process. However, it should not be the only measure of acceptance. For example, a new type of application delivery mechanism that is cheaper than the corporate intranet, such as delivery over the Internet, may prove to be a more beneficial solution to the organisation. Testing technology on the basis of a number of parameters is important for any organisation.

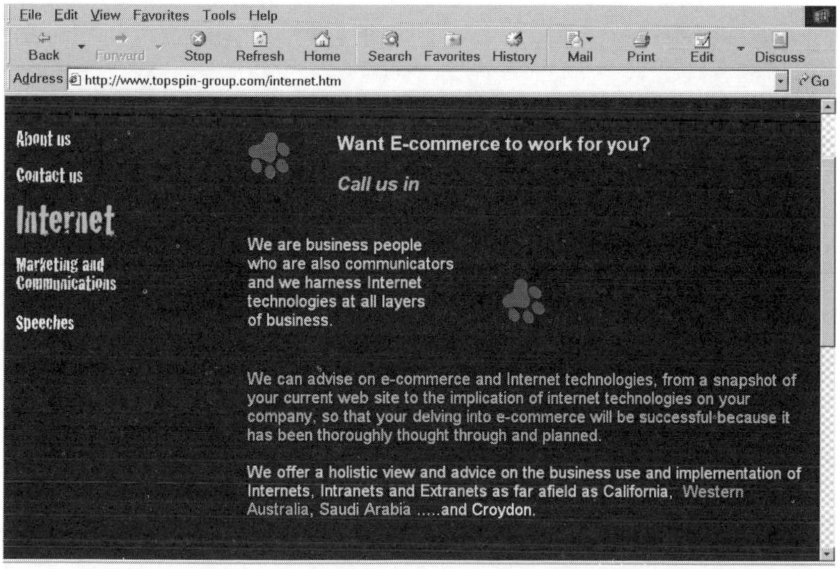

Figure 3.4
Consultancies on e-commerce and internet technologies are plentiful

All of these standards when combined will help you define a technology template that can be used to provide some level of assurance that a new application is appropriate for the company. It doesn't guarantee that the technology won't fail; it simply provides you with some assurance that the technology is likely to provide a benefit to the company. It is also important to understand that even with a comprehensive template, some new technologies will not be easy to assess and will have to be studied by the business. The best solution is to develop a technology test lab or contract out these services. A template can be provided to the testing facility, which should be able to return an opinion of applicability.

Where Do You Start?

When you've finally convinced yourself that you want your company to be an e-commerce powerhouse, where do you start? You start by looking at where you are and where you want to go. This is not a very easy task because it requires something that no book can provide: business savvy. It is the whole reason you are in business in the first place. You either have it or you don't, and the most important application of business savvy is deciding where you want to go.

Whether you decide to take your little store to the Internet will depend a great deal on whether you have the resources and expertise to do so. If you do set that as a goal for your company, the path to get there will be filled with website development, computer upgrades, distribution agreements, e-commerce technology, and e-commerce strategy. On the other hand, you may simply want to make your back office more efficient so that product flows more quickly to your customers. This goal may be as basic as implementing a new order entry system and using an Internet courier delivery application (*see* Figure 3.5).

Figure 3.5 *TNT provides worldwide delivery services using an online tracking system*

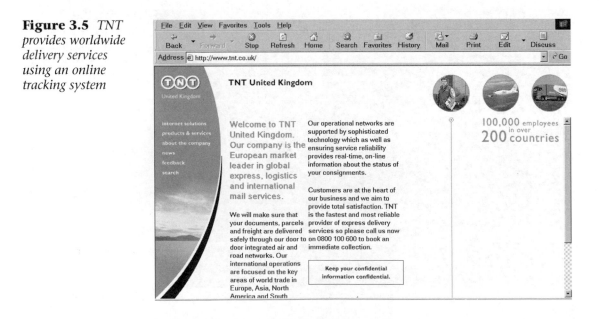

The best place to start is to decide how you would like your operations to change based on the concepts outlined in this book. You can then map a path to this goal by setting milestones, such as restructuring your internal operations, building a web presence, doing application development or partnering, and obtaining partners and affiliates. Always ensure that you do not stretch beyond the capacity of your resources or else you will make timing mistakes that may be costly or critical. These mistakes may include generating buzz and traffic before the website is available, approaching the market with an IPO before your Internet application is ready, and generating online sales without a fully functional back office to take orders or implement a technology before it has attained critical mass.

Developing Strategies

A strategy is essentially a game plan – one that is going to increase your chances of a win. The process involves setting a single corporate goal and then establishing smaller goals that will lead to the attainment of the corporate goal (called a route map). You will also need to place times or dates beside these smaller markers so that you are aware of how close you are to your goals (or the path).

The Least You Need To Know

➤ Any company can capitalise on e-commerce today.

➤ You must clearly understand the impact of e-commerce.

➤ The new age of communication will directly impact your company.

➤ You must carefully analyse new technology and its future direction.

➤ Don't forget to include WAP in your deliberations.

➤ You can build a technology strategy.

➤ Technology templates define the technical standards for the organisation but are only one tool used when evaluating an application.

LEMME BREAK IT DOWN...

e-Commerce Defined

In This Chapter

➤ Why e-commerce is so important

➤ How to build a web presence

➤ What are back-office systems?

Who Put The 'e' In Commerce?

Many progressive companies are performing some level of e-commerce. A small company that types an invoice on a word processor is conducting some business electronically. So the buzz around e-commerce doesn't pertain to anything new, because companies have been using computers for decades. It has gained massive press attention recently only because of the explosive growth of the Internet and the pressure on all companies to join this cyberlinked world. Companies that are succeeding on the Internet are forcing other companies to give serious consideration to the jump to cyberspace.

The primary factor that has made the growth of the Internet so strong is that so many people have joined the Internet community. This large group of users (called critical mass) has drawn the business world like horses to water. After all, what business can refuse a large group of people located in one place? Well, not physically in one place, but more spiritually in one place. The Internet is essentially a community or gathering place. We all go to the Internet to get, give, or exchange information, and the

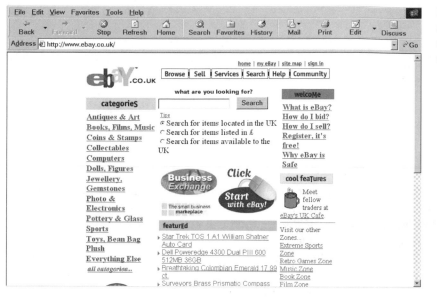

Figure 4.1 *ebay is a successful online auction site that uses e-commerce*

How Big Is The Internet?

The total number of internet users in May 2000 was more than 304 million.

137 million were in North America, 83 million in Europe, 69 million in Asia, 11 million in South America, 2.5 million in Africa and 1.9 million in the Middle East.

www.nua.ie/surveys

communal nature of the web is the main attraction for businesses hungry for opportunities to advertise or sell.

The Internet goes one step further than your average communal information watering hole. It maintains detailed and very highly controlled information about who is at which part of the watering hole. This makes it very easy for companies to target their advertising to their customers by either placing the advertising where their customers 'hang out,' like banner advertising (*see* Figure 4.2), or by attracting customers to their side of the watering hole, called 'generating traffic'.

Figure 4.2 *Banner advertising, often promoting goods that are not related to the host site, is commonplace on the internet*

What's All The Buzz?

The big buzz about e-commerce today is the substantial cost savings that will occur if a company's business were entirely electronic. This includes functions such as buying and selling, shipping products, or producing financial statements – and all without human intervention. This is the real 'e' in e-commerce. Humans, of course, will not disappear entirely. They will simply move to other tasks that generate real value, such as personalised customer service, sales, corporate development, or new product research. They will no longer do those tasks that can be handled faster and more efficiently by a computer, such as creating journal entries, sending purchase orders, or confirming shipments. If a company uses computers extensively to perform internal functions, we say it is e-commerce ready or capable.

One of the biggest underlying costs in any organisation is labour and the support of that labour by maintaining office space, travel expenses, telephones, and so on. Most of the individuals working in organisations throughout the 1970s and 1980s did not generate any actual revenue. These positions supported the generation of revenue but did not earn any themselves. To make matters worse, the majority of tasks were related to communications such as typing memos, managing information, or producing reports.

The Internet started as a way for large computer installations to share electronic information, but it rapidly attracted individual users who were able to share personal electronic communications. It didn't take long for companies to realise that they could communicate over this network with their satellite offices and reduce their long-distance expenses, travel charges, mail costs, and the typing pool (first human casualties). e-Commerce was born.

Go Play On A Busy Highway

The Information Superhighway (as the Internet is sometimes called) is easily accessible by anyone with a computer and a phone line. By connecting to a local ISP through a modem, any user can become a member of the Internet community and is able to send and receive information at a very low cost.

Figure 4.3 *E-mail is an excellent way to communicate with customers*

File   Edit   View   Insert   Format   Tools   Message   Help

Send   Cut   Copy   Paste   Undo   Check   Spelling   Attach   Priority   Sign   Encrypt   Offline

From: info@topspin-group.com   (Topspin)

To: Judith Mills

Cc:

Subject: confirmation of info

Arial   10   B   I   U   A

Violins Unlimited Ltd
West Yorkshire

Invoice/Receipt/Confirmation - *please do not pay*

Invoice number 002000/0001   **Account number** 00026

Date 10 August 2000

To Supply of goods on approval

Item	Description	Quantity	Unit Price	VAT	Total
antique bow	well played	one	£40,000		

What's An Internet?

A net or network is two or more computers that are connected so that they can communicate. An inter-network is simply a collection of these networks. So the Internet is nothing more than a collection of networks connected together so that the computers on each network can communicate with one another. Large-volume telephone lines and fibre optic cables provide the links for all these computers, and the total capacity of a line is called its bandwidth.

There Is No Free Lunch

Any free Internet connections, email services, web page hosting, etc. often come with limitations that force the 'free' subscribers or users to view advertising whether they want to or not. But in exchange, anyone can access and use these services, and in some cases, free services even make more sense than the pay services. For example, if I travel the world, I can usually find free access to the Internet through a library or a cyber

Figure 4.4 *Access to the Internet can be obtained for little cost or for free from numerous ISPs*

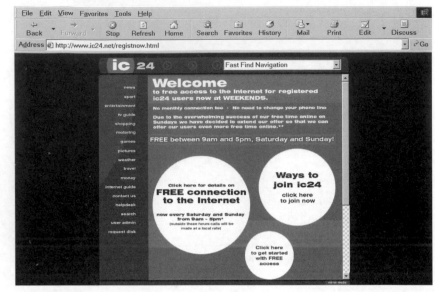

café, but I won't be able to get my email unless I use one of the worldwide free email services such as Yahoo! mail or Hotmail (*see* Figure 4.5).

The first step in choosing a name for your company is to research whether it exists on the net. We will skip the lessons on name choice, marketing, trademarking, patenting, how to run a company, and so on. You can get this information from a variety of books.

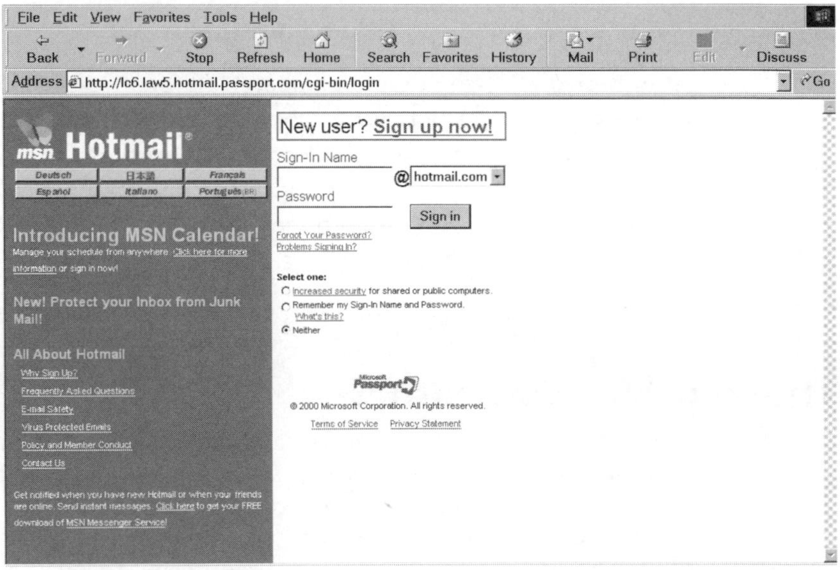

Figure 4.5 *You can obtain a free email account that can be accessed anywhere in the world from many different providers*

The Main Uses Of The Internet

➤ Email

➤ Viewing information on a website

➤ Presenting information on a website

➤ Shopping

➤ Newsgroups

➤ Chat

➤ Obtaining information through forms

➤ Providing information through forms

Email

An ISP agreement to host a domain should allow your organisation to set up multiple email IDs with your own domain name. If your original email was mycompany@ISP.com, it can now be changed to yourname@mycompany.com or webmaster@mycompany.coom or sales@mycompany.com.or all three. Email can also be set up as aliases, where email sent to these addresses all goes to the same mailbox. Multiple email boxes present the impression of a larger company but also help separate mail when the company eventually does grow.

Searching The Net

We can now search for our new proposed name in a number of ways. The first thing to do is to see how frequently the name occurs when you do a search using one of the large search engines, such as AltaVista, Hotbot or Google. It can be surprising to find out how many other people think like you do!

The big search engines search in a number of ways:

1. Some search engines look at keywords (called meta tags) which are embedded in the site by the designer.

2. Some search engines use advanced algorithms or calculations to locate the most popular site.

3. Some search engines list sites that have paid a fee, followed by non-paying websites. The problem with this technique is that if I am searching for information on 'mice', I don't want to see the Disney site listed first.

The next search mechanism is at a domain name registry – depending on your preferred domain suffix and territory. For instance, if you go to www.register.com you can check out names with a variety of suffixes, including the most common:

➤ .com

➤ .net

➤ .org

➤ .co.uk

➤ .org.uk

Figure 4.6 *Search engines provide a good springboard to find anything on the net*

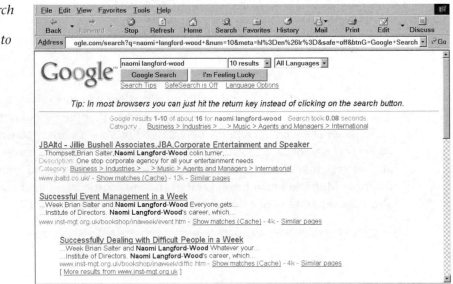

and so on. Very quickly it will allow you to see whether your domain name is available and will even come up with suggestions of alternatives if your choice has already gone Then you should check with the patents and trademarks people – www.register.com allows you to do this for the USA and Canada. Only then should you register your domain name – in all guises of suffix so as to stop the competition from being able to pass themselves off as you.

Spoof ... Now They're Gone

'Spoofing' is a term used to describe an Internet activity in which an unscrupulous organisation mimics another website. The site may look like a real website, but in fact it will be a false site designed to get your business. Some sites are designed only for the purpose of obtaining your credit card information. Be very careful how you access sites and be even more careful about supplying credit card information.

Figure 4.7 *What on earth has Demon got to do with Italian fashion?*

Building On The Foundations

Now that we have started the process of creating our e-commerce company, we can start working on the actual business. Remember that prior to this point you should have identified what your company was going to do and who your market would be. This process should have resulted in the company name and some initial agreements to do business with suppliers, etc.

Let's say that our game plan for going on the Internet is a contract to sell books for a publisher. I could potentially send emails to everyone on the Internet in an attempt to advertise the books. This technique is called 'spamming' and is considered to be the Internet equivalent of junk mail (*see* Figure 4.8). Another much less intrusive and more lucrative e-business model is to present the information to the public and try to get them to come to your website. Trying to get customers to visit your site is called generating traffic, and it is a key concept in most of the e-commerce business models that we will study later in the book.

Spam ... Email, Not The Luncheon Meat!

The act of sending bulk email is called 'spamming,' and it often results in the termination of your Internet account at your ISP or a darn good torching (otherwise known as 'flaming'). The term 'flaming' is used to describe the act of sending thousands of pieces of 'hate email' back to a 'spammer' site. If a few hundred flamers do this, it may be enough email to collapse your ISP's server and make your ISP very, very angry. We don't recommend spamming or flaming, although there are companies and individuals on the net that do nothing else.

Traffic Jams

When is a traffic jam a good thing? When it happens on the Internet and the site they are coming to is yours. Each server on the Internet has a limited capacity for hits. That is, they have a set limit to their bandwidth, and if everyone tries to access a website at the same time, they may well receive the equivalent of an Internet busy signal, or a 'site is not responding' message. This occurs because the pipe that brings visitors to your site has only a limited capacity.

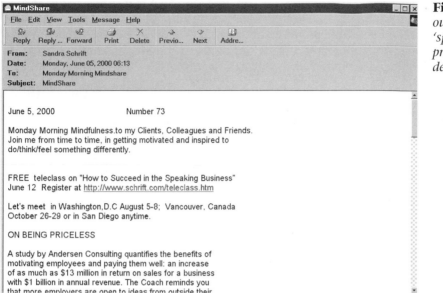

Figure 4.8 *One of our most frequent 'spammers' who has problems with her delete button*

Mechanics Of The Net

The Internet, as we already know, is a collection of networks that are linked together. There are a number of key elements that function together to make the Internet work. First, assume that we have two internal networks and that we would like to connect

The Wizardry Of IP

When we said that the Internet is a collection of networks all linked together, we meant linked by high-speed phone lines. When an ISP sets up a network to connect to the Internet, it gets a high-speed line from the phone company (such as a T1 line) and requests an IP address (or group of addresses) from a central IP registry organisation. The IP address is like an Internet phone number that allows communications devices on the net, called routers, to locate your ISP's network. When the ISP's router receives the message, it forwards the message to your computer or email box.

them in an external network of some kind. The first thing we have to do is run some sort of communication medium, like a wire, between them. This would not be difficult if they were located in the same building, but we can't string wire between two cities. Luckily, the phone companies have already done this, and they can supply one of these high-speed lines right to the server of both networks.

The second piece of required equipment is the hardware that will allow the networks to communicate. One type of connection to a high-speed phone line is a high-speed modem, but for a direct connection to the Internet, the piece of hardware needed is called a router. A router is essentially a computer that takes the message from one network and sends it out on the net to another network using an Internet protocol (IP) address. Another key function of a router is to know the fastest way or route to get to the other network.

I Am Master Of My Domain

A domain name is a web name that is centrally registered and belongs exclusively to you or your company. When you register a name with a domain registry organisation, the name is linked to an IP address on your ISP internal network. You then contract with your ISP to host your domain. Hosting will allow other users of the Internet to view your web page by typing in your domain name.

On each machine that is connected to the network a protocol operates with a piece of hardware called a network adapter (connector to the network) and a little configuration, and will result in messages being sent to or received from another computer. 'To' and 'from' IP addresses are attached to each message sent on the net,

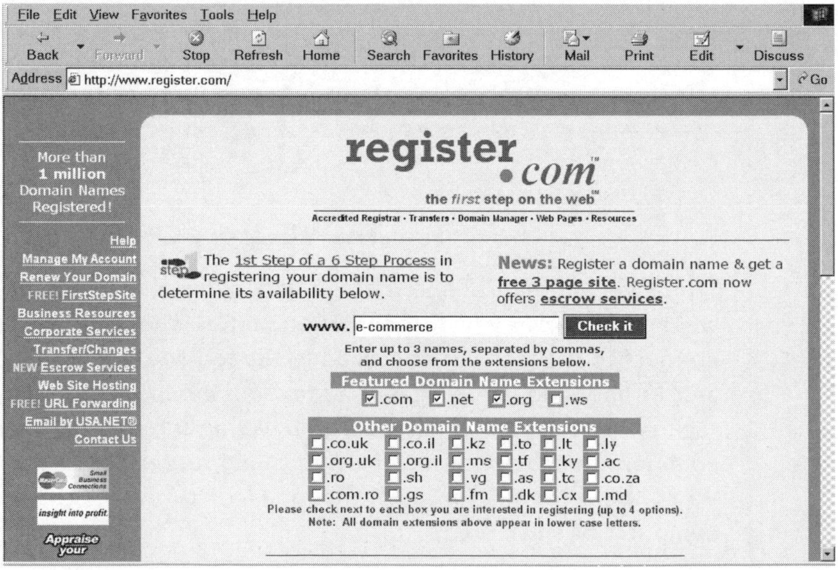

Figure 4.9
register.com is one of the best places we know to search for whether your preferred domain name has been taken – and it comes up with alternative suggestions

and all routers look at or 'sniff' the messages that pass by until they locate their own IP address. The router will analyse and hand off to a web server those messages that will be allowed through the network firewall. Usually, all these pieces of the Internet puzzle are managed by your ISP.

Firewalls

A firewall is a piece of software that analyses an incoming network message and compares the IP address or message content to a database of approved parameters. If the IP address isn't listed (or is listed on a blocking list) or the message contains text that is not allowed, the message will be dropped. If the message passes the parameter test, it will proceed to the correct computer.

82% of businesses with external electronic links are estimated not to use any firewall protection.

Domain Hosting

Another service that your ISP will provide is domain hosting. Domain hosting allows other Internet users to connect to your domain name by entering a URL (uniform resource locator), such as http://www.topspin group.com, in the URL search box on their browser. This will cause the central domain registry and all the Internet routers to send the message to your ISP.

After you have established a web hosting agreement with your ISP, it will allocate storage space on its server that will be accessed each time a request comes in. You are now ready to create your first web page, or home page, and load it into this 'storage space'. Web pages are created by using one of the many web design software packages such as Macromedia's 'Dreamweaver' (*see* Figure 4.10) Microsoft's 'FrontPage', or by utilising the services of a web designer. Most, if not all, web pages utilise the main software language of the Internet, hyper text markup language (HTML).

After the web page HTML file has been uploaded to your ISP's server, other users of the Internet will be able to see the page by typing in your URL. Your company is now conducting e-commerce. Electronically, your customers can see your website to get information about your company or products, as well as to send emails.

Figure 4.10
*Macromedia's
Dreamweaver is one
of the most popular
web development
programs around*

Index And Default Pages

When you create a home page, the file name attached to the first page is
default.htm or index.htm (or even html). When the domain is accessed through a
browser, it will always go to this page first.

Links

After you have created a home page and provided your customers with an address to find you on the Internet, you can continue to add pages of information. You access these pages by creating links on your home page that allow visitors an easy way to view another page. One way is to insert a text hyperlink that will allow visitors to click on the actual text and link to the other pages. Often, these links are part of the functions of an image. Images such as GIFs (graphical interchange format), JPEGs (joint photographic experts group) or image maps often include tags or links that will link to another page on your website when the graphic is selected. You can also link to other sites on the Internet or link to email addresses. This is a very powerful tool that is an important component of any e-commerce model, as we will see later.

Image Map

An image map is a special graphic. Well, the actual graphic is nothing special, but by using mapping software, you can segment or define areas on the graphic and create different links for each section. When a visitor selects a section of the image, the browser will process the link associated with that area.

A Form Takes Shape

You can also add a page that allows your visitors to send information without using email. A form is a special web page that uses various types of on-screen boxes to permit your visitor to enter or choose information (*see* Figure 4.11). When the visitor completes the form, the information is sent to your email box. This is another extremely powerful tool that is also a key ingredient of any e-commerce model. Most of the 'shopping carts', credit card payment pages, or registration pages are forms. The creation of a form is not difficult and most website software will offer this functionality. The tricky part will be in entering the processing parameters that will be provided by your ISP.

Figure 4.11 *Many retail sites offer forms which are easy to complete*

File Edit View Favorites Tools Help

Back Forward Stop Refresh Home Search Favorites History Mail Print Edit Discuss

Address http://www.smartbras.com/ Go

smartbras.com

choose a style -- Balconette Bra GO!
search by style GO!

About
Security
Help
Basket
Checkout
Fitting Room

Gift Finder

Receive a FREE Newsletter
Add email here
GO!

Delivery Details

Please enter your delivery details in the boxes below
Note. Items marked '*' are mandatory

* Title Ms
* First Name
* Last Name
* Address

* Town

e-Commerce – More Than Just Websites And The Internet

Most of what we have discussed is commonly known as e-commerce. But e-commerce is a term that has a much wider definition. We know that if business is conducted electronically, we are talking primarily about companies that use Internet technologies to perform all or the majority of the back-office functions with minimal or no human intervention.

Online Retail Sales

Sales on the internet of $2.77bn in 1999 are estimated to grow to around $167bn by 2005. Online sales will represent 7% of all retail sales in Europe by then.

Forrester Research

Hold On ... Back The Office Up

The term 'back office' refers to functions that support the operation of an organisation. Answering phones, creating orders, producing financial statements and so on are all part of the back-office functions. They are critical to an organisation but can often be performed by computers with greater efficiency, accuracy, and at a significantly lower cost than by humans. If you are able to automate your process then you will be able to compete on an equal footing with other companies that do. The use of the Internet is driving costs down dramatically across the world. Of course, people are still required for personalised service functions such as sales, support, etc., but the best-designed website can even eliminate these functions without any negative impact on sales. In fact, this is an opportunity for people to be more creative instead of just automatons in some processes.

Convergence Of Systems

The most important aspect of designing an e-commerce operational model is an exceptional ability to organise the operations of a company and clearly understand how all the pieces of the corporate puzzle work together. In view of the emergence of new distribution channels, all accessible through the Internet – television and telephone as well as the computer – it is essential that your company's plans include these multiple platforms at the customer or user end. The mobile phone looks to be a dominant force in user access and the move towards the personal portal.

Mobile Phone Users – By Region

➤	Western Europe	155 974 790
➤	Asia–Pacific	151 586 050
➤	US/Canada	86 744 700
➤	Americas	38 253 270
➤	Eastern Europe	14 441 670

Source: www.emc.com

Enterprise Resource Planning – Monitoring Your Resources

Enterprise resource planning describes the modelling of the operations of a business by back-office software. The goal is to eliminate multiple systems and the links between the systems by implementing one integrated solution. An integrated system is one that processes information without the need to send it to another type of software. An example is a customer order that generates a sales journal entry automatically in the nominal or general ledger.

Most ERP software does not integrate well with other systems. For all systems to converge, standards must be established and agreed to by all the software companies. The Internet is successful because it has been constructed by using standards.

So, this is what the buzz on e-commerce is all about. And if you don't believe that it is important, just remember that your competitor down the street is already halfway to becoming an efficient e-commerce company, and when they're finished, they'll probably start a price war ... just for fun.

The Least You Need to Know

➤ How to obtain information through forms.

➤ How the convergence of systems works.

➤ What is a critical mass on the Internet?

➤ How to generate traffic and the importance of doing so.

➤ Links can make your website more informative and interesting.

Chapter 5

The Virtual Company

In This Chapter

➤ Defining the virtual company

➤ Building a virtual company

➤ How to transfer information from systems to websites

➤ Migrating to a virtual company

The Virtual Company Defined

What is a virtual company? The main difference between a virtual company and a regular one is the degree to which the operations of the company are electronic. A truly virtual company does not carry inventory and has no staff, but still generates revenue. How? By utilising the power of new systems and the Internet.

In Figure 5.1, you can see a simple example of a web page with a single link to an online retailer who pays either a commission or a micropayment for sales or hits. After the website is running, no additional intervention is required to operate the organisation, and if a visitor to that site links to an affiliate's retail site and then makes a purchase, the virtual company will receive revenue. Amazon is one company that pays a commission for sales referred to its site in this manner. In this example, the virtual company does not carry any inventory or utilise any staff. However, to generate significant revenue, it will require website promotion as well as book-keeping to track revenue or file tax returns. Both of these tasks may require staff and other physical resources (unless these functions are outsourced).

Figure 5.1
This web page has a simple link to an online retailer who pays commission for sales

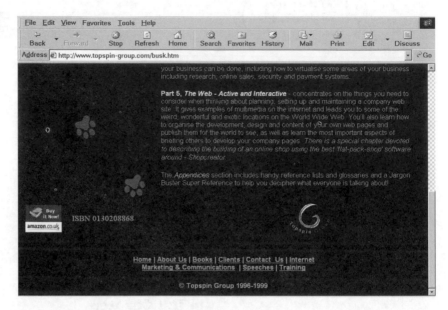

The word virtual is often linked to 'virtual reality' gaming systems that provide an electronic world to play in. With the use of goggles, specially designed gloves and body sensors, you can achieve the sensation that you are inside the game in a false or 'virtual' reality. The virtual company is much like the artificial world created by these gaming systems. It has a structure and it conducts commerce, but without a physical location or people. The concept of an entirely virtual company is an unattainable goal

Virtually An Oxymoron

The term 'virtual reality' is almost an oxymoron (a phrase that contains contradictory or incongruous words). Reality is either real or it is not. We say it is 'virtually real' because the systems are approaching reality or the image of being real. But when we talk of a virtual company, we are discussing a company that is already real but is going backwards to 'almost becoming' a company in the modern sense of the word. A company that is almost a company or 'virtual' is moving away from having physical operations such as offices, staff, or physical assets.

for most organisations and deserves the same level of respect as the paperless office. However, many companies are starting to incorporate virtual concepts into their operations as part of a general movement towards e-commerce.

Why Build A Virtual Company?

Do we really need to build a virtual company? Let's turn the question around and state it as 'Do we really need to invest money to reduce our costs?' Believe it or not the answer is often 'no'. There will be thousands of businesses next year that will spend more on e-commerce than they will ever receive back in profit. Many of these companies would be better off financially if they invested their money and focused their operations on tasks that provided the greatest return on investment.

However, there are hundreds of thousands of companies that can redirect staff towards value-added tasks, such as sales, through the greater use of automation. They can also reach new customers in other locations or more effectively communicate with their existing customers by using the Internet. The bottom line is higher sales as a result of implementing some level of e-commerce initiatives. So, although you may not need to 'build' a new virtual company, using the concept as a long-term goal can produce significant financial rewards for your organisation.

The Top 10 Benefits Of e-Commerce

➤ Higher revenue

➤ Reduced overall labour costs

➤ Reduced inventory expense

➤ Faster external access to ineternal information

➤ 24 × 7 (24 hours a day, 7 days a week) customer support features

➤ Faster information dissemination

➤ Reduced communication costs

➤ More valuable goodwill and shareholder value

➤ Better external information gathering

➤ Reduced operating expenses through supply reductions

The Top 5 Costs Of e-Commerce

➤ Higher per capita salaries for more sophisticated staff

➤ Higher technology costs

➤ Ongoing system upgrade costs

➤ Promotion for companies that are expanding their area of operation

➤ Coffee expense ... lots and lots of java ... in fact, just install a Starbucks

Building A Virtual Company

Building a virtual company from the ground up is far easier than converting or re-engineering an existing company. The greatest single benefit from building the company from scratch is that you will not have to deal with legacy systems or systems that the organisation is currently using. When re-engineering a company for e-commerce, these old operational systems usually have to be connected to the newer e-commerce systems or have to be retooled to provide real-time processing capabilities. This can be such a difficult process to complete that some organisations start entirely separate companies to manage new e-commerce development (sometimes outsourcing these functions can also be financially beneficial).

The first step in building a virtual company, after completing the business plan, should be to define clearly what tasks your company will perform to complete its business on a daily basis. This 'mapping' of operations can be done quickly to show the general tasks necessary to conduct a single transaction. However, don't dwell on unique hypothetical situations: KISS it (keep it simple, stupid!). These tasks should also follow the overall business plan that you develop to define what your company will do. For example, if my company's business plan is to sell a specific set of products on the Internet, a 'high-level' map of the process may include such tasks as the following:

e-Commerce Software

By the year 2002, $2.8 billion will be spent on e-commerce software, with the largest amount going to supply chain management software.

DataMonitor

1. Order new product from vendor.

2. Receive and update inventory availability.

3. Warehouse the product.

4. Process customer orders.

5. Deposit receipts.

6. Pick and ship the product.

7. Confirm delivery.

8. Pay the vendors.

The second step in the e-commerce development process is to decide which of these tasks can be automated. Systems can automate tasks 1, 4, 5, 7 and 8, but to 'virtualise' the inventory management tasks in 2, 3, and 6 will require either outsourcing the function back to your vendor or a third party, or the installation of some very expensive warehouse robotics. Most vendors will deliver the product to a third party at your request. This function is called 'drop shipping' and although on the surface it

Top 10 Web Retailers

In April 2000 (March 2000 positions):

1. amazon.com (1) 1 506 000 projected buyers and 16 260 000 unique users

2. ticketmaster.com (from 3) 633 000 projected buyers and 5 674 000 unique users

3. barnesandnoble.com (from 4) 439 000 projected buyers and 5 663 000 unique users

4. cdnow.com (from 2) 367 000 projected buyers and 6 797 000 unique users

5. sears.com (from 29) 303 000 projected buyers and 2 627 000 unique users

6. buy.com (from 5) 302 000 projected buyers and 2 493 000 unique users

7. drugstore.com (from 7) 261 000 projected buyers and 1 900 000 unique users

8. staples.com (from 38) 236 000 projected buyers and 1 654 000 unique users

9. jcpenney.com (from 9) 210 000 projected buyers and 2 032 000 unique users

10. more.com (from 22) 172 000 projected buyers and 1 218 000 unique users

Source: www.cyberatlas.com/markets/retailing

appears to be an easy way to reduce inventory, it may require a higher rate of compensation to your vendor. This higher rate must be less than your costs of storage and processing for you to successfully increase your margin or per-order profit. In those situations where your operation is small and your vendor will ship only in bulk, a third-party warehouse and shipping service may be appropriate.

A Virtual Example

The basic e-commerce supply chain model is the start of the 'virtualisation' of organisations, and many companies are beginning to take advantage of the cost efficiencies to be gained. In this model a customer can place an order by viewing real-time information about an inventory over the Internet at the same time that a vendor is notified that your inventory has to be restocked or that the shipment should be sent to the customer.

Managing And Displaying Inventory

Your first construction project beside the information highway can be an online store. Start by adding links to websites that meet two criteria:

1. They will help you attract visitors to your site.
2. They will pay a revenue stream for hits or sales.

Next, to attract customers to your online store and generate revenue you will need to provide them with a reason to visit the site. This will be provided, for example, by a store that will carry goods that can be purchased by visitors to the site through online shopping software. These transactions can be processed without any human intervention to manage the inventory, the web catalogue, or orders.

To achieve this goal successfully, you will require a system that can manage both a real inventory stored in a warehouse and a virtual inventory stored at your vendors' or partners' premises. The virtual inventory will be either a direct link to vendors who want to use your website to sell their product or an online posting mechanism for partners who don't have sophisticated systems. The real inventory will be an actual supply of goods. In both scenarios, you will need a way to manage the financial aspects of the business, such as accounting for sales and inventory. In addition, all information should be real-time, and all inventory systems should be capable of storing and uploading images of the products that are sold.

Accessing Information Not Stored On Your Website

There are two ways to present 'content' or information on a web page. The first is to put it on the web by creating and uploading new HTML pages. The second is to purchase software that will load the content for you. The first method could require an extensive number of staff to create the new web pages while the other method automatically loads dynamic (changing) information.

Figure 5.2
*This website features
static HTML pages*

To load information automatically will require software capable of accessing a dynamic file or a database of information, as well as software to load the information onto the website. Most current back-office inventory systems are based on relational databases and are already dynamic or, put more simply, when a product is purchased, the inventory numbers change automatically. The trick is to have this information loaded to your web page in real time so that posted inventory levels and pricing remain current. Of course, another option is to build the database as part of your website.

A Way Out There ... Like Way ... Way Out There

XML stands for extensible markup language, and it will be the new standard for Internet communications designed to replace HTML in the coming years. Documents on the web are currently distributed and viewed using HTML. XML is a wider version of HTML that allows for more flexibility in designing web applications, while still supporting older HTML development. Companies that exchange electronic information, such as invoices, have used electronic data interchange (EDI) for many years. Development is also under way to combine EDI and XML so that business documents at one company will flow easily over the Internet to another company.

Transferring Information From Systems To Websites

One of the first problems that you will face is how to store, process, and manage information between your website and internal systems. In the previous section, we discussed the use of forms to accept information from a customer. A customer who visits your website is viewing an HTML page. The hyper text markup language is

Figure 5.3
This website features static HTML pages

essentially a document 'displayer' and it displays information according to a set of standards. A form can also be displayed to a customer through HTML, but a form allows the customer to enter information or select information from a look-up list. When the customer uses the Submit button, your ISP's software will send the information to you as an email.

Using a simple example, you can hardcode a product on your web page and use a link to a form page to allow your customer to enter delivery information, account numbers, etc. Then, when you receive the 'form' information in your email, you can enter the order into your existing back-office order/entry system. A more sophisticated system would accept the order information from the form and process it in the back-office system without any intervention. This can be as simple as copying the text in the email to input media such as MS Word or Excel or by saving the text file as a delimited file (separated by commas or tabs) for direct upload into an order/entry system input.

Online Shopping

There are much easier alternatives to creating an online inventory/shopping site, such as using the services of companies that are online providing any company with the opportunity to list their inventory and prices. When a customer completes a purchase, email confirmations are sent to both the customer and the company retailing the product. The company can then sign onto the third party server and get the customer's order information. Although these are e-commerce alternatives, they will still require the administration of the web data by your staff through a browser.

Online Credit Card Purchases

Let's face it. You can't take cash with you, and you can't spend it over the Internet, so
you will have to use some form of online credit payment system (*see* Chapter 11). Most
credit card payment systems are form-based systems that are maintained on a secure
server. The data is encrypted or scrambled using software such as SSL (secure sockets

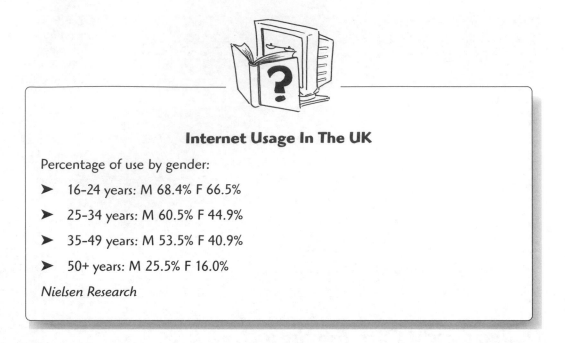

Internet Usage In The UK

Percentage of use by gender:

➤ 16–24 years: M 68.4% F 66.5%

➤ 25–34 years: M 60.5% F 44.9%

➤ 35–49 years: M 53.5% F 40.9%

➤ 50+ years: M 25.5% F 16.0%

Nielsen Research

layer). You can tell that you are using a secure site when the URL changes from http:// to https://, and there is an unbroken key or closed padlock in the bottom corner of the browser. There are a number of companies that will process these credit payments for a fee or other services available that will accept credit payments from the customer but won't forward them to their member companies until the customer receives the product.

Migrating To A Virtual Company

The migration from a regular organisation to a virtual organisation can take a number of different forms. Like building a new virtual company, the first step in the process is to analyse or 'map' the tasks that your company performs and then decide which processes can be automated. The next step is to decide whether these tasks will be outsourced or not and what new systems will be required to complete these tasks in a virtual manner.

One of the most difficult barriers to this 'virtualisation' process will be the attitude of the staff. As humans, we tend to stay with the comfort of 'that with which we are familiar'. Fear of the unknown is a great barrier to change and will require very careful management. Without the 'buy-in' of your staff, their resistance will slow the process of change and could result in the failure of the organisation to capitalise on the financial benefits of 'virtualisation'. In some cases, this resistance has caused the failure of entire organisations.

Things That Can Be Made Virtual

Virtual office space	Employees work at home or on the road and take any available workstation or communal space when working in the office.
Virtual order entry	Orders are entered by the customers online without the assistance of any staff.
Virtual stock control	Inventory, or stock, is listed online for customers, and orders are automatically sent to manufacturers or suppliers. The product is shipped directly from the manufacturer to the customer.
Virtual service	Customers are provided information through Internet search engines and FAQs (frequently asked question) seven days a week and 24 hours a day (7 × 24).
Virtual delivery	Many couriers handle the task of shipping anywhere in the world, complete with web-enabled tracking systems and guaranteed delivery.
Virtual procurement	Purchase orders can be generated automatically either when a customer orders the product or when your inventory falls to a certain level. Also, orders can be shipped directly from the vendor to the customer (drop shipped) to eliminate the need for inventory and warehousing.
Virtual banking	Credit card information can be processed automatically for deposit by a number of financial institutions, such as www.indianabank.com

Outsourcing

Outsourcing has been around since the earliest companies. Technically, any necessary function to the organisation is outsourced if another company performs the task. Today, this usually implies hiring an external company to do the regular day-to-day tasks of the organisation, such as accounting or computer maintenance. One downside of this concept is that the company often loses control over the task that has been outsourced. This can be disastrous if it involves a critical function such as customer service or sales. Also, more companies are finding that 'farming out' tasks to larger organisations has left them at the mercy of these external companies, sometimes to their own financial detriment.

Theoretically, outsourcing should reduce the cost of doing business or at least allow you to focus resources on those tasks that provide the highest return on your investment. However, you must ensure that any outsource agreements clearly and concisely define the responsibilities of each party and the ongoing cost of the agreement. Always be prepared to bring the task 'back inside' should the partnership become unfavourable.

To Web Or Not To Web

When you have decided to become an e-commerce or virtual company, you will have to make some serious decisions about the path that you would like your organisation to take. The most prevalent model of a current operating structure still follows the old Henry Ford assembly line theory, and most systems have been developed to manage information in a similar way. Processing information in batches is still the order of the day for most large organisations, but the problem is that computers allow us to capitalise on even more efficient business methods by combining elements from Ford's model with our capacity to process information one transaction at a time.

The old systems were designed on an old model, and now they need to be retooled. In the Ford model, limiting customer choice led to efficiency and, in general, this rule still applies. However, thanks to faster computers, e-commerce systems, and the Internet, offering your customers more choice doesn't necessarily lead to any significant inefficiency in production. So the tough decision is, do you stick with the same old systems that you have used in the past, or do you develop your business for the next phase by retooling your systems for e-commerce?

The Least You Need To Know

➤ Be able to define a virtual corporation.

➤ Know how to map a basic set of tasks.

➤ Be able to determine what to outsource.

➤ Choose what to automate.

➤ Know how to start building an 'online store.'

➤ Be able to define a basic e-commerce supply chain model.

Killer Apps

Converting Apps To e-Commerce Apps

Applications are not just program but concepts, products or ways that a company conducts business or performs a task. Implementing an e-commerce programme is an ongoing process of converting your normal day-to-day business processes into e-commerce enabled processes.

e-Commerce is a way of looking at the entire environment of an organisation by using some old concepts such as 'the paperless office' as well as some traditional killer apps concepts like 'critical mass'. None of these concepts is particularly new, but they are becoming increasingly important in defining and achieving success with e-commerce, because e-commerce is essentially a way of automating process.

What Is a Killer App?

In their book of the same name (Harvard Business School Press) Downes and Mui define a killer app as 'a new good or service that establishes an entirely new category and, by being first, dominates it, returning several hundred percent return on initial investment'. Essentially, the killer app is the next big thing, the new wave, the hot tip. It is this way because of the very simple principles that in 1998 were identified and commuted into 12 rules for building killer apps.

Before we get to a brief overview of killer app concepts, it is important to reiterate that the killer app rules outlined in this book are not necessarily new concepts. A great deal of praise should be given to the salesmanship abilities and the 'right place, right time' dumb luck of the inventors or founders of these 'apps'. Bill Gates has achieved a great deal, but computer operating systems were already around before he learned how to use a spoon. His success was in having IBM to distribute DOS with every PC, thereby creating critical mass. Jeff Bezos sold his first Amazon book long after you could buy used texts on almost any university network and gaming software on any BBS (bulletin board system). Even the Ford assembly line was an ancient concept because most of the great structures of the world used similar methods in their construction. What made these entrepreneurs and inventors successful was the combination of timing, perseverance, and a mix of the 12 rules.

The 12 Rules For Building Killer Apps

These concepts drive many of today's most successful technology companies and can be used by both new e-commerce companies and older companies that are changing to the newer e-commerce way of thinking.

Rule 1: Outsource To The Customer

Outsourcing to your customer is a relatively simple concept. Get the customer to run your company and don't pay her a thing. Now you can just imagine a banker throwing the combination to the safe over the desk and walking out the door. But what if he could somehow restrict the customer so that she could access only her own money. He might convince the customer that she could watch her own money and still get all the benefits of banking, such as security and centralised clearing. If the banker succeeded, he could take an extended holiday and return only to count the revenue from service charges.

This is exactly what 'outsource to the customer' implies. One of the most common examples of this concept in action is a bank's hole in the wall or automatic teller machine (ATM) where the customer, with the assistance of the bank computer, performs her own banking transactions. This was actually the public's first taste of e-commerce, way back in 1984 – though they didn't realise it at the time!

Another common implementation of this concept is the online 'call centre' (discussed in Chapter 10, 'The Customer Is King'). The customer accesses a company website to obtain information about products or services, tutorials, or general help, all without the assistance of a company employee.

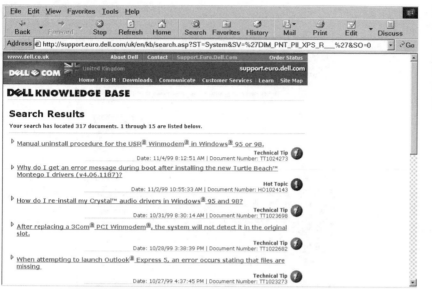

Figure 6.1
Computer manufacturer Dell provides customers with loads of valuable and easy-to-find information

Rule 2: Cannibalise Your Markets

'Build an e-business that steals customers from your current business to capture brand loyalty, reach new markets, or obtain critical mass.' This one is a very tough pill for most businesses to swallow. Hurting your existing operations for the sake of new operations is not something that has been taught in business schools. The concept is that if you don't take advantage of the Internet now, your business will suffer later.

The Internet provides anyone with the ability to 'take over' a category of product or service, and the rule of the day is eat or be eaten, even if it's your own leg. If you hedge your bets by attempting to cannibalise only areas of the market in which you are not active, then when someone else does sacrifice the whole market, they will become dominant. An example of this concept is the electronic version of the *Daily Telegraph* that was so successful at providing online information free over the Internet that most other UK newspapers had to follow suit (*see* Figure 6.2).

Here is a hypothetical example. Let's say that I sell books from a chain of stores. I don't want to hurt sales in these stores, but I want new sales. Libby, the kid from the computer room, says she can build me an online retailing empire as big as a jungle. I tell Libby to go ahead and start an Internet sales company that will only ship to customers where I do not have a store and to set the prices so that they are the same as in my high street outlets. After all, I don't want to hurt my existing operations. Libby quits, mumbling something about a rain forest.

The next week Libby opens libby.com (this is a fictional domain name; any resemblance to a domain name real or imaginary is purely coincidental). She has an old warehouse and the same titles that I carry, and she ships using a courier. She

Figure 6.2 The Times *is one of many British newspapers offering interactive news on the web*

doesn't just cannibalise my operation, she eats it whole as an hors d'oeuvre and spits out the pips. I, of course, could have stopped Libby in her tracks if I had been a bit more ambitious and less fearful of hurting my existing operations. The problem is that businesses see all that they have invested in a company and fear losing it or, worse, upsetting the shareholders. The cannibalising concept implies that you should make the investment in the new operation and abandon the old model if it can't compete. If you are really good, you will make both concepts succeed.

Rule 3: Treat Each Customer As A Market Segment of One

Yahoo! Online News

To see a customised news page, surf to www.yahoo.co.uk and find the My Yahoo! link.

This concept is about the ability for e-enabled companies to provide each customer with her own unique product or service. Remember in the old days of Henry Ford that customers could have any colour Model T they wanted, just as long as it was black? Now, in today's killer app world, customers can receive exactly what they want. For example, many information supply companies with websites, such as online news organisations, offer their customers the ability to customise the information they receive. Customers log on to the website and have the opportunity to customise and personalise a page that will reappear every time they sign on. They can also choose the content that they will view on this page. We will see in later chapters how this concept can be extended beyond bits of information to hard products, such as books, with the implementation of real-time systems.

This customisation allows companies to perform a marketing technique called 'niching' that involves breaking down customers individually by traits and rebuilding them into unique groups called 'communities of value'.

Rule 4: Create Communities Of Value

Creating communities of value by valuing communities is another relatively easy concept to understand. What companies have to do to create a killer app is gather customers together into discrete communities by creating an environment where they want to get together. For example, let's say that I want to gather computer-using-gastronomes who are turned on by that northern delicacy, black pudding. I can create a web page at www.iluvblackpudding.com. Now let's say that I offer very easy-to-use cooking instructions together with a list of shops where one can buy black puddings, and even online support for frustrated purchasers. What I am doing is supplying both helpful information and an environment where like-minded individuals can get together and later be mobilised to purchase products.

This is the second part of the niching concept described previously. After customers have been identified by individual traits, they are recombined into customer groups.

Rule 5: Rethink Your Customer Interface

In the past 50 years customer service has taken a bashing. Not only do we have to contend with rude shop assistants who would rather talk to each other at the other end of the counter than collect the money you have proffered by the till, but the dreadful organisation of many call centres – whose sole purpose is to save their parent organisations money – leaves many of their customers, who they should be trying to woo, vowing that they never want to deal with them again. This seems to be a British disease and is in stark contrast to the 'have a nice day' syndrome in the States.

One solution is to provide an electronic interface for customers. The benefit of this approach is that the organisation maintains complete control over the interface, because if my customer service clerk is 'having a bad day', he may take it out on my customers and indirectly on my future sales figures. An electronic interface doesn't have 'bad days,' and not only captures information but can instantaneously provide better responses by using this information to learn and memorise. However, just like call centres, this solution will succeed only if the depth and breadth of customer enquiry is thought through. We will be looking at this in more depth in Chapter 10.

Rule 6: Ensure Continuity For The Customer, Not Yourself

Within all companies there is a temptation to manage change for the sake of continuity within the organisation. The continuity that companies are trying to hold onto is the way that they currently do business. In fact, killer apps upset this balance and can cause 'the way businesses do business' to change so dramatically that older companies fail. So organisations would be better off managing the continuity of their customers' world, regardless of changes in the way business is done. The way they do this is by building interfaces to new ways of doing business that mirror what the customer is already familiar with. As long as there is this familiarity, customers will use the company's new technology instead of a competitor's.

Online Share Brokerage

To see an online brokerage, surf to `www.schwab-worldwide.com` (*see* Figure 6.3).

For example, let's look at share trading which was until recently a very traditionally run business. One of your customers calls your stock broking business to ask for information about a hot share tip they have heard about. They may want information such as price, market news, company data, and your opinion. Most of them also use computers and the Internet. You could manage the company's continuity by discounting the need to build an online trading facility with excuses like 'trading over the Internet is a fad because customers want current information and opinions from live brokers.'

Your competitor, however, has already reasoned that most brokerage customers have computers and Internet access and by supplying broker information online along with a share price look-up facility and a news search engine, your competitor will be able to

Figure 6.3
Schwab Europe is one of many borkerages appearing on the web

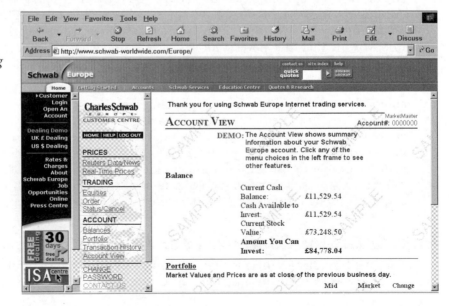

provide an interface that the customer is already familiar with. In this scenario, your competitor will steal your customers because the customers will try the system and find more concise and current information 24 hours a day.

Rule 7: Give Away As Much Information As You Can

Information is relatively free and available. If you are hiding or hoarding information with the view that it provides you with a competitive advantage or keeps your customers faithful, you may have missed the boat. There are a number of companies that 'missed the boat' when the Internet grew in popularity because they faithfully treated their internal information as an asset that would provide a greater return. This included the specifications or standards for their products.

But nothing is secret, and the first casualties of the new information order were the companies that failed to gain a 'first-to-market' advantage by enticing customers with free information. Customers now have access to free information everywhere, and they will always gravitate towards free information, products, or services and away from proprietary or fee-based information services. They will even pay in other more subtle ways for this content, and since they attach a value to information, that is what attracts them to a website. If enough customers can be attracted, concepts such as critical mass and creating communities of value will start to have a significant impact on the market value of the organisation supplying the information. The bottom line is that if you hope to 'sell' information or provide some sort of proprietary access to the information, customers will go elsewhere. In most situations, providing free information will result in greater benefits for your organisation.

Consider two companies, one that provides home help information over the net as a subscription and one that provides it for free. Company A, the pay-per-view company, signs up some customers and immediately has the resources to edit and write data. Company B, the free company, adds a way for visitors to post information for free. It is clear that visitors to company A will be limited but profitable, while visitors to company B will be vast but non-paying. Now let's say that Company B calls a DIY chain and tells them that a 'vast' number of customers (maybe in the thousands) come to their site for free information and asks whether it would like to advertise. Eventually, the growth in company B's website would even attract company A's customers and lead to the latter's demise. The moral: give away the information for free and capitalise on the other benefits of critical mass.

Rule 8: Structure Every Transaction As A Joint Venture

The virtual corporation is a company without infrastructure. But how does a company without infrastructure operate? Simple: it forms partnerships and joint ventures with other organisations that do have some form of structure or with other virtual organisations. Even more importantly, it forms partnerships and joint ventures with its users. The killer app often consists of a buy-in by the users even before the corporate partners. Java, Sun Microsystem's killer app, was released on the Internet and grew over time to the status of a standard simply because the users of the Internet accepted its open standards concept and because it was free. Once the users were jumping on the Java bandwagon, it became very easy to attract corporate joint ventures.

This concept of joint venturing is now at the point where new companies with no physical structure can compete more effectively than large, older organisations simply by choosing a series of partners that provide the missing physical structure. The advantage is that the virtual corporation can change instantaneously simply by altering the mix of partners. In addition, partners can be brought together on short notice to grow an app that already has increasing user support. This type of process can be made so efficient that each transaction could be structured as a joint venture, although at some point you will need a partner with real assets. Luckily, most 'asset-based' companies are not organised enough to compete effectively with the virtual company. (*See* Chapter 5 for more information on virtual businesses.)

Rule 9: Treat Your Assets As Liabilities

New technology-based organisations have little in the way of physical assets, creating powerful competition from a financial perspective simply because the return on investment is astronomical for any revenue. If your company doesn't have any physical assets, such as real estate, there is less pressure to provide a return on that investment. The downside of course is that with no physical assets you are providing a service only and will be ineffective at competition unless you attain brand recognition.

Not all assets, however, should be dismantled. Assets that are used in production that is not threatened by digital technology should be kept. However, asset-based companies must move to the e-commerce model by building or valuing digital assets. If they don't, virtual competitors will develop these virtual assets, and the physical, asset-based company will be left on the sidelines as a supplier to a large virtual market with very tight margins.

The Online Auction At QXL

An example of a digital market is QXL, which allows anyone to sell or buy products. Surf to www.qxl.com for a look.

Let's say that company A is a producer of industrial products with a significant investment in plant and equipment. Let's also assume that it has a traditional marketing network of brokers and salesmen. Company B is creating a virtual marketplace that provides customers of heavy industrial equipment with a place to view and compare information, prices from partners, and a way to communicate with the rest of the community. Its customers can order online, cutting out the middlemen and significantly lowering costs. For company A to avoid becoming just a supplier to the market and competing with other manufacturing partners on price, it should beat company B to the digital market by creating that market.

Rule 10: Destroy Your Value Chain

A value chain can be defined as a series of functions that create and distribute an organisation's goods and services. Conducting business in a traditional supply chain model can be a risky proposition. There are numerous competitors who are after your market share, and they intend to upset the market through the use of new technology. The concept of destroying your value chain is simple: take the risk and upset your partners, give away value for free, and essentially do what it takes to reposition yourself as the leader of the destruction process. Why? Because leaders control the process and can define standards or limit damage. Regardless of what your value chain is, use the power of the digital world and new technology to position the company for the future.

How Can You Destroy Your Value Chain?

➤ By giving away proprietary information or products so that they become the standard for an industry

➤ By eliminating middlemen and using the customer to create orders

➤ By outsourcing functionality (such as delivery) to new partners

➤ By automating the process where possible

Rule 11: Manage Innovation As A Portfolio of Options

Innovation is expensive, risky, and hard to put into terms such as projected return on investment or impact on shareholder worth. Borrowing a page from financial portfolio managers, it is possible to identify a sure fire method for minimising the risk of investing in innovation – the diversified portfolio. Remember that if your company doesn't pay careful attention to innovation, it can be run over by it.

Just ask any major bookstore if Amazon is a concern. The problem is that innovation is risky, difficult to quantify, and often expensive. The easiest way for a company to participate is to take a small position in the new technology so that the company is an active participant with a relatively low exit cost. Microsoft continually invests in emerging technologies as a minority partner only. That way if the technology fails, its loss is minimal. If the technology succeeds, Microsoft is a participant with an inside track. The key is that any failure is likely to be offset by a successful innovation somewhere else. This is how innovation is managed as a portfolio of options.

Rule 12: Take On The Youngsters

Finally, we have one more rule for building a killer app. Taking on youngsters does not mean giving a teenager the title of director just to keep him off the streets. However, hiring him to give his input into development is a great idea if he is under the age of 30. Children and young adults of this age group have been brought up in a different world from their '40-something' parents. The way they interact with technology is totally different from older adults, and their frame of reference or understanding of technology is also totally different. In many cases they drive the first initial interest in killer apps.

Children have learned by playing computer games that textual information is slow and inefficient, that interfaces should be straightforward to use regardless of what they do, that things should be fun because attention spans are short, and that somewhere out in cyberspace is what they want or need for free. These concepts are vital to the success of your killer app, and are easily understood by youngsters. As a killer app builder, you cannot afford to ignore their insight.

Land Mines On The Road To A Killer App

As well as the 12 basic rules to killer app success, there are without a doubt a number of serious land mines on the killer app slip road to the Internet. They are:

➤ Internet usage drop.

➤ Apathy.

➤ Clutter/rubbish.

➤ Obvious advantage of asset owners.

➤ Fragmenting of the net.

➤ Duplicate function.

➤ Selling off the net.

➤ Control of the net by industry/lockout.

➤ More effective and efficient coverage – brute force advertising.

Internet Usage Drop

The volume of traffic on the Internet has risen dramatically in 2000. New users of the Internet accounted for the vast majority of this traffic. Their usage levels rise significantly in the initial year of use, sometimes to the level of an addiction. However, over time, the usage decreases and levels off. Usage can rise again if access is provided at work, but never up to the levels when the Internet was a new toy to the user. This is because user interest wanes and because their access process is made more efficient.

They will start to go to sites only when required and only if the process is fast and efficient. This decline has been documented in numerous studies.

Remember that this phenomenon is related only to existing Internet users and will undoubtedly become more of an issue when the growth of new users levels out. Since this plateau is still a little way into the future, the net impact on e-commerce organisations will be minimal for company models that attract new users to the net. If your model is based on the return of existing users, this information will have to be carefully considered during the business plan design process in order to entice your customers to return on a regular basis. The best examples of this technique are websites that allow users to customise the main access page for news feeds. This encourages repeat visits to the site on a daily basis to 'get updated' on current news, sports scores, stock quotes, and other information. Many of the major search engines, such as Yahoo!, provide this type of customisation.

Apathy

One of the reasons that customers do not return to a website is apathy. Customers' attention spans are very short, and if the information changes, they will stay tuned. But if the information doesn't change, they will lose interest. Let's say for instance that you buy a new car, and it is delivered to your house. Do you drive the car at a set and constant level over the next few weeks? In fact, most people can barely leave the vehicle alone the first night, but as the weeks wear on, the interest in 'taking the car for a spin' diminishes. The same thing happens on the net. People initially get hooked up and spend the first few weeks surfing, but then gradually lose interest in surfing. They may still use the Internet, but not at the same level as when it was new. In the example of the new car, they are getting less new information that is of any value since the smell is fading, the newness of the driving experience has gone, and there are other new things that tug at one's attention.

This information is also valuable to e-builders since keeping customers' attention is tough. How tough? Just ask television advertisers who found users switching channels during their commercials or fast forwarding past the commercials that were recorded by VCRs. The interest level of users in commercials was waning until sounds and images were more carefully constructed to quickly attract and keep viewers' attention. This is even a greater threat to the Internet since it also requires the users to expend an effort to interact, as opposed to television, which requires little effort. The best remedy for apathy is to provide customers with something new and interesting on a regular basis, make it easy for them to use, and carefully construct the sounds and images to hold their attention. Strive to make your website highly entertaining while requiring minimal effort from the users.

One supermarket chain is working with an American organisation to develop what they charmingly call a snortal. Thus the idea is that when you are cyber-shopping from their site you will be assailed by the aroma of freshly baked bread which, as all retailers know, induces the customer to buy. (No – we did not write this on April 1st.

Figure 6.4
Snortals – no we weren't joking! But do you really want to smell that freshly baked bread from a supermarket when you order online?

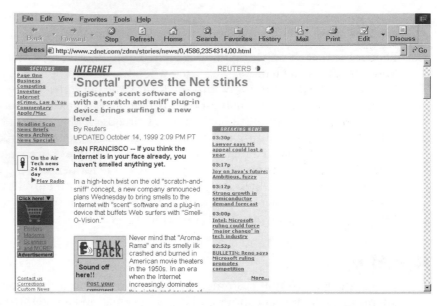

There are at least two organisations experimenting with smelly shopping set-top boxes. *See* Figure 6.4.)

Clutter And Rubbish

One of the biggest contributing factors to apathy among users of the Internet is the increasing level of clutter and rubbish on the net. Anyone who has surfed the Internet for information over the past few years will have noticed the steady increase in websites that appear on search engine lists for specific searches that have very little to do with the information in the search. A large number of these sites have advertising and sales as their number one priority, providing lots of information about sponsors and products without making it easy to find the information you are looking for. Combine this with the concept of short customer attention spans, and you have a recipe for apathy.

The downside of this problem is that there is no solution. Companies hungry for business and profit will continue to pound out more and more advertising, promotional material, and links without any thought as to the overall consequence, which is declining usage rates for the average user. This presents a great opportunity for companies to capture a large piece of the market with a killer app that cleans and sanitises the net for content so that users get high value. This, however, flows against the premise of the open nature of the Internet and could prove to be a significant Internet land mine for future e-commerce companies.

Obvious Advantage Of Asset Owners

An asset owner is anyone who owns a physical asset, such as plant and equipment used to manufacture products, or content such as movies or music. One fact that any Internet builder will have to face is that the owners of hard assets have the advantage and over time will capitalise on that advantage. The race to the net is intense because of this very concept. If your organisation doesn't own its assets, you will have to own the customers. You own the customers through branding (creating a widely known brand), familiarity (making the customers familiar with your site), and standards (becoming the standard). If you can attain these goals, the owner of the hard assets will be relegated to the role of supplier.

However, do not underestimate the power and wealth of organisational asset owners who have the physical assets you need to conduct business. You can open a retail site, but will have trouble selling at rates less than a manufacturer's website. The point is that if your technological and marketing savvy and operating methodology were comparable to your suppliers', they could blow you out of the water because they own the product.

The solution to this threat is to own the customers by gathering their loyalty into a cohesive community. Customers will be naturally suspicious of websites that promote one manufacturer's product, and suppliers are unlikely to support their competitors. This single piece of information should help you compete with asset owners regardless of their wealth as long as you beat them to the market.

Fragmenting The Net

Fragmentation of the Internet is a growing problem that will command more attention in the coming years. Part of the problem comes from one of the 12 rules we talked about earlier. Creating communities of value will cause the fragmentation of the Internet into successively smaller groups as more and more companies attempt to gather customers into their own community. Customers will feel less like moving to new communities if two requirements are provided:

1. The clutter and rubbish on the net make finding new communities difficult (familiarity).
2. Everything that they need is provided at their current location.

Customers will always venture around the Internet, and this will make trying to build a critical mass of customers into a community of value more and more difficult. Another aspect of net building that will contribute to this problem will be the race to be 'the first to market'. Each new successive venture on the Internet will continue to fragment customers into smaller and smaller groups because each venture will strive to be 'new' or the first to market. Obviously, promotion will be the main growth engine of new Internet communities in the coming years. The implication is that unless the concept you are building is so innovative that customers will come to visit your site by word of mouth alone, you will have to find a promotional bankroll as big as that of a large corporation to attract enough traffic to make your venture viable.

Another possibility is that users of the Internet will hunt for goods or information internationally, but deal locally with organisations that they are familiar with. In creating communities of value, the organisations that have the ability to add a physical aspect to the group, such as a local meeting place or physical location near the group, will continue to cross-fragment the market. Members may occasionally leave the group to surf outside, but the community app will still command the lion's share of the transactions. This assumes that the two rules are not met by the organisation behind the group. If it is sophisticated enough to provide for its customers, then these external excursions will be smaller in number.

Duplicate Functions

As each new venture is started on the Internet, cross-over and duplicate functionality are likely to be more prevalent. Every customised web page offers news, sport, and stock price information, and they are all essentially duplicates of one another. Is Snap better than Yahoo!, or is AOL better than ICQ? This duplication of function is a serious limitation to the growth of any new organisation since the only way customers will change from their familiar surroundings will be through differentiation. If my website offers exactly the same functionality as yours, I will probably stay with my site. If your offering is significantly different, enough that I value it more, I will move. If I am new to the net, I will most likely start at the most popular sites.

Duplication of functions is not easy to manage. In the case of restaurants, more locations in closer proximity can often generate significantly more business than a single restaurant by itself. The same concept on the Internet will not necessarily offer the same benefits since the first example deals with a physical location and the second deals with a virtual location. However, partnering with your competitors to turn them into your suppliers is often the best solution. Using your competitor's site as the foundation of your own organisation is the best defence against duplication. Moreover, they have already done the hard part of building their site, and this allows you to focus on your own special add-on functionality. If the add-on brings you more clients, it will also bring your partner more clients, and everybody will win.

Selling Off The Net

Everybody today wants to be an e-tailer. Just try a simple, general search for product information and see how many responses you get for online retail organisations. Most general product information searches will result in links to the web pages of companies trying to sell products. These links often force users to scroll through various advertisements and promotions before they successfully access simple product use information. This is greatly adding to the time that users have to spend on the net to

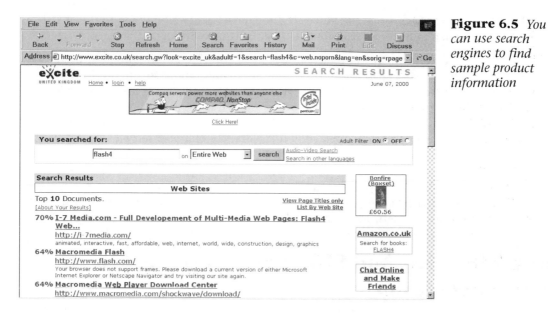

Figure 6.5 *You can use search engines to find sample product information*

find something of value, and it has started to cause users to put down the keyboard in frustration. At this rate, the attraction and utility of the Internet is likely to diminish for seasoned users. However, to offset this decline will be the continual rise of new users and net shoppers. This information should be considered when designing any new e-commerce company or website as it will have a direct bearing on traffic levels.

Control Of The Net By Industry Lockout

There has never been an industry that has such potential for growth as information technology, and this usually attracts the big established corporations such as Microsoft and Disney. However, large global competitors don't like to share their toys, especially with fledgling upstarts. The exception is Microsoft, whose strategy is to 'buy in' to emerging technology that fits its vision of the future. Disney, on the other hand, rarely shares. One thing these titans do have in common is the need to control. Almost all large organisations have gained this control through size and branding, but the Internet has caused some of them to shake and shudder at the thought of losing control. This is why the most valuable Internet hot property, such as the search engines, are being bought up by the big corporations.

The plan is not new: they use money to purchase these virtual assets and then work to control the market. Step two in the plan is to keep out the small fish by creating an overwhelming presence through advertising or by buying the smaller guys out. The Disneys of the world also have the money to buy the right knowledge assets so that just as you are reading this book, so is the Disney war department. The downside of all this is that even if the net looks like it is free, portions are slowly being swallowed in the background by the big companies and once they have narrowed it down to the 'usual suspects', it's back to business as normal. Unless, of course, new giant killers emerge.

Even if they succeed in controlling the Internet, so what? Well, the problem with companies like Disney is that they don't share their toys, and they are not likely to keep running things for free. Eventually with size, you will start to see attempts to capitalise on the free content of the Internet. Content is the power of the future, and copyright and trademark are powerful allies to the big company. So, if Disney and friends own the search engines, they may not blatantly charge a service fee, but they may start charging companies to submit URLs or just relegate those that don't pay far down the result list. Most search engines already offer 'services' that allow companies to list their names at the top of a search list, and this is bound to continue. So by capitalising on their Internet assets, these large organisations can make short-run gains (or long-run if no competitors emerge) at the expense of the openness of the market.

More Effective And Efficient Coverage – Brute Force Advertising

Let's say that you and I were going to release the same killer app on the Internet. The only difference between us is that a major partner bankrolls my company. If the two apps were identical and entered the market at the same time, they would initially have an equal chance of becoming the 'standard'. However, since I am funded by very deep pockets, I have the advantage of attracting visitors or generating traffic by a large international advertising campaign.

All else being equal, traffic would flow faster to my app, thereby increasing the chance of its acceptance as the standard and relegating yours to second place. Your only hope

Figure 6.6 *The web has a plethora of active and successful search engines, some dedicated to particular products or geographical areas*

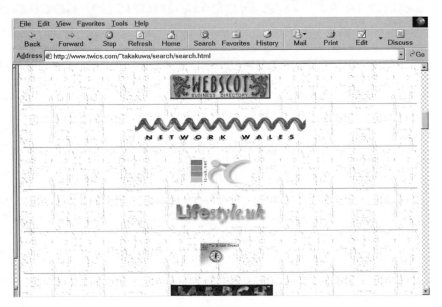

would be to attract enough backing to capture a significant piece of the market to make the app viable.

However, just because you are the first to market doesn't necessarily give you all the advantage. For instance, there are a number of search engines that are active, viable, and profitable as well. In fact, you could change your app enough to surpass my app's popularity, depending on the change that was made. However, as more and more large organisations enter the fray, it will make it more difficult for the upstart to compete if the business models are the same or similar.

The good news is that by being aware of the world of e-commerce, you can easily outmanoeuvre your competitors to avoid each pitfall.

Avoiding Land Mines

Knowing what land mines exist and where they are is extremely important information that you should use in the development of your e-business. Steering clear of land mines or making your business land mine-proof will protect you from the scenarios noted above.

1. Keep the content fresh and interesting, change it often, and provide ample help and assistance.

2. Provide new value by adding new functionality, information or offerings to your market; if you are really effective at this, you will attract new slices of the market to your site, all within the same community (called creating sub-communities).

3. Become indispensable to your customers by providing applications that they must use on a regular basis, such as links to search engines, share prices, news, etc.

4. When dealing in physical products, be prepared to have a physical location in the future.

5. Make your business fast, efficient, easy to use, and fun.

6. Provide links that add value to the community. If you don't, users will consider them as nothing more than annoying clutter.

7. Limit the amount of advertising allowed into your community and strictly review links and affiliate sites for content and advertising levels.

8. Use the three-click rule (i.e. everything on the site should be accessible from everywhere else within three mouse clicks) as a testing guideline or go to www.e-biz-pro.com for a free online assessment.

9. Keep the information useful and relevant, clean the site often, and ensure that the amount of useless information is minimal.

10. Ensure that help functions such as FAQ search engines return efficient and clean answers. You can provide detailed archives elsewhere in the site with an appropriate warning of content clutter.

11. Never allow your partners to clutter your site or over-approach your customers (i.e. spam).

12. Control access to customer information so that they will continue to patronise your site.

13. Avoid killer app competition with asset owners unless:
    - ➤ You have long-term contracts.
    - ➤ They are woefully slow or technologically illiterate.
    - ➤ Your killer app is better than their offering.
    - ➤ Your aim is to sell out to them or their competitor.
    - ➤ The competition between asset owners limits their flexibility.
    - ➤ They don't have this book.
    - ➤ Your app is based on the community and not the asset.
    - ➤ You're in it for the short term.
    - ➤ The app is a stepping stone to take over the hard assets.

14. Avoid duplicating another killer app unless yours has better functionality, or you are attempting to steal market share or split the market.

15. Use subtle methods to sell and avoid overselling to your own market.

16. Develop an organisation or killer app that has the potential to attract or recombine fragmented markets.

17. Promote your app as a standard or as a critical mass by imaging it as a community of value.

18. Partner with compatible organisations and work to lock out the big organisations by continually hitting them where it hurts with high-quality free content. This could be called 'destroying their value chain'.

19. Counteract brute force advertising with savvy net promotion. One advertisement during the Cup Final will not generate as much traffic as a well-placed Internet story.

They say that a moron makes a mistake and continues to make it; an average person makes a mistake once or twice and learns not to make it again; a genius learns from the mistakes of others. By knowing the land mines that lie ahead, you can become the genius in your market by simply avoiding them, using them to your advantage, or building a killer app that can withstand them. There are undoubtedly other land mines and pitfalls on the horizon, but by staying informed and keeping in touch with the world of e-commerce, you will greatly increase your chances of spotting them long before they will do any damage. Our best advice is to hire an on-site e-commerce guru – or retain an e-commerce and Internet adviser to the board – to continuously scan and report on changes within the world of business and e-commerce and how these changes affect or alter your plans. The money will be well spent.

Knowing what it takes to build a killer app and where the land mines are will provide a solid foundation for your business plan to help you create a new e-commerce company or move your existing functions towards the e-commerce model.

The Least You Need To Know

➤ Define what a killer app is.

➤ Outline the 12 rules to building a killer app.

➤ Identify potential land mines lurking on the killer app road.

➤ Understand how to avoid land mines and pitfalls.

Chapter 7

The Laws Of The e-Commerce Jungle

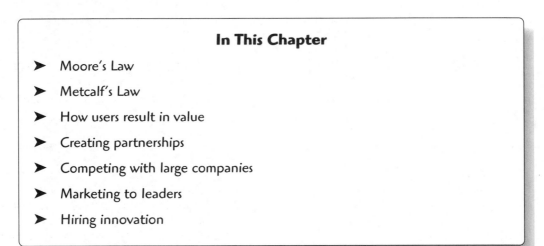

In This Chapter

➤ Moore's Law

➤ Metcalf's Law

➤ How users result in value

➤ Creating partnerships

➤ Competing with large companies

➤ Marketing to leaders

➤ Hiring innovation

There are a number of laws that define the e-commerce jungle. And don't be fooled. It is a jungle out there where companies either eat or are eaten. Some of the older ones are even hunted for sport. However, in the midst of all this overnight growth, chaos and big apes can be found certain laws that apply in this jungle. Knowing the e-commerce laws can help you avoid those nasty elephant traps and things that hide in the grass just waiting for your company to come along. These laws are not particularly new, but they are very relevant, and knowing them will go a long way towards helping your company survive and succeed in the wilds of the Internet.

There are a couple of things to consider. First, all laws will eventually be broken, and even though you may want to religiously follow a law, remember that as the world changes, so do laws. Often, this strict adherence to a principle can lead to inflexibility and an inability to change quickly, which can have dire consequences for organisations. Second, remember that laws attempt to define a precise principle, but with the exception of mathematics or physics, laws rarely last or stay the same over time simply because the world changes. So, you need to understand these e-commerce laws and principles, but remember that there is never any black and white, just various shades of grey.

Moore's Law

In the 1960s, Gordon Moore, Intel's founder, predicted that every 18 months chip processing power (as established by chip transistor density) would double while the costs would stay the same. This simple law has held true in general. Transistors were created in 1949 at Bell Laboratories. They are merely very-low-voltage, electrically powered switches.

Placed in the chips of computers, millions of these switches control the functionality of the computer. In order for Moore's law to be true, more and more of these switches would have to be added to the CPU of the computer for it to become faster. However, if these chips were simply added inside computers, we would be

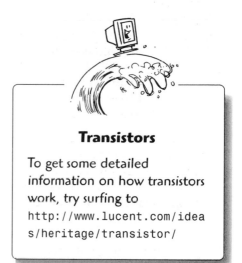

Transistors

To get some detailed information on how transistors work, try surfing to
`http://www.lucent.com/idea s/heritage/transistor/`

Figure 7.1
35 years on, Moore's Law appears remarkably accurate

back to rooms full of machinery and the cost would not decline. What Moore saw was that the technology would advance that would allow for transistors to decrease in size and for more of them to fit onto the silicon wafers of chips. Even though the cost of the plants and machines necessary to make these chips would increase, the actual cost per chip would remain constant since more and more would be produced.

This, of course, has had a significant impact on the world. It keeps the cost of computers constant, which over time implies that the real cost, given inflation, is actually falling. Economies of scale, or buying supplies in volume, help to further reduce the cost, which makes computers accessible for almost everyone. The more people who use computers, the greater the 'critical mass' and the benefit of this 'mass', which we will discuss in the next law. So, Moore's Law incorporates an assumption that even though it would cost more to make the chips that have increased speed, this speed is necessary to make computers more functional and therefore more widely useful. If there were no need for greater and greater speed in computers, there would be no market to justify the investment in chip technology and Moore's Law would 'hit the wall'. We have not reached that point – yet.

There is, however, a growing size and weight limitation requirement that is still pushing hardware manufacturers to obtain fully functional computers that are progressively smaller and lighter. This causes pressure to be placed on the chip manufacturers to increase speed while maintaining or even decreasing the size of chips. Smaller devices are required for everything from personal computing devices, the integration of mobile phones with computers, networking devices that must be carried by staff, and so on. So the law basically says that computers will get faster, but will remain the same price.

Metcalf's Law

Robert Metcalf, the founder of 3com, made an observation that a network increased in value with the addition of each new user and that this value could be defined as the square of the number of users: utility = (number of users)^2.

Often, the value of something is measured by its utility. Utility roughly equates to how useful something is. The point of the equation is not to provide a number that we can impress people with; instead, the utility of a network formula is used to show the concept that as each new user is added to a network, this mysterious value or worth of the network increases at a faster rate than the number of users. So, if I have a network with one user, and I add user two, the number of users would double or have a growth of 100%, but the utility would grow by 400%.

What constitutes a network in Metcalf's Law? Well, since he was the founder of Ethernet powerhouse 3com, a network was likely to be a network or a group of computers connected together. We are all familiar with a regular computer network, such as the local area network in our offices, the Internet, or bank hole-in-the-wall machine networks, but there are a variety of other networks to which Metcalf's law

applies. Phones are essentially networks with network interface devices (pho
attached. Other types of networks include utilities that deliver electricity or g
pipelines that deliver oil, road systems, satellite TV networks with dishes, cre
networks, and so on.

Worldwide Internet Users At The End of 2000

Expected to total 374.9 million, the numbers of users by country is estimated as:

1. US – 135.7m with market share of 36.2%

2. Japan – 26.9m with market share of 7.18%

3. Germany – 19.1m with market share of 5.10%

4. UK – 17.9m with market share of 4.77%

5. China – 15.8m with market share of 4.20%

6. Canada – 15.2m with market share of 4.05%

7. South Korea – 14.8m with market share of 3.95%

8. Italy – 11.6m with market share of 3.08%

9. Brazil – 10.6m with market share of 2.84%

10. France – 9.0m with market share of 2.39%

11. Australia – 8.1m with market share of 2.16%

12. Russia – 6.6m with market share of 1.77%

13. Taiwan – 6.5m with market share of 1.45%

14. Netherlands – 5.4m with market share of 1.45%

15. Spain – 5.2m with market share of 1.39%

Source: eTForcasts

Value In A Crowded Network

When Thomas Edison made his now famous phone call to the Mayor of New York, there were two users on his network. But if he had taken that network and tried to sell it, everyone would first have said, 'What's a phone?' followed by 'What use is it to me?'

Now, imagine if I put the current worldwide AT&T network with its millions of users on the market at the same time. How much would that network be worth? And if we included the entire worldwide telephone network, it would have an even higher value. The value of the larger network is derived from the fact that everyone knows what a phone network is, and therefore appreciates its value. These larger networks have achieved 'critical mass'. Edison's two-person network would have minimal value to the average person. So what's the point? The point is that the value of a network is the square of the number of its users, and this rule also applies to applications on a network such as websites, software, or retail sites. If you are going to build an e-commerce business, this point is very important. The value of the organisation will grow significantly as more users are added to the company's network or community of users. This can include visitors to an e-commerce retail site, intranet, or users of a distributed application.

Web Traffic

To see a posted count of the traffic that visits the top websites, surf to www.mediametrix.com — then use the links to go into the Press Room and Press Releases.

This sounds like an obvious statement from a sales perspective because it is obvious that if I add more customers, the value of my company will grow. But what if the application or access to my website is distributed for free? We would think that the value of the organisation in this scenario would fall to zero, but actually the opposite is true. Amazon loses money, but its market capitalisation is more than $23 billion; Yahoo! doesn't charge its customers, yet is worth billions of dollars; and Ask Jeeves is worth in excess of $1 billion, even though it provides nothing but links to other websites. Their values are derived from the millions of unique visits to their websites each year by net surfers. These users or 'traffic' create value according to Metcalf.

How Do Users Result In Value?

The real value created by traffic is not just the potential of sales and advertising, but the potential of being the lead killer app in the category and becoming a market standard. If your application becomes the standard for a market, as in the case of the Windows operating system, competitors have a difficult time competing, and you will, in effect, control the market. This provides the ability to dictate changes and control what affiliated or compliant applications are included with your killer app.

An affiliated application may be a link in a website, a plug-in to software, and so on. What is most valued by the market is the potential to make money in the future, not through sales of the original application but through sales of the other add-ons, such as training, affiliate sales, software, and so on. The more users that use an application, the greater the value of the application will be. Easy, isn't it? We will see how this applies in real e-commerce life at the end of the book.

First To Market Wins (Usually)

This law is true only to the extent that the first killer app to market has the greatest potential to win, but doesn't guarantee a win. What they will 'win' is the chance of becoming a standard and the value associated with this position. But being the first to market does not imply that everything should be held in secrecy.

Secrecy Is Not The Answer

In fact, holding everything in secrecy usually can't be done because there are always disgruntled employees and suspicious vendors ready to spread the news. Even if you are successful, it probably indicates that you have not shared your ideas with the market. When the application is released, you will have to spend a fortune in promotion to get traffic to come and see your site, Internet users will be wary of this phoney promotional buzz, and your resources will be smaller because most of your budget will be spent. Also, if you don't share your ideas with the market, you will lose out on the valuable associations that can be gained from partnering organisations on the same wavelength.

By keeping things 'under wraps', you may, in fact, be smothering your killer app to become the 'killed app'. A better approach is to worry less about the secrecy of your project and concentrate more on getting it to market first. This is especially relevant when we discuss applications that aim to take advantage of a deregulated market, such as the telephone market. The first-to-market law doesn't guarantee success to the first participant. In fact, any of the following aspects can negatively impact your first-to-market benefits:

➤ If the application is deficient to the number two entrant.
➤ If you mismanage the entrance to the market.
➤ If you attempt to capitalise too soon on the value.
➤ If you ignore your partners.
➤ If you ignore the market.

The best way to get to market first is to have a clear battle plan that will take you there complete with promotional strategy. But you shouldn't dwell on the plan – it is much better not to tweak it to death but get out and get on with the business.

First Out Of The Gate Doesn't Guarantee A Win

Remember that first to market doesn't guarantee a win. This is especially true if the second to market is Microsoft. The great Bill Gates Internet miss was his underestimation of the importance of the Internet that caused him to delay development of Internet Explorer. He should have studied Metcalf's law more closely because if he had, Internet Explorer could have beaten Netscape to the market and would have been distributed through that locked-in market of the Windows 95 operating system. (This doesn't count the fact that the American courts felt otherwise and determined that Microsoft had abused its near-monopoly status by 'forcing' its users to use Internet Explorer rather than Netscape.)

This also would have given Microsoft a stranglehold on that little upstart Sun Microsystems and its Java application (*see* Figure 7.2). In fact, Internet Explorer was next in line behind a number of other browsers and yet today owns the top usage spot. It's not a killer app, nor does it have the status of a standard, but that was Bill Gates' folly. If Microsoft had been first to market, just imagine what it could have done, and for so much less investment.

Want To Download A Browser For Free?

To download Netscape, surf to www.netscape.com. Want Internet Explorer? Go to www.microsoft.com. Want a Java browser? Go to www.sun.com.

Figure 7.2 *Sun is the home of all things Java*

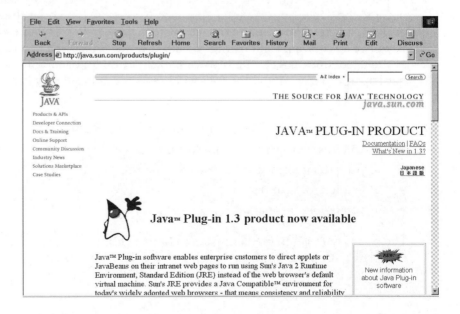

A Small Piece Of Big Action Is Profitable

In the early 1990s, the deregulation of the phone industry started to generate a number of interesting developments. Smaller competitors were starting to get into the business of sending data over phone lines or their own finer networks. As phone switch-building companies developed new switches that would carry both voice and data, these smaller upstart data companies started to prepare to move into the phone business.

All it would take was fibre optic cables, network interface devices (switches), and a way to get critical mass on the network. Investors who funded the fibre networks in critical areas, such as cable TV companies, completed the first requirement. Phone network supply companies such as Nortel that built the digital switching systems handled the second requirement. The third requirement was fulfilled by the deregulation of the phone industry and rules that forced incumbent phone companies to provide access to their networks so that all calls would be carried, regardless of the originating company. This created instantaneous critical mass for the new companies since they could now put a call through to any owner of a telephone. The business plan of the start-up phone companies was simple. They were to be the first to market with a new infrastructure and the latest technology in a deregulated industry that already had critical mass. They had nothing to lose.

This concept, however, doesn't just apply to large deregulated industries. It can also apply to any industry that is dominated by old, slow-moving corporates with massive infrastructures. Your company will have an advantage if you can supply the same service with better technology than a larger incumbent organisation. Although bigger companies usually have a larger amount of cash to compete with, they often cannot move fast enough to compete with newer technology. They also don't want to bring in new technology too fast because they are trying to protect their existing infrastructure, as we noted in Chapter 6 on the killer app. That implies that industries such as banking, utilities, retailing, insurance, estate agents, publishing, entertainment, and media are all open to the attack of the killer app. Just think about all the steps that are involved for these companies to get a product from supplier to customer. Then decide how you can do the same thing faster, cheaper, and without a distribution network.

Get Partners, Lots And Lots Of Partners

You can do it alone. You can raise the money, create an awesome killer app, spill it onto the Internet and be an overnight web sensation. But you probably want to last more than 15 minutes, and you probably don't have years to build the perfect app, given the previous example. The next best thing is to develop partnerships with companies that can add value to your app.

This provides two main benefits. First, they can pass traffic to your killer app in exchange for traffic from your site. Second, your partners can provide an actual piece of your virtual organisation. Let's say that you run an Internet retail outlet that focuses on selling software. You may also want to link to another website that provides reviews and tests of software. The goal is to provide your own user community with the added value from the second website without having to add and manage this functionality yourself. Now, if you continue to do this a number of times, you will build an organisation with significant functionality for your customers without the overhead. The downside occurs if your partner turns out to be unreliable by providing poor service or a poor-quality application.

Large Companies Are Large And Can't Move

The fact is that most large companies are unresponsive to changes in the world around them. They have huge infrastructures with committees, budgets, and managers that are incapable of movement. By the time they have changed, the market has moved, and the technology has become obsolete.

Not all large corporates are this way, however. Some very inventive entrepreneurs have created large organisations that can turn on a sixpence. How do they do it? They follow a few basic rules:

Changing Technology

You can get information on changes in technology through websites such as those found in the links at `http://dir.yahoo.co.uk/news_and_media/technology/`

➤ Pay attention to the world around you. The only way to do this is to actually get out into the world around you by learning new technologies, talking to companies on the cutting edge, and spending a great deal of time researching technology. There are some ways to make this process more efficient by using electronic news delivery services, by hiring research staff, or by using test labs.

➤ Test new technologies when they are available. Many companies are now using in-house and contract test labs to test new technologies for both functionality and a detailed synopsis of a particular technology's capabilities.

➤ Hire technologically forward-thinking people. Individuals who think outside the box are a rare breed. They are difficult to find and even more difficult to keep. However, good companies endeavour to satisfy these employees because they are the lifeblood of the new company.

Large Companies Have Less Talent

This is a growing phenomenon as new firms start attracting talent through pieces of ownership that large firms would never give up. Giving a stake to its employees is not a new concept. Many organisations have provided share options for employees for a number of years. What is new is that these plans were originally given only to senior individuals. Now the talent is becoming increasingly younger, and in order to entice the very best individuals, companies are starting to acknowledge that the young stars are the ones who need the share options. The problem in the UK is that the government is still catching up with the information age and the implications of the Internet. Many believe that current tax-raising schemes are not in line with the government's desire to promote and support entrepreneurship and e-commerce ventures.

Attracting The 'Rising Stars'

Most of the new start-up Internet companies have very limited resources. This causes them to search for talented individuals who will accept an equity position in a company in exchange for wages. However, very few established organisations accept the theory that people should be given 'a piece of the action' if they don't own the business. Companies such as Microsoft have never followed this old style of management. Instead, it has rewarded its employees with generous options that have resulted in a number of millionaires – many of whom continue to work for the benefit of Microsoft and themselves. The philosophy that no employee should ever be paid more than an executive is absurd in this rapid-paced world of technology. It becomes even more ridiculous when we realise that older executives who have risen to the top over many years do not fundamentally understand the new technological world order or their place in it. In the UK, however, do watch out for the ceilings in share options for employees which can cripple a forward-looking and generous company with National Insurance (NI) clawbacks on benefit in kind.

Young 'star' employees are realising their worth and many are abandoning the old corporate structures for the new environment of the virtual organisation. No limits, no boundaries, fat share options, and generous signing bonuses are becoming the rule of the day in the technological world, and it will become even more commonplace as the complexity of the technology grows.

This doesn't apply to all technology employees and, in fact, sometimes the level of compensation does not warrant the investment. Many optioned employees are not worth the value of their options: for example, executives who are incapable of effective organisation, technology employees who cannot think 'outside the box', and employees with extensive experience but none that is applicable to the current world. Companies have to be very careful in applying the equity of the organisation to the talented individuals who will add significant value and then provide those people with higher levels of compensation. At the same time, companies have to strike a balance by ensuring that too little compensation is avoided, or the impact on the organisation will be extensive.

Options Are An Option

Options are essentially agreements that obligate the company to sell a certain amount of its shares at a certain price level. The intent is to encourage the employees to work hard so that the value of the organisation will increase and thereby increase the market price of its shares by making the options valuable. At the same time, delays in the vesting of the options ensure that employees stay with the organisation until all benchmarks are complete. For example, a company may give a star employee 10,000 options at the current market value of £15 each and set three benchmarks at one year, two years, and three years. This means that the employee will be able to cash in one-third of the options, if he wants, at each benchmark. This is called vesting. The goal is to keep the star employee from leaving the organisation. The downside of options is that if the employee is a poor choice, there is no way to fire him without 'paying out the options' or allowing him to continue working. Legally, unless termination is written into the option agreement as grounds for expiration of the options, the company will either be stuck with the employee or with paying him off.

A second problem is that often organisations supply mediocre employees with excessive options. These line employees do not necessarily provide any growth potential to the organisation and will often cause the 'stars' to leave for greener pastures. For example, if the chief accountant has more options than the chief technology officer, the company will run the risk of losing the employee who provides a higher value. To keep employees with the organisation, the company will have to update the option agreements to add options to the employee compensation package in later years. Also, for the options to be of any value, the company must be, or plan to be, public in the near future.

The bottom line is that large established organisations are loath to give up share ownership to attract star employees and are even more loath to provide options worth millions to young employees. The result is that these established organisations will have a deficient talent pool in the future that will add to the risk level of the organisation. By rights, the value of the organisation should reflect this level of technological risk, and as investors and traders wise up to this measure, stock values will fall. The exception will be organisations that employ talented individuals, reward them to stay, and promote this fact to the world. This is called managing intellectual assets.

Twenty Percent Know, Eighty Percent Follow

The 20–80 rule was established by marketing specialists decades ago. They quickly realised that 20% of the population were likely to try a variation on a product or a new product during its introduction. They also found that within this leader group there was a subset of super leaders who adopted the newer technology first, regardless of price or complexity. The remaining 80% were laggards who adopted innovations after the first 20% had proven the use and popularity of the product. This particular rule is very applicable to the world of new technologies such as e-commerce – 20% of companies and individuals within companies will accept innovation, 80% will follow behind.

This has never caused too much difficulty until the era of the killer app. Now, organisations that were always exceptionally consistent at generating revenue are under siege from the new upstart virtual organisations and their ownership talent. The result is that the leviathans are effectively caged by their lack of a technologically advanced talent pool. The standard solution of paying higher salaries may not succeed in attracting the talent needed to compete.

Herein lies a true dilemma. If you hire a talent pool, the board of directors must approve the outlay. What they are approving is the outlay of both cash and equity to other people. Only a board with a majority of 20-percenters is likely to approve such an arrangement. But, statistically speaking, your chance of getting the majority of individuals on a board who are innovators is astronomical. What this means is that the new killer app organisations have lightning-fast reflexes and carefully developed talent pools motivated by the fact that they will become rich if they bump off your company. On the other side is your staid old board of directors.

The 20% innovators are often the most valuable people to have as customers. They will tend to pay more for the technology just to be leaders. These individuals are called the cream of the market. New technologies steal these individuals away simply because they want to be the innovators in the marketplace. The downside of this for the incumbent organisation is that these people usually supply a large piece of the overall corporate profitability. The second problem is that they will eventually drag the other 80% with them.

Targeting Market Leaders

Competing with established retailers and e-tailers is becoming a very difficult task and the odds against new online retailers are growing. Some companies have chosen to take the approach of targeting the leaders of regional buying groups in promotion and advertising by identifying their traits and actions. Placing ads on websites about new technology attracts higher-income individuals in the 20–40 age target range that these companies are trying to capture. They are not interested in attracting the whole market (it's unrealistic), but instead they want to attract just the leaders willing to try to accept the new approach to online e-tailing.

Nature Giveth And Nature Taketh Away

There is no perfect employee. Exceptionally smart employees can often be arrogant, sarcastic, and difficult to keep challenged, while upbeat employees can often be inefficient and unfocused; technologically brilliant individuals sometimes have difficulty thinking outside their own box, and charismatic individuals are difficult to manage. Developing e-commerce requires a mix of all these talents. You need charismatic individuals to sell, technologically savvy staff to implement the complex technology, upbeat individuals to add drive and spark, and intellectually intelligent individuals to pull it all together and create innovation. If you choose your team members from only one type of discipline or with only one of the above personality traits, you are losing out on the potential rewards of the others. It is like building a cricket team full of great bowlers. Who's going to wicket-keep, slip-field, or hit the sixes?

Diversity In Employees Is Key

e-Commerce is a marriage of technology and business. The subtle nature of both must be clearly understood in order for your e-commerce company to efficiently make it to market or for your old company to become an e-commerce company without collapsing the existing business. The likelihood that your network guru is also a marketing guru is remote. Therefore, the move to e-commerce will require an assessment of your existing talent pool's strengths and weaknesses. Back-filling these weaknesses with outside talent is the best option, but to really gain significant benefits, make sure that these individuals bring a wealth of different perspectives to your operation. For example, the combination of a web application builder, logistics specialist, and customer support specialist will produce a stronger e-commerce application than three programmers.

Staying Innovative

A sure sign of an innovator is someone who reads about, writes about, or studies advancements in his or her field and in other fields. You can easily stay on top of innovation at online technology information providers such as
`www.silicon.com`

Innovate, Innovate, Innovate

It is also important to recruit innovators. Innovation is a true talent because very few individuals can see the wood for the trees and even fewer can tell you what's beyond the woodland. Yet innovation is so essential to the world of e-commerce technology that ignoring it could be catastrophic to your organisation. The case of IBM is a classic example of a company that nearly collapsed in on itself due to a lack of innovation coupled with corporate arrogance. Old ideologies allowed people such as Bill Gates to gain vast control over areas such as operating systems and the world of client server computing. Yet even Microsoft nearly missed the

Figure 7.3 *There's plenty on the net to keep you up to date in the fast-moving world of internet technologies*

Internet innovation. Innovators are a rare breed, and yet they are essential to divining the direction of e-commerce technology.

It is important to understand that individual intelligence manifests itself in different ways. Some incredibly gifted musicians are autistic, some great artists fail maths, some great mathematicians cannot write, and most of us fall somewhere in the middle. Effectively mixing the types of intelligence inside your talent pool can lead to some amazing innovation.

People Fear Change, Machines Don't Care

One fact of life is that, with some notable exceptions, the vast majority of people avoid change. It is a simple fact that we feel comfortable with things we know, and the only time we change willingly is when we have become bored with the existing status quo. This isn't to say that people won't change; it's just that people are usually unwilling to change as an act of free will. They often have to be enticed or coerced. This has an immense impact on the development and implementation of e-commerce applications from both an internal and external perspective. Internally, employees are usually most open to change when they are young or new to an environment. That is simply because they have not had the time to build a comfort level or familiarity with their environment. They are open to gathering as much information as possible to climb the familiarity curve as fast as possible.

The second place in which the acceptance of change will have an impact is with external contacts. Customers will have to be enticed to visit your e-commerce company and suppliers will be wary of any changes that they will have to make. Unfortunately, you need these individuals to accept your innovation in order for you to succeed. This aspect was covered briefly in the rules of the killer app in Chapter 6 related to 'Ensuring Continuity For The Customer'. The underlying reason for ensuring continuity for the customer is to avoid the reluctance of your customers towards change. If they are familiar with the new interface, they will be more likely to use it. As for new customers, they usually have to be coerced with clever promotions or by following the leaders.

Fear of change goes hand in hand with the previous law of the e-commerce jungle regarding innovation. The primary reason for lack of innovation is fear of change. If we avoid change, we are likely to see only minimal benefit from innovation. This fear is also largely generated by our personal fear of not understanding the innovation and our growing lack of leisure time in our busy lives. Basically, change takes time and effort. Who has any of that? However, change is essentially not just to stay ahead of the competition, but to stay ahead of the workload. Pouring money into e-commerce development will yield savings in one of the most precious commodities: our time. If we free up some time, then maybe we will be more willing to study change and the vicious circle of more work, lack of time, no innovation – and more work will finally cease. This investment in technology will also yield a side benefit: since machines don't fear change, change is easier to implement. The more technologically advanced your organisation is, the less you will have to deal with aspects such as the fear of change.

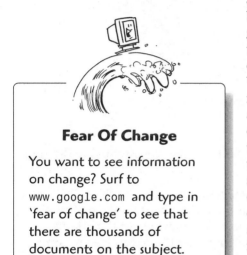

Fear Of Change

You want to see information on change? Surf to www.google.com and type in 'fear of change' to see that there are thousands of documents on the subject.

Spend On The Future, Not The Past

Companies spend an enormous amount of time and money on looking back or just keeping up with change. Accounting departments spend a great deal of time and resources to produce financial statements and analyses that review what has happened, sometimes months ago.

Although accounting is an essential way for any organisation to track its performance and even provide indications of future trends, spending resources on producing another report is one less resource available to push ahead. Accounting does, however, provide the skeleton of any organisation, and it is essential to implement systems that will reduce the resource requirements of this back-office system. Large companies are notorious for maintaining complex accounting structures that provide minimal benefit but use a great deal of resources.

Consistent procedures are the key to building a successful real-time accounting system. Real-time accounting systems capture information on a transaction-by-transaction basis from point of capture through to the general ledger without human intervention. This then allows management to obtain information quickly and in real time so that resources can be spent looking forward.

Once you have implemented the networked skeleton of your organisation, you can spend more time looking ahead and far less time looking back. Getting your employees to change will be more difficult. Many managers protect their personal interests by building extensive empires of undocumented complexity. Many major corporations have hundreds of legal entities and as many bank accounts to manage their operations.

The same functionality can easily be managed by using a fraction of the entities and bank accounts at a significantly reduced level of overhead. Often the response from executives and managers is that the entities are needed and cannot be reduced. However, some of the largest organisations in the world operate with a handful of entities and bank accounts. It is worthwhile, therefore, to revisit the old habit of budgeting and see how little of it is really necessary to run the enterprise – rather than stifling creativity by doing as much as possible.

Tie It All Together

In order for a company to survive in the demanding, fast-paced world of e-commerce, it will require a number of things. It must have a mix of talented people who can produce a wide-ranging and forward-thinking viewpoint and yet have the ability to complete goals and understand complex technology. It must have a focus on efficiency that eliminates waste and redirects resources to value-added tasks while focusing the organisation on looking ahead. It must gather traffic to its website, its products, or its innovations in order to become the leader of its industry to create critical mass and become the standard. It should endeavour to be the first to market with innovation in order to lead the competition. It should ally itself with like-minded organisations and go after the established titans' high-profit markets with a low or no overhead structure. It should not fear the big established organisations because they are slow to move and short of talent. It should hire the best people and reward them for being the best. It will succeed.

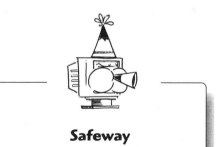

Safeway

At one time the Canadian division of Safeway Store International operated a $14 billion annual treasury flow through two legal entities and fewer than a dozen bank accounts.

The Least You Need To Know

➤ Moore's Law – every 18 months chip processing power doubles while the costs stay the same.

➤ Metcalf's Law – a network increases in value with the addition of each new user.

➤ It is imperative to get partners.

➤ Find the leaders in the market.

➤ Go after the lucrative markets.

➤ Big companies have weaknesses.

➤ Hire innovative employees.

➤ Companies should look ahead, not back.

Part 2

Opportunities In e-Commerce

It's wide open and new, fast and exciting. It's the world of e-commerce, and the opportunities are endless. In this section, we will go into some of the details of what you have to do to become an e-business. First, we will discuss the concept of real-time and integrated systems, particularly as they relate to the back office. Then we will discuss the supply chain and how you can automate your company in order to drop significantly the cost of doing business. We'll look at some of the things that Amazon.com did and provide you with some online examples that you can link to.

We will look at how to manage your customer relationships better by using e-commerce and how to build an online customer service centre. Knowing all about managing your electronic payments is critical to e-commerce, and we'll also discuss the latest technologies and security.

We will close the section with a look at how to build and manage a virtual workforce and work environment, and the last chapter will look at the concept of data mining, including how to store, retrieve, and analyse your operational information to make better decisions.

At the end of this, you will be able to build the foundation of your e-business and be ready for the next section on marketing in this new world.

Chapter 8

It's Just A Matter Of Time: Real Time vs Batch

In This Chapter

➤ What real-time systems are and how they can work for you

➤ How systems can create near-zero transaction costs

➤ Why batch systems are dinosaurs compared to today's technology

➤ Real-time back-office systems and why you need them

➤ Things you should know about information storage

Real-Time Systems Defined

There are basically two types of software: those that process information on a transaction-by-transaction basis and those that store data for processing at a later time. The first is called a real-time system and the second a batch system. Originally, computers were expensive, slow, and required offices full of programmers and operations staff, yet to process a single transaction could often take a room full of hardware many minutes to complete.

It was during this period that the Henry Ford mass production model was inadvertently used as a basis for programming. The goal was to gain enough speed and cost efficiency to make the use of computers justifiable for large organisations. Remember that the old behemoth mainframes required a great deal of a company's resources for everything from special ventilation to permanent maintenance and operations staff, and it was only the arrival of the mini-computer, followed by the PC, that removed the necessity

Internet User Accounts

25 million 1996

95 million 1999

304 million 2000 (first quarter)

540 million 2001 (est.)

for such people-intensive computing. (In fact, it was only in 1977 that the chief executive of DEC predicted that 'no one would ever want a computer in their home'!) Thus, the concept of grouping the transaction data and applying a programmed routine to this batch of information was born. In that era, before the 1980s, the computers could be scheduled to run at more advantageous times when the office staff were not present, and apply programming routines that repetitively processed high volumes of information such as month-end accounting data.

The Batch Era And The Introduction Of The PC

As the years progressed, the cost of hardware fell, new software and operating systems reached the market, and the speed of computers significantly increased. In this environment, these batch programs actually performed even better and allowed the programmers to focus their attention on new processes, such as capturing document data typed in letters and memos, improving data communications such as file and data transfers, and providing greater data analysis.

With the introduction and acceptance of the desktop PC, an entirely new 'world order' emerged. The power of computing was instantaneously distributed to users, and software was created that allowed them to produce documents and ad hoc reports from their very own computers. Batch systems that ran on mainframes still commanded the bulk of computing resources, but new online processing such as automated banking and order entry was starting to emerge and produce significant operational cost savings. In the distance was the rumbling of a new technology called distributed computing – or networking – that was about to change everything.

The introduction of networking software to the general public was simply an extension of the project by DARPA to connect large mainframes at various government defence departments and educational institutions. This project was the forerunner of the Internet, and the distributed or 'spread-out' nature of this environment gave rise to the greater use of transaction-based processing (processing information one transaction at a time) such as email and file transfers. Even the basic premise of sending a 'packet' of information over a network between two computers lent itself to the processing of information one transaction at a time.

Object-Oriented Code And Databases

As the cost of computers continued to fall and their speed increased, programmers found two avenues to explore. The first was the storage of data in a series of indexed files or tables called a database, and the second was the development of object-oriented code. In an object-oriented coding environment, variables (data storage capsules) are passed into an object or piece of programming code that processes the contents of the variable and returns either a new variable or some other type of output. The goal is to create an 'object' that performs an action on a type of variable, regardless of the value or content of the variable.

How The Internet Was Born

The Internet started life as a project of the United States Defense Department's DARPA (Defense Advanced Research Projects Agency). It wanted to link the computing environments of major government agencies and universities involved in defence research to a network that would provide continuous communications and processing capabilities should any part of the network be destroyed by an act of war. The primary focus was on the long-distance transmission of packets of information and the routing of these messages around 'damaged' areas. The project was called ARPANET (Advanced Research Projects Agency Network) and focused on the transmission of data over a network using a new suite of protocols called TCP/IP (transmission control protocol/Internet protocol).

In 1985 the NSF (National Science Foundation) introduced a new programme to establish Internet access across the USA through the implementation of a high-speed, high-volume backbone called NSFNET. Then, in 1989, British scientist Tim Berners-Lee developed a set of hypertext standards for CERN (the European Laboratory for Particle Physics), and the net was born.

To read more about the history of the Internet, surf to www.e-biz-pro.com

For example, it is easy to write a piece of code for a robotic arm that accepts a number and converts it into a signal to move the arm the same number of millimetres as the number. The small 'snippet' of program code can be referenced from elsewhere in a program or by other programs to move the arm. The alternative, which was widely used in the 'old days', was to code the distance into the program whenever the arm needed to move. As you can see, to make a simple change to the distance would require recoding the program. The concept of object-oriented code is an essential

121

element of most programming performed today, and it is the basis of programming languages such as Java and C++.

And where were all the batch programs? Alive and well, still trudging along, and oblivious to the world around them. That is until two events converged. The first was the Y2K threat – the Millennium Bug, which with hindsight can be regarded as over-hype, hoax, or Armageddon (take your pick). Inside these old batch programs were the first noted Y2K threats, and this started the greatest process of software replacement in the history of computing. It is interesting to note that most of the problems originated with code that was not object-oriented.

The second event was a small Internet company called Amazon.com. Amazon was started in 1995 to capitalise on the growing use of the Internet to purchase books online with a credit card. It was always an Amazon corporate mantra that its internal systems would allow for this process to occur online and in real-time – 10 million Amazon customers later, the stodgy world of retailing was being stopped dead in its tracks. Customers at Amazon enter their orders for books online as easily and efficiently as if they were shopping at a store. They also pay for the books immediately by using credit cards. This is not significantly different from any other retail operation except that the customers are doing the work of order entry.

Where the most significant change occurred was in Amazon's ability to process these orders in real time. The minute an order is entered into the Amazon website, the highly automated process of picking, shipping, and restocking the books begins. This is far different from the old batch world of gathering all the orders for a day to run an overnight process that would print warehouse picking lists or re-order reports. The per-transaction cost of completing a purchase at Amazon is a fraction of the cost

Figure 8.1
Amazon's books pages are linked to its internal real-time operating system

of completing the transaction at a traditional retailer, and it does not require expensive retail space.

The Near-Zero Transaction Cost

So what does all this have to do with e-commerce and you? Simply that e-commerce is the movement towards real-time and fully integrated systems and away from batch systems and batch-processing methodology. You must decide how your organisation will do this if you have any hope of competing with the Amazon.coms of the world.

A real-time system processes a transaction instantaneously from start to finish. There are no information flow stoppages or holding of data or intermediate delays for human processing. This drives the per-transaction cost (the total cost to complete a transaction) to an extremely low level.

Just What Time Is It?

There is an extensive body of research related to real-time systems. Many of the universities in North America have dedicated their intellectual resources to the study of real-time systems, and most of this science studies machine and work processes. e-Commerce, however, is more concerned with back-office functionality or how efficiently the internal systems process a transaction or perform a function. The goal is to reduce the resource expenditures on a per-transaction basis. For example, if a customer enters an order, there is no reason why the income statement should not reflect this transaction a few seconds after the order has been placed.

The following list includes traditional costs to complete a single order (a per-transaction cost can be calculated by dividing a total cost figure by the total number of orders received over a set time period such as a year):

➤   Monthly telephone expense   To receive orders.

➤   Bulk expense   For 0800 (Freephone) lines.

➤   Staff wages customer service   Customer service clerks.

➤	Rent/Utilities CS	Customer service centre.
➤	Desk/Supplies CS	Customer service centre.
➤	Desktop – PC	CS hardware costs and software licences.
➤	Desktop maintenance costs	To keep customer service PCs running.
➤	Staff benefits CS	The cost of benefits provided to the staff, such as health care.
➤	Server and networking expense	Inclusive of hardware/software/maintenance/depreciation.
➤	Payment handling charges	Staff costs, as opposed to automated payment systems.
➤	Order printing	Paper, toner, printers, maintenance, physical order storage.
➤	Staff wages and benefits WH	Warehouse staff for picking and packaging order and preparing shipping documents.
➤	Shipping expense	Packaging and courier expense.
➤	Rent/utilities WH	Customer service centre.
➤	Warehouse supplies	Racks, bins, etc.
➤	Other corporate overhead	Administration/accounting/management staff, insurance, bank fees,etc.
➤	Stocking costs	Lost interest earned on the value of stock.
➤	Marketing and promotion	Expenses related to attracting customers.
➤	Credit/fraud/loss	For fraudulent credit card usage.
➤	Returns and damage	For damaged or returned goods.

Obviously, the more costs that can be eliminated through the use of systems, the greater the advantage you will have over your competitors. Approaching zero cost is attainable, but only if your systems can process a transaction with very limited human involvement. To achieve a near-zero cost level will require the additional benefits and time savings provided by real-time systems. By making all your company's systems real-time, you will provide the business with a very solid foundation from which to grow.

Real–Time Systems In The Back Office

One of the easiest places to start the process of moving to real-time systems is the back office. The back office comprises all of the functions that support the 'visible' or 'production' operations of the organisation. Production processes are actions, such as manufacturing or construction, and visible processes are external functions, such as sales and service. The vast majority of the back-office resources are dedicated to accounting and finance.

There are numerous accounting packages available that operate in a real-time mode. However, the greatest difficulty with any of the existing accounting systems on the market is their legacy–old programming methodologies that have been given a fresh coat of paint, and old batch methodologies that are fired up one transaction at a time. Yet the consumer would not accept waiting for a batch process.

The Need For Speed And Storage

Operating a real-time system requires two important components: very high-speed processors and large storage capabilities. The whole purpose of the old batch-processing strategy was to capture the speed and efficiency of a repetitive process, much like the efficiency of an assembly line. These concerns were very real issues in the 1970s and 1980s, but now those issues are not as prevalent due to the low cost of processors. The ability to complete transactions one at a time requires a great deal of processing speed from the computers that will perform the

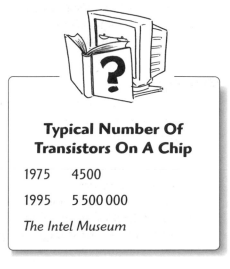

Typical Number Of Transistors On A Chip

1975   4500

1995   5 500 000

The Intel Museum

tasks. Today, a 750MHz chip set for a server costs less than £750, and the introduction of programs and systems that can perform multiple tasks simultaneously (asynchronous processing) and distribute the workload over one or more processors in the same server has reduced the processing time required by these applications. The power of a web server running true multi-thread operational software built with true object-oriented programming on a system that has multiple processors is more than adequate to start the creation of a virtual back office for your company.

The second important element is storage. As each customer enters data into your system, you will need to store this information for a variety of reasons. Data mining

The Data Mine

Data mining is the process of using stored data to assist current operations for financial benefit. The most common of these is to analyse customer sales information to adjust product mixes (which products are carried). However, data mining can also be used to assist in creating sales promotions, manage inventory levels, cash flow requirements, etc. Capturing and storing all operational information is the key to the success of future data-mining activities.

(*see* Chapter 13, 'There's Gold In Them Thar Hills: Data Mining') is a concept that is based on the collection and storage of all transactions and information. This is particularly valuable when the information pertains to customers.

Storage

There are a number of storage methodologies and hardware available in the market today, and each method has different benefits and costs. When implementing a real-time back-office system, the existing storage capabilities of the organisation must be reviewed. This is especially true when an organisation moves towards the storage of objects within a database (code and information together). A simple full-colour graphic of an inventory item can take up a significant amount of space on a disk. Hundreds or thousands of these items can swamp it. In addition, newer technologies, such as video, are likely to play an increasingly important role in business and will require even greater amounts of storage (*see* Figure 8.2).

Storage Terminology

➤ IDE hard drive – a single storage mechanism; multiple IDE drives can be installed on a server

➤ SCSI (small computer system interface) – takes the concept of IDE one step further by allowing more drives and more functional sharing

➤ RAID – a storage architecture in which multiple disks operate as if they were one

➤ Optical – CDs are an example of an optical storage device

➤ SAN (storage area network) – where data is stored over a distributed network in different locations

➤ Data warehouse – a large centralised storage area such as a database

➤ Data mart – smaller, distributed data storage areas

➤ Online storage systems – storage at another location, usually run by a third party

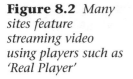

Figure 8.2 *Many sites feature streaming video using players such as 'Real Player'*

The Least You Need To Know

➤ Define what a real-time system is.

➤ Know a very brief history of computing and the Internet.

➤ Review the concept of object-oriented software.

➤ Decide why we need real-time back-office systems.

➤ Know something about the near-zero cost transaction.

➤ Comprehend the need for speed and storage.

King Of The Jungle - The Automated Supply Chain

In This Chapter

➤ Defining the supply chain

➤ Automating the supply chain

➤ Getting supplier buy-in

➤ Automating warehouse and delivery systems

➤ Defining the customer-driven supply chain

Defining What A Supply Chain Is

A supply chain is simply the combination of tasks that a company performs to move services or products from suppliers to customers. This basic definition is simple, but it becomes far more complex when we try to build a model of a generic supply chain that can be used by all companies. Your company may sell software, but that is a significantly different supply chain from a company that drills for oil. Or is it?

We need a model to assist us in defining standards that will drive the development of our e-commerce automation. Without these standards, we run the risk of developing inconsistent and incompatible systems or systems that won't work together. Microsoft Windows is successful because its software is a standard for operating systems. Microsoft originally pushed its way into delivering its software to users for what appeared to be no charge (it was bundled with the PCs) and because users could easily pirate the software, its use grew to critical mass.

Why It's Difficult To Define A Generic Supply Chain Model

Trying to define a generic supply chain that is applicable to all types of organisations is very difficult for a variety of reasons.

Supply Chain

4% of UK companies had an e-supply chain in the first quarter 2000.

1. There are almost as many variations of supply chains as there are companies.

2. Each organisation participates in the supply chain to varying degrees.

3. There are physical supply chains (actual physical product moves through an organisation) and virtual supply chains (no physical product moves through the organisation).

The Generic Supply Chain

At one end of the spectrum are companies that control the entire chain from the production of basic materials right through to the delivery of the end product to the customer. For example, a large energy company that explores and produces natural gas may also ship the product through its own pipeline to its own power-generating station and deliver electricity over its own grid to its own customers. This is an example of a highly controlled supply chain.

At the opposite end of the spectrum are companies that open a website with some form of content to attract customers and then link to a sales organisation such as Amazon.com. They provide their customers with the capability to order products through their website, but never manage the actual physical flow of the product. This task is managed by the online sales company (we will discuss this e-commerce business model in a later chapter when we look at sales-linking organisations).

This model is general enough to apply to all businesses, regardless of their products or services. If I run a modelling agency, my product is the service of providing human clothes horses, and my employees are essentially vendors that are supplying an input (their labour). Microsoft supplies software, but it doesn't own the packaging company that makes the box or the plant that supplies the CDs (at least, not yet). These products are considered inputs into the software production process so Microsoft both orders and manufactures products. Both these examples fit the model.

Why do we even need a generic model? Because it provides an easy starting point for understanding how to and why we would want to automate a supply chain. We have just defined the process in general, and now we can define how to automate the process. It's that simple.

A Generic Supply Chain Model

Suppliers	Accept orders from company.
	Supply inputs or final products.
	May ship product direct to customer.
Company	Send purchase order to suppliers (purchasing).
	Manufacture final product if needed (operations).
	Present product to customers (marketing).
	Accept orders for product (sales/customer service).
	Ship product to customer (logistics).
	Receive payments/pay suppliers (bought and sales ledgers or accounts receivable and payable).
Customer	Order product.
	Receive product.
	Pay for product.

Note: When we discuss products, we are including both products and services

Breaking The Chain – Automating Your Supply Chain

If we keep in mind the simple supply chain model cited previously, we can see there are two main flows to automate.

1. The flow between the supplier(s) and the company.
2. The flow between the customers and the company.

Step One: Automating The Flow Of Supply

The supplier/company flow consists of sending an order to the supplier, receiving a product from the supplier, and paying for the product. The first thing to do is automate the communication process that occurs between the company and the supplier. One of the easiest ways to automate this process is to email your orders direct from your purchasing system to the supplier. It is usually a relatively easy task to get a purchasing system to dump purchase order information into a text file that can then be sent to a supplier inside or attached to an email.

A more complex solution is for your supplier to design an ordering system that accepts order information directly from the Internet. Your company could establish an account with the supplier and sign onto a secure server on the supplier's website to complete orders. Another automation method would be for your company to send the data electronically in a file that can be processed by the supplier's system. This may involve a direct link to the supplier or the delivery of an encrypted order file over the Internet. The drawback to this particular scenario is that each supplier will probably have a different order/entry system, each with its own unique file format for processing the information. Building a different interpreter for each supplier would be time-consuming and costly.

Electronic Data Interchange

Electronic data interchange (EDI) was developed to solve this exact problem. Using a set of standards (ANSIx12 or UN/EDIFACT), companies were able to send their information in formats that the vendor could then interpret by using the same standards. The problem was that most companies did not have the capability to interpret their information into ANSIx12 so the services of an intermediary were required to act as a translator. This task earned companies such as IBM and the major banks a healthy revenue and severely limited the growth of EDI.

A New Blend Of EDI And HTML

In 1997, a W3 working group started on the development of a set of standards that would combine EDI and XML. This combination is presented as a needed standard for electronic commerce transactions so that net developers will be able to design e-commerce solutions that communicate easily with each other. The drawback to this approach is that standards are by their nature inflexible, and e-commerce systems at this time require a great deal of flexibility. The risk is that any new attempt to tightly regulate format and content is likely to receive limited acceptance. For more information on this initiative, you can surf to http://www.w3c.org/ECommerce

Figure 9.1
Turn to W3C for information on web standards

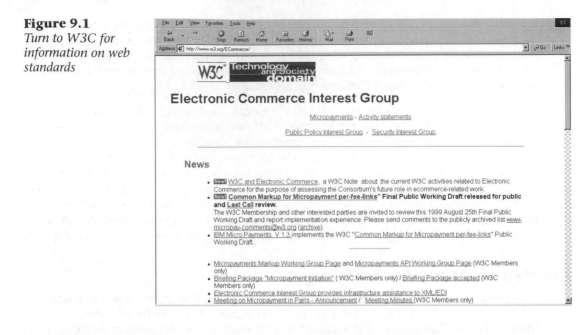

Supplier Buy-In

In general, people resist change, and people want control. These are two of the biggest roadblocks to successfully automating the supplier portion of the supply chain. Most of your suppliers have systems and operations that are no doubt unparalleled in efficiency and effectiveness. Or at least that's what they believe. If you now tell them that you want them to change these processes, you are likely to receive significant resistance to this effort. Simply put, people resist change and want to be in control so that unless your orders are of significant size, your ability to change your suppliers' operations will be limited.

The best approach is to give them a dozen copies of this book, try to persuade them to your way of thinking, and provide them with options that are easy to implement or adjust. Some of the most successful supplier automation programs start with the vendor as a development team member included in the process from the start. This assists in lowering supplier resistance and leads to the design of better systems.

Step Two: Automating The Receiving Process

Now that order information is being captured and processed automatically, the next step is to automate the receiving process. This step consists of two pieces:

1. Receiving the product into stock.
2. Confirming and tracking the shipping of products delivered directly to customers.

What will drive this process will be the receipt of goods at the warehouse or the confirmation of delivery to the customer.

A Standard Model For Receiving Stock

➤ Order product.

➤ Set up a supplier information object.

➤ Set up a stock information object.

➤ Create a purchase order using the supplier and stock objects as inputs.

➤ Deliver the purchase order information to the supplier.

➤ When the product arrives or is delivered, add items to the stock as received.

➤ Create the payment file (this can be automatic or based on an invoice).

➤ Create the final product (the new stock item may include multiple old stock items).

➤ Transfer items between types of stock (raw material to finished goods).

If every input into an organisation is treated in a similar fashion, including the application of labour and overhead as an instantaneous stock (the costs flow into a pool and then get allocated to the final product cost), the ability to create a real-time financial system is relatively easy.

To automate the receiving process, the information used to produce the purchase order (PO) can also be used to acknowledge receipt of the product. In older receiving models, a purchase order is printed and mailed, and the receiving information is keyed into the system when the product is received. You can automate this process by having re-order information posted to a secure server for pick-up by the supplier, allowing your supplier to view your stock levels online to automatically ship the product, or by pushing re-order information to the supplier's website or system.

In our automated supply chain, barcodes could be attached to products that are shipped from the supplier if your supplier agrees or has standard codes already affixed to the product. However, having the supplier barcode such information as the PO number, product count item number, and even bin locations on packages would greatly aid in the automation of the receiving process. When the product arrives at the warehouse, the receiver can simply scan the code with a reader, and the system will

The Barcode

A barcode is a series of vertical black lines of varying width separated by white spaces, most commonly used on grocery products. A barcode can be used to represent various alphanumeric information, such as stock item numbers. This information can then be attached to a product and read by a scanning device that uses lasers to read the dark and light areas of the bar code. A computer interprets the data for use by an application. Organisations set standards so that product manufacturers and suppliers can read the codes on all products regardless of the hardware and software used.

match the item to an order, update the stock level, release the PO for payment, or cause an automated warehouse to store the product on a shelf.

The Automated Warehouse – A Hypothetical Example

The automated warehouse works like this. A product is received on the loading dock, is read into stock by a barcode reader, and then is placed in one of a series of standard plastic bins by the receiver. An automated placement system controls a series of belts that accept these standard plastic bins and pass them to a tagging system (larger products are stored on pallets and placed by forklift robots). The tagging system reads a barcode card that is attached to the bin, and the bin is then sent along a series of belts to narrow storage isles where a placement robot will store the bin and transmit the location to the inventory system. Multiples, or groupings, of product are placed in dynamic bins that are reset when the warehouse staff takes an item from the bin.

Figure 9.2
Barcodes allow computers to scan information directly from labels. This barcode is for a book (all book barcodes begin with the numbers 978)

ISBN 0-13-020886-8

9 780130 208866

When a customer places an order for a product, the system knows exactly how much of the product is available and where the product is stored. It uses the reverse of the storage process to extract the items for shipping, automatically prints and attaches delivery information to the box, and then sends it to the loading dock.

Automating Delivery Systems

Another area that can be easily automated is the delivery of product. Many of today's largest courier companies are already a great distance down the e-commerce path, such as FedEx and its Internet shipping service. Its ability to track a package is unrivalled by other industries and relies heavily on real-time systems, extensive use of barcoding, and automation.

FedEx

FedEx ships in excess of three million packages per day.

FedEx

It is highly unlikely that these companies will change their systems for your company, but as a customer, they will provide you with a variety of alternatives such as Internet access and software, and if your company is large enough, they will build an interface to your logistics systems.

Luckily, these couriers have made this quite easy for their customers by limiting the amount of information required for delivery through the use of customer account numbers and standardisation of the dynamic information such as delivery addresses. By using these standards, you can easily mirror the information within your system to

Figure 9.3 *UPS is one of many shipping and courier companies to be found on the web*

produce a delivery note. Tracking packages through the Internet is an easy way to provide your customers with a low-cost method for following their orders simply by including a tracking number from the courier in the order confirmation email and by providing a link to the courier's tracking system on your website.

If you choose to use your own delivery system, you can automate the delivery process by using tablet PCs for your delivery staff (computers that resemble the screen portion of a laptop and use a stylus or electronic pen for entering data). A tablet PC allows you to load shipment delivery information, obtain a digital signature from customers with a stylus, and easily transmit delivery information back to your system for web access by your customers. You can even incorporate GPS data (global positioning system data from satellites) into the mix by automatically tracking delivery truck positions against a database of GPS delivery locations.

GPS

Global positioning systems use a series of low-level satellites that transmit messages back to earth, comprising the satellite's position and a special digital code used to calculate the message travel time. Three of these signals can be received and used to triangulate the position of the receiving unit, called a GPS receiver. This information can then be transmitted by radio or mobile phone to a computer to track the progress of a delivery vehicle.

At this point, automated systems should allow you to order product from a supplier, receive and store the product in an inventory, track product as it moves through different inventories, and ship the product and track the movement of the package through the delivery system.

The Customer Flow

The second major type of flow in the process of automating the supply chain is the flow between the customer and the company. This flow is also known as the order/entry flow.

Customer-Powered

In the current world of order entry, customers are rarely required to enter order information. Call centres are staffed often with hundreds of operators who key in the details of customer orders and the information to establish customer accounts or payment details. Call-centre staff provide an important link to the customer and, in some instances, have been shown to add to the volume of sales. However, in most instances they provide only minimal incremental value to the organisation and are simply high-level key-entry clerks.

Standard Model Of Order Entry

1. A customer chooses to purchase a product.

2. A sales order is created or derived from a quote.

3. Stock is checked and reserved.

4. A back order is created if required.

5. Product is shipped.

6. An invoice is sent to the customer.

7. The payment is received and deposited.

8. The payment is applied to the invoice.

A better solution is to move the organisation towards an automated environment where the customer enters the order and account information directly into your system. This can be accomplished through the transmission of order information online for high-volume customers or through Internet order systems for low-volume transactions. The key to the success of this type of migration is simplicity of use. If your customers find it complicated or time-consuming, they will not use your system.

The major benefit of this type of program is that your call-centre key-entry staff can now be directed to perform value-added functions, such as help desk, service, and sales or data mining. The downside is that you will still require some level of call-centre

Figure 9.4
EasyJet's order-entry screen allows customers to choose their preferences before being automatically handled by its back-end systems

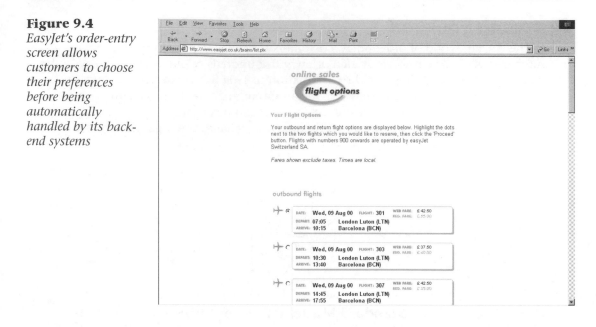

operation for those customers who refuse to deal with a machine or are not sophisticated enough to place their own orders. You will also have to dedicate staff to assist customers who want to transfer bulk information electronically (this should be easier when standards for e-commerce ordering are set and accepted).

The Simple Online Order System

➤ Step 1: Create a web page form that is comprised of:

– A series of check boxes beside a list of your product's description, prices, and an image.

– A series of entry boxes for customer information.

– A link to a secure credit card server.

➤ Step 2: Wait for orders via email.

e-Commerce Solutions

Businesses have created systems that customers can access directly through phones or dial-up software, but these are restricted either to those customers who have the accessing hardware and software or by the limitations of phone systems. So the obvious choice for effective automated order entry is the Internet, and it is such a good option that it is the only one we will discuss. Almost everybody in Europe has access to it (or knows someone who has), and the standards used in the Internet, such as HTML and forms, make it an ideal automation solution.

We will discuss some aspects of marketing in later chapters, but for now let's assume that customers are interested in doing business with your company. The first step in the order/entry automation process is to create a method for allowing your customers to create accounts or access existing account information. This is the personal information related to a customer, and it is essential in order to complete the order and to manage and mine the information related to that customer (we will discuss data mining in more detail later).

Another critical function is the presentation of decision-making information to the customer. This includes everything from a catalogue of items and prices to detailed company or product information. Your website will provide the medium for data presentation, and it should be built in such a way that the data can be easily updated or automatically updated in real time by your internal systems.

Your customer must also be able to assemble an order easily. This is usually accomplished by purchasing either shopping cart software or by utilising the services of an online shopping company.

The final piece is the capture of payment information, usually processed through a secure connection to a secure server so that others are unable to see your credit card information. All of these technologies are available and easy to implement.

The Least You Need To Know

➤ Define what a supply chain is.

➤ Understand how to automate the supply process.

➤ Know how to automate the receiving process.

➤ What options are available to automate the delivery process.

➤ How to automate the customer order-entry process.

➤ Identify e-commerce solutions to managing customer orders.

The Customer Is King

In This Chapter

➤ Defining on–demand customer service

➤ Different types of call centres

➤ The virtual call centre

➤ The web information model

➤ Outsourcing your customer service

On–Demand Customer Service

In the previous section, we discussed briefly some of the issues related to automating the call centre, specifically the order-entry functions. On the surface, the goal of automating the call centre appears to be the reduction of staff levels, but in reality the goal is to reduce the cost of activities that provide little or no return on investment. These costs are associated with employees whose primary task is to enter order information into an order-entry system. Most organisations will still require some form of call centre, depending on the size of the operation and the success of their website, to provide easy and clear assistance to their customers.

Tasks Handled By A Call Centre

There are a variety of tasks handled by a customer call centre that all pertain to the interaction between a company and its customers. These include the following:

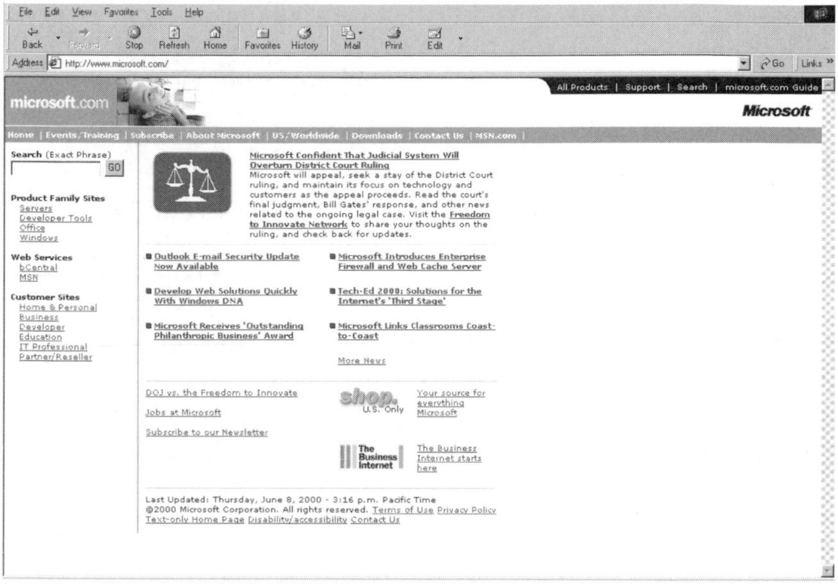

Figure 10.1
*Microsoft provides
plenty of online
customer
information at its
website*

➤ Entering customer orders for callers unable to complete an order online.

➤ Providing information about the company, products, or services.

➤ Customer product assistance (help desk).

➤ Contact management (directing incoming calls).

➤ Investor relations.

➤ Emergencies.

Most of these tasks can be handled online over the Internet by an effectively designed website. However, larger organisations and those with critical support programs (emergency assistance) may still require a 'live' call centre. A visit to the Microsoft website will show that it provides an extensive amount of online information, but no two-way, online sales support for potential customers. Support shortcomings such as this won't impact the Microsoft bottom line, but they will significantly impact the bottom line of other organisations that have stronger competition.

Why A Call Centre?

Should you have a call centre at all? This is a difficult but essential decision for any organisation. The trade-off is simple – a call centre provides your customers with a human voice to talk to for service, support, and sales information, but the downside is the very high cost of staffing. Some of these costs can be reduced with the use of an online or virtual help centre to handle some of the questions from customers.

The balance between the costs of the call centre and financial rewards that are derived from customer satisfaction must be weighed carefully. Just to make the decision a bit more complicated, consider that the larger and better known your organisation becomes, the easier it will be for customers to get satisfaction from an online website. Smaller organisations may need a 'live' voice to close sales and build trust with new customers.

The 24/7 Call Centre

The term 24/7 refers to call centre coverage that is provided 24 hours a day, seven days a week (and nothing to do with July 24th!). This level of coverage is usually created by providing a fully staffed, 24-hour call centre. It is essential to have a 24/7 service centre if the assistance it provides is critical, such as emergency services, or if you are operating across international time zones. In most cases, however, the 24/7 call centre is a luxury that returns minimal value in the middle of the night.

The Shifting Call Centre

The shifting call centre is a term used to describe the relationship between two locations in different time zones. For example, a call centre in the UK could handle the bulk of the call traffic from 8am GMT. Then gradually throughout the day the calls could shift west starting at 4pm GMT to a call centre based on the west coast of America. The west coast call centre could close at midnight GMT and a similar operation could start off in Bombay. This so-called 'follow the sun' system could provide your worldwide customers with 24 hours of coverage using regular day shifts. The key to the success of shifting call centres is telephony management software that can distribute calls between all locations throughout the day based on the level of calls.

The Online Information Centre

Information Search

4% of UK consumers use the internet to obtain information about companies and services.

Deloitte Consulting

The real focus of automating call centre functions for e-commerce is the development of the online or Internet-based information centre. Its greatest benefit is a 24-hours-a-day virtual operation. The greatest problem is that the information is either static (unchanging) or delayed (online responses via email). The structure that you use to build the virtual information centre will define its effectiveness and success. It is usually broken into a few main areas.

Information

The information section provides static information about the company, products, services, pricing, and delivery or contact information. It is simply a series of searchable web pages of general or specific information.

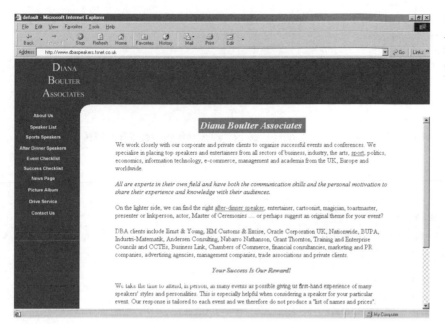

Figure 10.2
A website is normally made up of a series of individual web pages

Frequently Asked Questions

The second piece is a frequently asked questions (FAQ) section. This section is also a group of HTML documents or series of organised links that list the previous questions asked by other customers and the answers provided by the company. This section should also be linked to a form that allows your customers to send their own questions. Most ISPs provide auto-response software that will confirm that the form has been received.

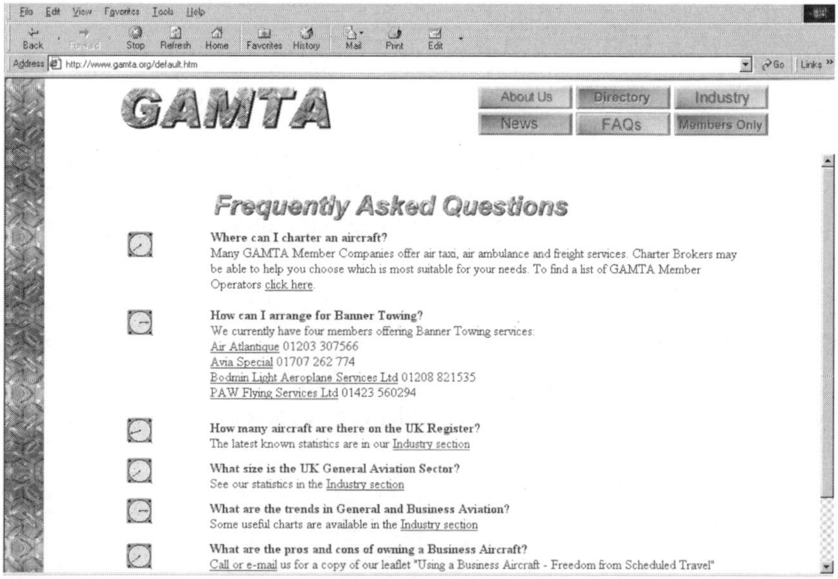

Figure 10.3
Frequently Asked Questions is a standard method of supplying easy navigation to all the information your customers might normally be seeking

Fastest And Slowest e-Commerce Websites In The UK

May 2000 with the average web page download time in seconds ...

Fastest

1.	lycos.co.uk (search engine)	8.34
2.	excite.co.uk (search engine)	8.43
3.	easyjet.com (travel)	10.78
4.	thetrainline.com (travel)	11.41
5.	go–fly.com (travel)	14.71

Slowest

1.	hmv.co.uk (CDs and videos)	51.42
2.	bookshop.blackwell.co.uk (books)	47.87
3.	yahoo.co.uk (search engine)	47.7
4.	egg.com (financial services)	47.6
5.	sony.co.uk (electrical goods)	46.29

Source: www.cacheflow.com

The Chat Room

Often, companies will provide an online chat facility to allow customers to meet to discuss issues or to meet online live technical support staff (*see* Figure 10.4). This is an excellent way to provide live assistance without long-distance telephone charges. Some organisations are even supplying video links.

The Site Search Engine

Another important piece of an information centre is a document search engine for locating specific references to a word or phrase, both in the company website and on the Internet (*see* Figure 10.5).

Figure 10.4
A chat room allows online visitors to post and read electronic messages

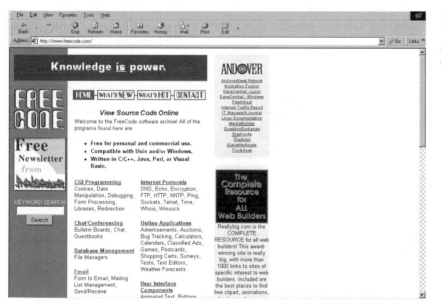

Figure 10.5 *Many websites offer keyword searches as a quick route through*

Customer Transactions

Customers should be given the opportunity to place orders, obtain downloads, or access functionality or online programs (for example, web casts) easily and efficiently. The instructions should be logical and simple, and online wizards should be provided for more complex orders.

The Online Help Desk

When customers have a question about your company or products, they usually expect a direct point of contact with your organisation. You provide this service either to encourage sales, in the case of those customers seeking product information, or to assist with product usage so that customers will be satisfied with your products or service. Dissatisfied customers have a direct negative impact on future sales in that they will be less likely to purchase new products from you – as well as telling all their friends!

So the two key functions provided by the help desk are answers to questions and product use assistance. One easy way to do this is to provide a well-organised series of online help tutorials that take a user through actions on a step-by-step basis. You can also link to online tutorials with online organisations. Answers to questions are most efficiently provided in a FAQ section with an associated FAQ search engine. Instead of answering the same question hundreds of times for individual customers, the FAQ provides one answer that all the customers can access.

When The Virtual Help Desk Fails

Nothing is more frustrating than having to spend an hour to solve a five-minute problem. Many of the online help functions available today are disorganised and use voluminous dumps of FAQs that can cause a user to spend hours searching for information. Embedded search engines especially often return results that are not related to the question.

A Bad Search

We had a question about the registration wizard in Office2000. The registration wizard forces you to register the product with Microsoft every single time it is installed. Our question was, 'What would happen if a user has more than one PC, loses a PC, changes a hard drive or upgrades, etc.?'

1. We started by surfing to www.microsoft.com

2. We went straight to the search option and typed 'registering more than one copy of office2000'. We got a 'no results' message.

3. We narrowed the search to 'registering Office2000'. We got a 'no results' message.

4. We returned to the main page and selected 'support', 'home customer', and 'online support'.

5. We chose 'search personal' and entered 'Office2000', 'registration', and 'go'. We received five responses, none with any reference to registering Office2000.

6. We tried the Office2000 troubleshooter and, after reading 20 responses, found there was no information on registration.

7. We returned to the main page and searched by product, selecting 'office', 'downloads & support', 'support online', and 'using Microsoft Office'. The result was a blank page.

8. We backed up and tried 'installing Microsoft Office'. The result was a blank page.

9. After a quick search, we found there was no place to submit a FAQ.

10. We gave up.

You can try this search by starting at www.microsoft.com to see whether they have changed anything.

A Good Search

1. We started by surfing to www.microsoft.com

2. We went straight to the search option and typed 'digital nervous system'.

3. We got 20 responses related to the 'digital nervous system'.

The only problem is that this isn't really a good search, just a lucky one.

Bad and Good FAQs

More often than not, long lists of FAQs force users to scroll through one page after another to find an answer to their question. Companies tend to dump information website, anticipating that its customers will magically find the answers, but the risk is that customer attention spans and tempers are very short. (This is one of the main sources of so-called 'e-rage'.) There is definitely a growing dissatisfaction with the ability to get good information from the Internet, and as companies heap more rubbish into their websites, customers will look elsewhere for information.

Clearly organising your data, providing a search engine that ranks responses, eliminating extraneous or old documents, and giving the customers an easy way to communicate a question and receive an answer are vital elements in building a

A Simple Web Information Model

1. Design the information in an outline before placing it on the Internet and design it for use from the user's point of view. There are a number of website design programs available to assist in the task.

2. Use graphical images that imply their function or indicate what they are linking to.

3. Use different categories to sort links so that customers can access the same information from different paths (for example, by product, by type of information, and by type of problem).

4. Use the three-click rule – in general, it should take no more than three clicks for a customer to access the information she needs.

5. Limit the total number of links per page while still trying to follow the three-click rule because too many links can make it confusing for visitors.

6. FAQs should have a way for someone to submit a FAQ and should have a ranking search engine that ranks searches by the most popular related request or by number of references to the search phrase.

7. Search engines should be accessible from every page.

8. Search engines should only pull up information that is relevant to the type of search (sales information should be only sales information). Extraneous web documents should be excluded.

9. Design the site so that the information has a logical flow. A customer should always know where she is in the site.

successful virtual call centre. This will result in good FAQ lists that are relevant
informative while reducing the amount of time for the majority of users.

Customer-Driven Service

The primary goal of automating a call centre is to get the customers to do the work of
order entry and searching for support information. They will perform these functions
as long as the process is easy, fast, and efficient. If the process is cumbersome, difficult,
and slow, you will get customer dissatisfaction and a reputation for poor service. This
will ultimately lead to reduced sales.

One definite disadvantage to the Internet is that customer dissatisfaction on the
Internet travels very fast and very far. Customers are becoming more savvy at using
online information from other customers to select products and services, and
newsgroups are an ideal festering ground for dissatisfaction with companies to be
publicly voiced.

Anticipating Your Customers' Needs

An important part of any information centre is the need to anticipate your customers'
requests. For example, if you design a software package with a new security algorithm
embedded in the code that will be frustrating to your customers, you can mitigate negative
customer feelings by adding help information to your website in a visible and easy-to-

The World's Mobile Phone Users By Technology

With all the different mobile phone technologies you can identify potential
target markets and trends by seeing who uses what and where ... to see where
the growth areas are (May 2000).

GSM	236 869 140	AMPS	69 378 380	CDMA	48 520 720
PDC	45 621 600	USTDMA	33 111 560	TACOS	10 665 630
NMT-450	1 571 400	NMT-900	1 092 850	C450	169 200
RC2000	0				

Source: www.emc.com

access area. This will help answer your customers' questions and reduce the number of direct calls that have to be managed by your staff. If you do not anticipate your customers' information requirements, the cost will be additional resources and lost sales.

Data Mining Your Service Information

One process that will add immense value to the information centre is data mining your service information to change the actual product or service, assist in the design of new products or services, assist in the design of web information, or to anticipate new problems. Some of the best research available to any company is in the information requests by its own customers. For example, if customers continually ask whether your product can perform a new function, changing the product to add this functionality may increase sales.

Outsourcing Customer Service

Many organisations are wrestling with the concept of outsourcing. There are numerous horror stories of companies that have outsourced internal functions, only to be later held to ransom by the outsourcing company. Also, critical functions, such as customer service, directly impact sales and therefore have to be closely monitored and controlled. By passing these responsibilities to another company, you limit your control and flexibility over functions that may be essential to achieve excellent customer service. However, it is clear that there is great financial potential to be gained from the efficiencies of using an outsourced call centre.

At this point your company has started to automate processes, defined how to process orders and ship product (supply chain), and now how to support those customers.

The Outsourcing Checklist

1. Carefully study your operations to determine any potential impact from outsourcing. For example, if you outsource your accounting function, determine the impact on such areas as daily management, customer service, etc.

2. Review outsourcing options, verify company reputations and financial stability, and check references (nobody supplies a bad reference, so ask for a

complete list of past customers and a reference list, and then cold call the customers not listed on the reference list).

3. Ensure that the terms of service are detailed in legally binding agreements that include clear and firm pricing, disaster recovery guarantees, the level of resources guaranteed by the outsourcing company, benchmarks and performance measures, reporting, tasks and responsibilities, rewards for performance, etc.

4. Develop a contingency plan to reintroduce the function into the organisation on short notice.

5. Carefully monitor the work performed by the outsourcing company and the results of this work, such as reports, programs, content creation, etc.

6. Make sure your customer and company information is secure at the outsourcing company by reviewing its security procedures and store backups of your company data and outsourcing systems at your site.

The Least You Need To Know

➤ How to define on-demand customer service.

➤ Learning the pros and cons of different types of call centres.

➤ The key is to understand FAQs, have a reliable help desk, and anticipate your customers' needs.

➤ Learn how to use a web information model.

➤ Learn how to use the outsourcing checklist.

Chapter 11

Show Me The Money

In This Chapter

➤ What electronic funds transfers are and how they help your online business

➤ Making and receiving payments electronically

➤ What types of security concerns exist

➤ Security solutions available to businesses, including SSL

➤ e-Banks: the new online banking alternative

Electronic Funds Transfer (EFT)

Perceived value is the foundation of any economy and forms the basis of all trade. We measure the worth of something by its value even when we do not use currency. If value was to disappear from an economy so would the economy. For example, the Internet is successful because we perceive that it provides something of value (information), and we pay for the right to use it. When we conduct business on the Internet, we are looking to trade something of value (cash) for something else of value (product, knowledge or service). But we will do this only if the value that we derive is greater than the cost. Even though the current primary use of the Internet is communications (email) and information gathering and dissemination, shopping is growing rapidly as a favourite pastime of surfers, and as long as people continue to perceive a benefit to online shopping, this growth will continue.

So what's the point? The point is that we will shop as long as there is value in lower prices, satisfaction guarantees for products or services, and very low consumer risk. The

Figure 11.1
*Maelstrom is one of
thousands of sites
offering visitors a
bewildering array of
products*

failure of any of these could shake the foundation of e-commerce. So businesses have to be very careful about how they conduct business on the Internet, especially where payments are concerned.

Businesses such as Amazon learned very early that the real value in the Internet was not just to provide information but also to provide access to products. One of the greatest hurdles to overcome was convincing customers to send credit card information over the Internet and trust the company.

Internet Customers And Payments

People are often afraid to send their credit card information over the Internet. What a surprise! With all the ways your information can be used against you, it is a wonder any business is done at all. Customers are far more wary about providing credit information than ever before. Originally, only computer software vendors that were well known in the tight-knit Internet community were able to succeed at getting credit card sales, but now every company that sells something is sporting a net address, and they all store credit and sales data. The greatest threat to Internet sales growth is the press story waiting in the wings about some company that has had its customer database hacked for credit card numbers, identities, expiration dates, home addresses, e-mail addresses, and even products recently purchased.

To reduce the threat of this potential disaster, a number of new companies have been trying some innovative approaches. Companies that pay the vendor through the Internet without sending your personal credit information or banks that use electronic payments are two examples of new services that are reducing the risk of providing credit information.

Payment Types

There are two primary flows of funds inside companies:

1. Payments received from your customers.
2. Payments made to your suppliers (including employees that supply labour and governments that supply bureaucracy).

As an incoming payment becomes due to an organisation, it is set up as a receivable amount or sales ledger item in the books; as an outgoing payment becomes due, it is set up as a payable amount or bought ledger item. When the actual payment is made, these accounts are reduced, and the offsetting entry becomes an outstanding item in the bank account. This simplified process is one of the largest contributors to overhead expenses in most modern organisations. The problem arises as a result of the differences between keeping track of the actual cash and reconciling this amount back to the general, or nominal, ledger as well as bank accounts. In addition, money has a time value that must be managed, and if you use different currencies, movements in these currencies will result in losses (and gains!). Large and expensive treasury and accounting operations have grown to fill the roles of cash and risk management.

One goal of e-commerce is to reduce these expenses by streamlining the cash collection and payment operations. In Chapter 9 on automating the supply chain, we saw that the receipt and payment processing functions could be automated along with the rest of the supply chain. The receipt of an actual product or confirmation of delivery to the customer could automatically produce vendor payment information, and customer payments could be automatically deposited when they are received through the use of credit card software.

Payments In – Receipt Of Payments

Payments come from three sources:

1. Retail customers.
2. Wholesale customers.
3. Various miscellaneous payments (i.e. everyone else).

Prior to the growth of online electronic payment methodologies, most of these payments were received in cash or cheques and periodically the organisation would make a physical deposit at a bank. Newer electronic methodologies allowed funds to flow faster through the use of telegraphic transfers that did not require a physical deposit. Although the funds were electronically deposited to the bank account, the downside was the high cost to use the service. In the early 1970s, major banks began a concerted effort to allow companies to transfer funds electronically direct from one bank account to another.

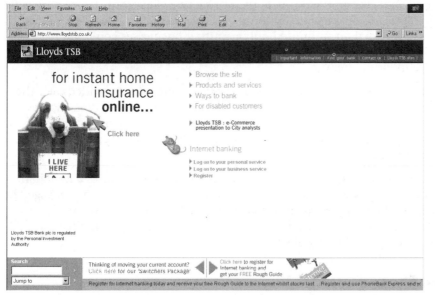

Figure 11.2 *Most UK banks are now offering their customers the facility of online banking*

Modern Payment Systems

The introduction of PCs and modems resulted in the development of externally accessible bank systems known as PC banking. Companies could sign on to the bank systems using PCs and transfer funds through EFTs or telegraphic transfers (TTs). In addition, electronic data interchange usually incorporated an EFT component that allowed an organisation to accept invoice documents and automatically generate payments after the documents were verified.

By the late 1970s, retail customers could make payments to companies through direct debit (automatic withdrawals from the customer's bank account) or ATMs. Payments using these methods transfer funds from the customer's bank account directly to the company's account. Today, there are numerous payment options available, most with an EFT component.

Credit Cards – A (Very) Brief History

The history of credit goes back as far as the beginning of trade. It is likely that promises of future payments were made early in the history of mankind and thus started the provision of credit – and probably the first bad debt!

In 1958, the Bank of America issued a blue, gold and white card in California that allowed a select group of users to pay for products at participating merchants without cash. The users would then pay the bank at a later date for the purchased items.

One of the advantages to using credit cards is that users no longer have to carry cash to pay for a product. In the early days, simply providing a credit card so that the number could be imprinted was enough to complete the transaction. Electronic processing was introduced later to provide online authorisation and depositing functions. In the late 1990s, the Internet provided an unlimited opportunity if businesses could get paid for products or services sold electronically. The inevitable marriage of the two technologies was a match made in virtual heaven.

At first, credit card numbers, user names, and expiration dates were provided over the Internet in insecure forms. This process has since been updated to include measures that ensure your credit data is not visible to other users (encryption) and a way to ensure that the party you are sending your information to is the only company receiving it (authentication).

To accept credit cards as a payment option, you simply have to sign on as a merchant with your bank or credit card organisation. You will be required to pay a percentage fee from 1% to 3% depending on your turnover and the products sold. There are also a number of vendors on the Internet that will process the credit information for you once it has been entered into their website.

Credit Card Processing

After a customer has supplied you with her credit card number, name, and expiration date, two things must occur to complete the transaction:

1. The credit card must be authenticated with the credit card company so that you can receive an authorisation number. This provides a limited guarantee that the funds will be made available to you when you complete your deposits by ensuring the user of the card is not over her credit limit and that the card has not been stolen.

Figure 11.3
Cybercash specialises in processing electronic payments on the web

2. The electronic credit card information must be turned into an actual deposit at your financial institution.

Some companies, such as Cybercash, provide Internet payment processing software that can accept and process credit card information to receive online authorisations (*see* Figure 11.3). They can also provide software for linking to your financial institution to create electronic credit card deposits.

Electronic Cheques

Electronic cheques are used to make electronic payments between two parties through an intermediary. This is not much different from the current cheque processing system except that electronic cheques are generated and exchanged online. The intermediary will debit the customer account and credit the merchant account.

Micropayments

Micropayments are cash payments that are made as a result of using a service on the Internet. They are also made between two or more Internet companies to help generate traffic through links. The way a micropayment works is that a company usually registers with an organisation that verifies and reports on traffic levels between sites. Next, a very small payment per link or per click is calculated and when the total owing reaches a specified threshold, the payment is released from either the customer's actual

The Traffic/Micropayment Model

Company A offers Company B a fee for each user it sends to Company A's website. The users will link to the A site from a link on B's home page. Company A can manage the process, or it can register with an organisation that will track incoming messages for it. When the number of visits reaches a certain threshold that makes economic sense, a payment is made from Company A to Company B. The main reason for using a third party to track pay-per-click micropayments is to reduce the potential of fraud. These organisations will manage the security aspects of these programs to ensure that the traffic generated is not repeat traffic or that it has not been artificially created by Company B.

or virtual bank account to the vendor's account. Micropayments are used to charge visitors to websites for using games, viewing pictures, and so on. They are also used between Internet companies to pass payments from one company to another for the generation of traffic to the website through the use of links.

Payment Security

There are a number of ways that criminals will attempt to steal or alter payment information. The intent is to capture personal financial information such as credit card numbers, the name on the card, and the expiration date. This information can then be used to purchase other goods online for delivery to a temporary address. By the time the fraud is detected, the perpetrators have disappeared. These techniques include spoofing, sniffing, content alteration, and denial.

Spoofing

Spoofing is the act of mimicking a legitimate website including layout, colours, and function to obtain credit card information or steal business. The technique involves registering a domain name that is very similar to a legitimate sales site, but is perhaps different by a single letter such as Amazin.com.

The illegal website then copies the text and graphics of the legitimate site and builds some functionality to mimic the feel of the links contained in the site. The next step is to offer a popular product at a ridiculous price to entice people to send their credit information. Of course, not all sites that mimic using the misspelling technique are

Figure 11.4
Unfortunately spoofing is all too common an occurrence by web fraudsters

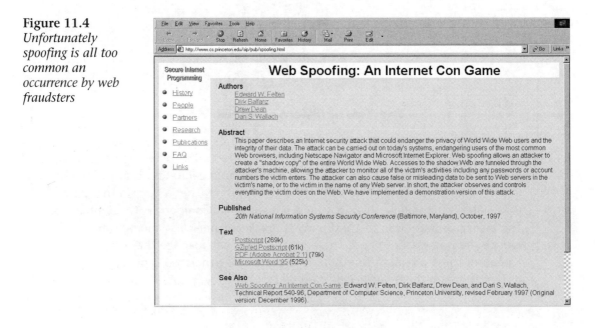

bad; some are just creatively diverting business to their legitimate site. Others are simply capitalising on famous phrases. For example, at the time of writing, www.whitehouse.com was a pornography site.

Sniffing

Sniffing is a term used to describe the act of reading unprotected packet information as it travels over a network. The act of sniffing packets is relatively simple with the use of various network-sniffing software programs that were originally designed to assist in network error detection. Sophisticated hackers lurk or watch for messages to and from certain IP addresses, and if they find something, sell the information to criminals or competitors.

Content Alteration

One method of diverting payments would be to intercept a bank account number and change it to another. This is called content alteration, and is used by sniffers who capture the packets, alter the content, and then send the new packet to its intended recipient. Another piece of information that could be altered is the shipping address for an order.

Security Breaches!

60% of organisations have suffered a security breach in the past two years, yet 63% have not carried out a risk assessment of security risks.

75% of those who suffered a serious security breach had no contingency plan, yet 40% of security breaches reported were actually down to operator or user error.

DTI survey

Denial

This illegal technique involves conducting business with an organisation electronically and then denying that the transaction occurred, or denying it was ever initiated. An Internet user may order product on a credit line and have it shipped to another location. Then, when the bill is received, the user denies that he ever ordered the product.

Security Over Networks

There are a number of ways to combat these fraud techniques by using existing products and technology available in the market. The goal is to implement enough security on your network so that it is protected without limiting the users so much that they are ineffective at completing tasks. Another concern is the high cost of managing the security function or the high cost of outsourcing. If you sell 100 T-shirts a year and lose one to a bogus order or fraud during the same time frame, it is unlikely that using an Internet security service will be cost justified.

Secure Socket Layer

Secure socket layer (SSL) is a technology that encrypts or encodes the packets of information sent over the Internet so that only the sending and receiving computers can reassemble and read the information. Encryption is used along with registered certificates that use a third-party registration service to confirm that your customers are actually connected to your site. The combination of SSL and certificates makes transactions very secure.

When you establish a connection to a secure server, the two computers will agree on an encryption algorithm and cryptographic keys that are used by SSL to scramble and reassemble packets of information. Keys (or codes) are provided to users in pairs, with one key kept private and the other made public. When secure communication is required, an external party will use the public key to communicate with you. Only the matching private key can decode a message that is coded by a public key, and a message coded with a private key can only be decoded with the matching public key.

Figure 11.5 *SSL connections provide online users with a secure connection to a website. Note the padlock at the bottom of the browser, and the fact that the URL begins 'https'*

160

An Example Of Keys

Let's say that two people each have a set of cryptographic keys, and they want to send each other a secure message. Party A would encode the message using her private key and then re-encode the message using the public key of Party B. The result is that when Party B receives the multi-encoded message, he will first decode it using his private key (so only he will be able to decode it) and then use Party A's public key to complete the decoding process. If a sniffer gets the packet, his ability to decode the message will be virtually impossible.

Certificates

Certificates are encrypted files that are stored on your web server and usually registered with a third party. The files then communicate with your customer's browser to confirm that the site they are accessing is in fact yours. These can also be used to authenticate users that access your networks from both outside and inside the office. In this instance, you would provide a certificate to a specific individual who would then store the file on her computer. When she signed onto your system, the server would search for the certificate before allowing access.

Public Key Infrastructure

Public key infrastructure (PKI) is the engine that drives certificates. It is essentially a mechanism for the storage of public keys along with a certificate that identifies the owner. Certificate authorities (CAs) perform the PKI management function by registering end users, validating their identity, revoking certificates, and distributing the CA's certificate widely through software such as browsers. For intranets, this task is sometimes performed by owner organisations, but for the Internet, the task is usually outsourced to an existing CA, such as Verisign.

Verisign Website

Verisign is one organisation that provides online certificates. You can get more information at http://www.verisign.com

Figure 11.6
Browsers can be set up to search for online certificates and to warn when authenticity cannot be confirmed

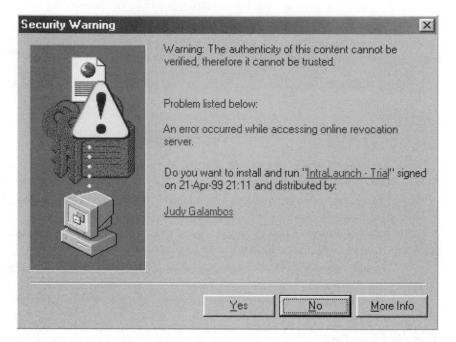

By implementing SSL on your servers and using certificates, you can provide a secure method for your customers to communicate with your website to exchange information, make payments, order product, and so on.

How It All Hangs Together

All of the preceding security measures can be used to tighten the security for electronic payments as well as all types of transactions and information distributed over intranets, extranets, and Internets. Maintaining security helps customers and website visitors feel more secure and this helps encourage them to buy products. It also helps keep your business information and transactions private.

Authentication (Protection Against Spoofing)

SSL and encryption technology will allow a user to obtain a registered public key to decipher messages from a particular source. The certificate authority will provide a certificate electronically when you initiate a secure transaction with a registered company. Most companies will post a link to a secure server, and the connection will cause a certificate to be sent to your browser. The certificate verifies the identity of the company that you are connecting to. In this instance, a spoofing site would not have the capability to provide the same information, and as the use of certificates grows, the ability to successfully spoof sites will decline. That is, until they find a way to spoof certificates.

Privacy (Protection Against Sniffing)

To ensure that information cannot be read, encryption will provide a method for sending information without any risk, as long as the dual-key, multi-key encryption technique described here is used. After you have obtained a public cryptographic key from the party you are communicating with and have stored it, you can encrypt a message using your browser's security function. Remember that in order to encrypt the message, the receiver must possess a corresponding key to decode it. Any public certificates will be automatically remembered by your system for later use.

Content Integrity (Protection Against Altered Content)

The use of encryption provides one of the easiest methods for determining whether the content of a transmission has been altered. In the first place, the only key that can decode a message is the public key of the sender. If another party alters the message, it will be decoded as garbage because he does not have the ability to code it (private key) or if he did encode it using the public key, you could not read it (you don't have the private key). Any attempt to decode an altered packet would result in garbage.

Non-Repudiation (Protection Against Denial)

If an encoded message is sent to you and you use a public key and certificate to decode it, it must come from the registered owner of the certificate. In fact, the certificate authority will guarantee its authenticity. That way 'he said, she said, we said' will never be an issue ... as long as you understand the language of the message.

Payments Out

The second type of payment that flows through an organisation is that made to your suppliers. For many years, organisations have had the capability to make direct deposit payments to employee bank accounts via BACS. All this required was the employees' banking details. Because the organisation created and controlled the payment information file, it was unlikely that there would be any of the difficulties usually associated with dynamic external payments (such as supplies). Payments for supplies require more work to verify the accuracy of the transaction, review invoices and shipments, and verify the total price. Employee information, on the other hand, is relatively static. The same amount of information is still required, but gathering it in the first place could take considerably longer.

Electronic Data Interchange

EDI allowed some organisations to streamline the payment process by making the invoice review task more automated. A supplier would send the invoice to your bank, and the bank would interpret the invoice into an EDI standard. This file could then be sent to your data processing department for processing by your internal procurement system. Once approval was received to pay the supplier, the bank would initiate an electronic funds transfer. Some banks even provided a matching service that would match supplier invoices to pre-approved purchase orders and then automatically pay the invoice through an EFT if a match was found.

Even though this process reduced the significant expense of processing cheques at the bank, very little of these savings ever reached the companies. Remittance forms still had to be printed and mailed, and the cost of implementing EDI interpreters or using the bank networks and services was very high. Usually, only the largest organisations had the resources to implement such a programme.

The Newest Arrivals On The Payment Scene

Payments can now easily be made through online banking programs that provide the company with the ability to send e-cheques over the Internet. Using this model, the company could transfer funds to another company's bank account using a method similar to telegraphic transfer. The process would include the registration of the payee (supplier) and the transmission of payment instructions using the security measures defined above. Remittance information would be emailed to the payee company at the same time.

A modification to this model could be for a company to establish an e-bank distribution account that disperses a deposit of funds to other registered e-bank accounts. Each vendor would sign up for a free account that would then automatically transfer funds to their main bank account or hold the funds in the e-bank for investment, etc. This allows larger organisations and trading groups legally to become banks without the usual regulatory approval (as they are simply managing internal payable accounts).

e-Banks

e-Banks are electronic banking organisations that provide banking services without branches, such as smile.co.uk or e-first.com. Accounts are usually created for users when they sign up. For payments to be sent, the account holder must transfer actual funds from her regular bank into her e-bank account. Those same funds can be transferred out of the account at any time. The goal is to reduce the transactional costs of traditional banking by eliminating the overhead of branches and cash handling. Lately, many variations on the e-bank model have started to crop up, including the following:

➤ Traditional banks that still charge the same fees.

➤ Entirely new electronic e-banks that charge no fees.

➤ Brokerage houses that manage electronic investment accounts.

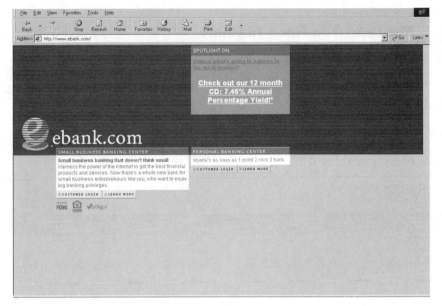

Figure 11.7
*Internet-only banks –
such as ebank.com –
are springing up all
over the place*

➤ Credit card companies that provide online credit facilities.

➤ Insurance companies that provide account operations.

➤ Crooks, conmen, and their ilk.

➤ All kinds of variations on the preceding bullets.

An e-Bank Warning

Be very careful of online e-banks. Some e-banks are fronts for organised crime, often from other countries. Some offer interest rates that sound too good to be true; and as many of them are not subject to the protection of UK jurisdiction you should be wary – unless they are now covered by the E-commerce Directive from Brussels on June 6 2000.

We suggest that you carefully check out any e-bank by doing the following:

➤ Researching the company through traditional methods (rating agencies).

➤ Verifying its existence by visiting or calling the bank.

➤ Verifying its claims with listed participants, such as official regulators, banking ombudsman, etc.

➤ Reading published articles from respected news agencies or journals.

➤ Reviewing associations.

➤ Ensuring that the site is not a spoof.

The Least You Need To Know

➤ Define various electronic payments types.

➤ Identify customer concerns regarding security.

➤ Be able to identify security risks.

➤ Understand SSL, encryption, certificates, and PKI.

➤ Identify solutions to security threats.

➤ Understand what e-banks are.

Chapter 12

The Virtual Workforce

In This Chapter

➤ Defining a virtual workforce

➤ Understanding the benefits of a virtual workforce

➤ What are virtual employees?

➤ Building virtual workspaces for virtual employees

➤ How outsourcing can help your company

➤ Building a staffless organisation

➤ The pitfalls of virtual workers

➤ Avoiding these pitfalls

What Is A Virtual Workforce?

A virtual workforce is the human resources of a virtual organisation. They are no different from any other HR group, except that they do not work on company premises. Being 'virtual' would imply that they are almost employees, but that is not the interpretation we apply to a virtual workforce. A virtual workforce is one that performs functions without a physical presence, or with only a partial physical presence, at the company workplace. They can be working offsite, or they can be working offsite occasionally and onsite occasionally. Sales or service staff who travel extensively can be considered virtual employees because they do not really perform tasks in a company-owned location unless you call their car a company-owned location.

That is the real distinction between a virtual staff and a regular offsite staff. Virtual staff do not have a physical location that they can call 'their' office. Instead, they work permanently or part-time away from the office in locations not paid for by the company. This can be a home office, an employee-owned shop, a car, or even their bed. There are three types of employees: those on company property, those who are not, and those who are a little of both – and this is a trend that is growing rapidly.

Beating The Traffic By Telecommuting

This concept of working away from the office is often called telecommuting. It is called that because the employees actually commute to work using telephone communications for computer connections and voice communication. Essentially, they are commuting through the phone to their place of work.

Telecommuting has a number of basic requirements from the company point of view. The employee must be able to communicate with the company through readily available public phone networks, and employees must have the capability to send and receive data such as emails and files, as well as access centralised applications. Essentially, this requires that the company has a network configuration capable of handling employee access whether by dial-up connection, dedicated line, or web access. It also implies that there must be a way to contact the employees if they are using the phone line, such as through email, Internet, and intranet telephony or a separate phone line. The goal is to allow the employee to work at a cheaper location than the rest of the organisation, whether that location is a satellite office or a home office.

Figure 12.1
European Telework Online is one of many sites giving useful advice for telecommuters

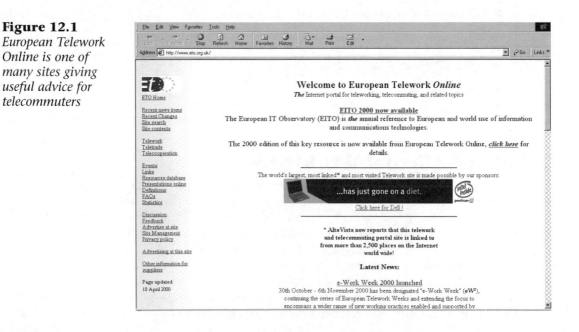

Home Office/Satellite Office

A home office is just that – an office in your home. Not the kitchen table, but an actual office or workspace off the beaten path and preferably away from the fridge and TV. Way, way away from the fridge and TV. No *Neighbours* while you work.

Satellite offices are smaller offices away from the main office, which have meeting rooms, equipment, and all the facilities of the larger offices without all the cost.

Examples Of The Virtual Workforce

Examples of virtual workforces are growing more and more prevalent. IBM, Hewlett-Packard, BT, and KPMG are some of the organisations benefiting from the move to virtual workforces. These organisations have had to overcome a series of problems associated with this way of working, such as the networking and communications logistics, the choice of employee candidates, changes to the way managers evaluate and review employees, and even the difficulty in convincing shareholders that their investment was not being misspent. In each case, the company took on the task and realised both benefits and pitfalls, but recognised that, in general, the overall results would be favourable.

The positive impact on society of a move to a virtual workforce is relatively easy to measure. Some of these benefits include the following:

➤ Lower stress levels, leading to lower health costs (but equally many feel disenfranchised and out of touch with their colleagues).

➤ More efficient productivity, resulting in more free time for employees (while the converse is also true, depending on the people and their home circumstances; in Europe, houses tend to be smaller than in the US and finding space which can be permanently allocated as a work area is more difficult).

➤ Proximity to home, leading to more mothers with valuable skills staying in the workforce.

➤ A greater understanding of technology and communications by the virtual employees.

There is no doubt that employees have to interact in order to conduct business. Some organisations have tackled this problem through the use of meeting technologies such

Figure 12.2
Microsoft NetMeeting provides an easy way for virtual employees to keep in touch with head office

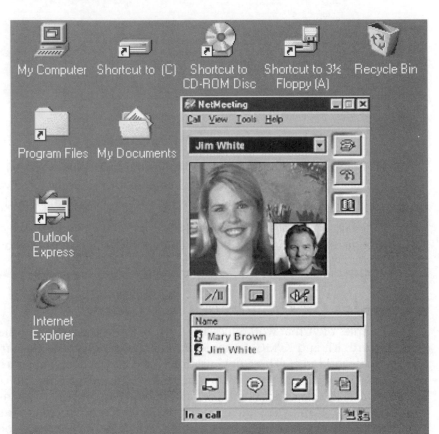

as Microsoft NetMeeting (video-conferencing software (*see* Figure 12.2) while others have approached the task by having employees coming to work periodically for 'meeting days'. The fact is that face-to-face communication is important, but does not have to happen every day. In fact, too many meetings can result in extremely low levels of productivity (if you don't believe us, read a Dilbert cartoon book). However, the sharing of ideas is an important concept in managing and ensuring the correct mix of offsite work and onsite work (video conferencing can be useful in this regard). In addition, most employees need interaction with other employees on a regular basis to make them content with their position and feel that they are part of the tribe.

The Benefits (And Downsides) Of A Virtual Workforce

There are a number of benefits from a virtual workforce for both the employee and the company. Employees who work offsite tend to appreciate the ability to focus on their tasks without interruption. This leads to a higher level of productivity without more time or greater effort. In fact, employees who have the correct environment often work in what are microbursts of productivity. During these times the employee is able to complete a significant amount of work in a short period of time. This is very similar to the effect of closing the door to your office and forwarding the phone to voice mail for a set period of time. Virtual employees also tend to have more mental space, or thinking time, leading to greater creativity. For the right employee, working virtually can result in the same or greater levels of work at a significantly reduced stress level. This results in a happier and more content employee.

Obviously these benefits depend on the personality type and motivations of the employee since the converse of the above is also possible. Some people become almost inert when left alone with no stimulus from other people. Also, briefing needs to be more comprehensive or you may find that tangential work is achieved which sets the company back instead of pushing it forward.

Offsite employees can provide a great cost saving to the organisation. Because the cost to the employee of commuting is significantly reduced, the move to an offsite work location is usually considered a significant cost benefit to the employee. However, even greater savings accrue to the organisation in the form of reduced office overhead.

Savings For The Employee From Telecommuting

The employee also significantly benefits from the 'virtualisation' of the workforce. A virtual employee can save on petrol and wear and tear on his vehicle, parking or public transport fees, fewer expensive business clothes, reduced expenses from buying restaurant or convenience lunches and drinks, and reduced costs in after-school day-care (a big expense for parents). Society benefits from telecommuting through less strain on the public

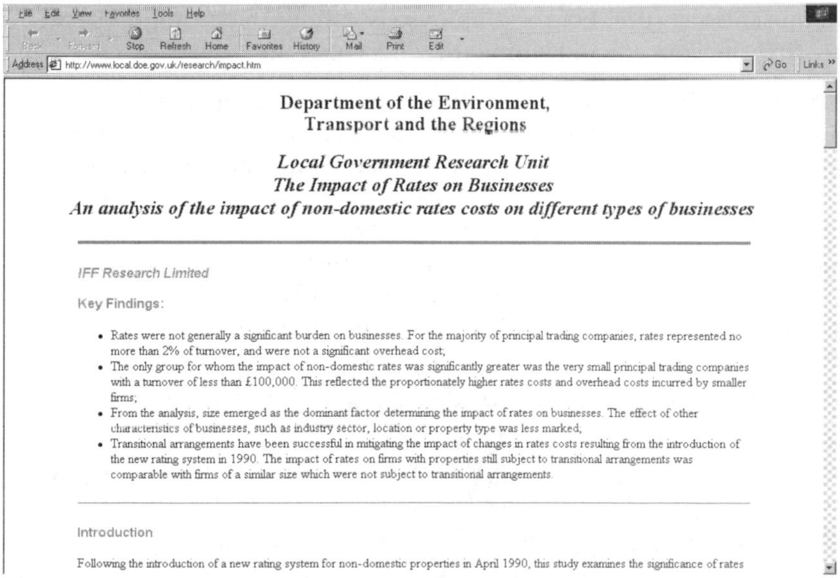

Department of the Environment,
Transport and the Regions

Local Government Research Unit
The Impact of Rates on Businesses
An analysis of the impact of non-domestic rates costs on different types of businesses

IFF Research Limited

Key Findings:

- Rates were not generally a significant burden on businesses. For the majority of principal trading companies, rates represented no more than 2% of turnover, and were not a significant overhead cost;
- The only group for whom the impact of non-domestic rates was significantly greater was the very small principal trading companies with a turnover of less than £100,000. This reflected the proportionately higher rates costs and overhead costs incurred by smaller firms;
- From the analysis, size emerged as the dominant factor determining the impact of rates on businesses. The effect of other characteristics of businesses, such as industry sector, location or property type was less marked;
- Transitional arrangements have been successful in mitigating the impact of changes in rates costs resulting from the introduction of the new rating system in 1990. The impact of rates on firms with properties still subject to transitional arrangements was comparable with firms of a similar size which were not subject to transitional arrangements.

Introduction

Following the introduction of a new rating system for non-domestic properties in April 1990, this study examines the significance of rates

Figure 12.3 *The government may conclude that rates are not a significant burden on businesses, but many would disagree!*

infrastructure such as roads, transport, and emergency services (as a result of fewer accidents). Society also benefits from having parents available for their children after school, lower stress levels in the population, and associated gains for the health system. The benefits from 'virtualising' the workforce are potentially clear and measurable.

However, beware the Chancellor! Many people do not realise that if they set aside a room for paid work they could be liable for universal business rates. Insurance for equipment, planning for health and safety requirements as well as suitable desks etc. all cost money and, if too many people work from home, the Chancellor is bound to look at this as a bonanza for clawback of benefits in kind. This, together with any anomalies which could create difficulties in the resale of a house, means that careful planning, both for the company and for each virtual employee in prospect, needs to be carried out.

How To Assess Who Can Be Made Virtual

Not every employee can be 'virtualised'. Some employees have functions that require close co-ordination with other employees or the operation of equipment that cannot be moved. Other tasks have to be situated close to customers, such as retail staff. More importantly, not all employees can be 'virtualised' because of their personalities. Some people need the interaction with co-workers, while other employees have a limited ability to focus on tasks well enough to be unsupervised.

You will also get employees who feel that if they are offsite they will not get recognition for their work and often have managers who confirm this pattern by favouring non-virtual employees. The old adage 'out of sight out of mind' is true and you must carefully evaluate whether an employee is capable of working effectively outside the office, and you must also evaluate his or her offsite work environment. The best scenario is a self-motivated employee who can work in a quiet home environment. You must also ensure that the employee is willing to become a virtual employee by discussing the concept and eliminating his concerns.

The next step in the process is to evaluate what the employee does on a daily basis to decide whether the tasks can be virtualised. Don't be too surprised if the first response from your managers is that the tasks cannot be virtualised. Managers who are afraid of losing control will meet the concept of managing employees who function outside the work environment with resistance. They will also fear that if you find out the employees can work by themselves, you will think the managers are redundant. Addressing these concerns prior to establishing a virtual workforce will smooth the transition to that state. In fact, the first people who should learn to telecommute are the managers.

When evaluating the tasks of an employee, try to decide how and when the employee will need to communicate and with whom. If these are face-to-face communications, ascertain whether they can be scheduled for onsite time periods without any impact on the performance of the task. Also search for the impact on other job-related functions that will occur because these tasks are virtualised.

The most important questions that must be addressed are whether the work can be done offsite and if so, can that work be effectively measured? If it can be measured, how will your managers set performance goals and ensure that they are being met? Measurement of the completion of tasks and work is critical. In the bricks and mortar world, your boss may call you in and give you some vague description of a task with no timeline for completion. In the virtual world, employees are considered suppliers and, as such, require a clear definition of what needs to be done, when the tasks must be completed, and what priority is assigned to the task. The implication is that your managers will have to be trained in how to make their expectations clear. One of the best ways to do this is to get those managers to start emailing project directives to employees. Once the employee is comfortable with complying with these email orders, he can start the process of becoming a virtualised employee.

One of the most critical factors is the workspace that the employee will use to work offsite. In most cases, simply letting the employee set up his worksite will be sufficient. However, to reduce the risk of working in bad environments, you can supply the employees with corporate guidelines along with a one-time bonus for equipment. Depending on the level of the work required, the environment will have a direct impact on performance.

Information On Designing Home Offices

There is a variety of information on how to design home offices at
`http://realtimes.com/rtnews/`
`rtcpages/19980304_`
`homeoffice.htm`

Quiet workspaces that are set aside specifically for the purpose are the best for virtual employees to allow them to focus on their tasks. They should also be clean, uncluttered, and comfortable. If the environment is set up to foster productivity, the employee is more likely to deliver that productivity. However, you will have to encourage some development of the offsite workspaces by providing information that helps your employees create the most productive workspace for them.

How To Manage A Virtual Employee

Managing a virtual employee is nothing like managing an onsite employee. For the vast majority of the time, you, as a manager, will have no contact with your employee. This is often a very difficult concept for a manager to accept, but the task need not be difficult. Training managers in how to set task goals and priorities, how to clearly communicate their expectations to the employees, and how to follow up with performance measures and personal discussions will reduce the problems associated with managing these employees. As long as everyone clearly understands the game plan, the team will perform up to expectations.

If the game plan is not clearly communicated, the managers should not expect goals to be met. The whole approach to managing virtual employees will require more work on the part of your managers. They will have to maintain better information on schedules and expectations. However, they can make this process easier by maintaining electronic performance templates that track the employees' incomplete tasks to a task schedule. The manager can add the tasks and the employees can maintain the information in the file.

Communicate Goals And Objectives

The key to successfully managing virtual employees is to clearly communicate goals and objectives for each employee and then identify milestones towards the completion of these goals. Setting goals is a difficult task, but can be made simple if these goals are identified and agreed to by both the virtual employee and the manager. The goals should be both attainable and measurable. If you are unable to measure the goal, you will be unable to tell how close you are to completing the goal.

The second piece of information that you will need is an estimate of the amount of time that will be required to complete the task. This is called a milestone or benchmark, and there can be one milestone per task or a number of milestones for larger tasks. Periodically, the manager of virtual employees should meet with those employees to evaluate their position in relation to these benchmarks. If the employee is 'off track', assistance should be provided to get the employee 'on track'. If missing benchmarks is a consistent behaviour and is not attributable to poor goal setting, that employee may not be suited to virtualisation.

Measuring Your Virtual Employee's Performance

Performance measurement is an integral part of goal setting. Virtual employees are given tasks and goals, and their performance is measured against these goals. However, it is also important that employees are motivated to complete these tasks by linking rewards to either individual performance or corporate performance. The obvious method for rewarding employees for corporate performance is shares or share options. The most effective way to reward employees for personal performance is a bonus. Examples of goals for employees might be to successfully complete the development of a part of an application by a specific date. If the milestone is met, the employee can be rewarded with credits towards a project completion bonus, shares, etc.

Obviously, if an employee is incapable of completing assigned tasks away from the office, the best thing is to reverse the virtual agreement and bring that employee back into a controlled environment. However, arbitrarily pulling an employee from a virtual assignment is likely to cause bad feelings. To avoid these situations, the employee's manager should outline a virtual working agreement that explicitly describes what constitutes a breach of the agreement and then clearly inform the employee that any breach will result in the cancellation of the virtual work agreement. Prior to an agreement being cancelled, the manager must make every effort to communicate and remedy any perceived problems. If the problem persists, the virtualisation agreement should be reversed or cancelled.

Partially Virtual Employees

Not all staff or functions can be made totally virtual. The vast majority of tasks in a corporation that are performed by employees will have to be completed on company property. In these scenarios, the employee and manager may opt for a part-time virtual agreement.

A part-time virtual agreement allows the employee to block hours or days that are spent offsite. Travelling back and forth between offsite and onsite offices is highly inefficient and should be avoided at all costs. Managers should also be made aware of this fact and held accountable for the impact they have on employee travelling time. Part-time virtual employees will save less in resources than fully virtual employees will simply because they will spend more resources on travel to and from the office and create higher overhead expenses while working in the office. However, they will tend to use fewer overall resources than the full-time employee does.

Reviewing Tasks For Part-Time Virtual Work

All tasks performed by the employee must be carefully reviewed for how critical they are to the organisation. Each one should be evaluated by simulating the impact of the task on the company as a result of an inability to communicate with the employee for two days. For example, if you have a part-time virtual employee and she manages entry and reconciliation of miscellaneous journal entries in the general ledger, what would be the impact on your operations if you were unable to communicate with that employee for two days? The likely answer is not much impact at all. However, if a network administrator is unavailable for two days, the impact could be devastating. This employee can still be made virtual, but contingency plans will have to be developed in the event that the employee is unable to communicate for a couple of days.

Be Flexible On Hours And Schedules

The key to a successful transition from a traditional work environment to a virtual work environment will be the ability to be flexible on hours and scheduling. The implication is that your systems and employees must have the capability to effectively and easily manage scheduling. If they can't schedule or prioritise tasks very well, any attempts to virtualise the function could fail. It is also imperative that the corporation and manager learn to be flexible with their work hours while still meeting hard deadlines.

An example of this type of scenario is the construction industry, which has one of the highest levels of virtual employees because most of them are subcontractors and most work offsite, usually out of their vehicles. Contractors learned a long time ago that hiring employees was a costly experience, especially during the economic downturns in the 1980s. The construction industry quickly adopted the concept of hiring individuals as subcontractors. This allowed these virtual employees to decide when they would turn up for work, choose what work would be done, and provide input into the timetable for completion of the work. When a house is constructed, work is scheduled to begin and end at certain times, and the contractor is rewarded with payment and future work for completing milestones. But if a contractor or builder, for example, wants to build a wall in the middle of the night, that's up to the subcontractor – subject to noise nuisance, etc. All the contractor is concerned about are the project deadlines.

These same concepts can easily be applied to the workplace as long as the communication infrastructure that the business relies on is working. In fact, virtual workforces can keep a company up and running even if disaster, such as a storm, strikes the company offices.

Subcontractors Or Employees

Subcontractors are individuals who are either self–employed or incorporate a company to do business, but usually have only themselves as employees. The advantage for companies that hire contractors is that the organisation can shed workers without having to pay severance packages. The benefit for the subcontractor is greater autonomy and usually higher wages. However, beware the pitfalls of IR35 and talk to your accountant before choosing a route!

When Can An Employee Be Virtual?

If we look carefully at what employees do in their day-to-day work, we can start to analyse what tasks they have to be physically present for. Someone who deals with customers on a daily basis at centralised premises such as a retail store may have to conduct the bulk of his tasks at that location. Therefore, part-time virtual work may be a solution, or part-time virtual work may be entirely inefficient. In most scenarios, scheduling the workload of part-time workers so that tasks that require their physical presence are performed on a single day will help provide some mix of virtual and onsite work. Some examples of tasks that will require non-virtual or onsite employees include the following:

➤ Face-to-face contact with customers at a company location such as a retail store.

➤ Work with specialised equipment that cannot be installed remotely.

➤ Manufacturing processes that must be maintained together.

➤ Work that requires a controlled environment, such as a call centre or systems operation centre.

➤ Work that will benefit from daily personal contact with co-workers, such as financial trading rooms.

The difficult part will be to admit that a person's function need not be onsite at all times. An administrative assistant (or secretary) can work just as quickly on a project from his home on a computer connected to the company network and can even forward his office phone to the offsite location. However, in most cases few executives would admit that their assistants could do this effectively. They would claim that the individual was an integral part of their own daily function and that they couldn't get the same level of responsiveness that they would get at work. The question that has to be answered is, does this 'level of responsiveness' justify the additional cost that the company must bear for this position? If you look carefully, the answer will usually be 'no'.

The Virtual Work Zone

At some point, the company must make some serious decisions about its environment and location. Historically, companies centrally located near each other. This was to facilitate interaction with suppliers, competitors, and customers. But today, with the rapid advancement in communications technology, this is no longer the case. Now, suppliers, competitors, and customers are so widely dispersed that the idea of locating in close physical proximity to them is proving less and less feasible. Also, rents in locations that were traditionally part of this philosophy, such as city centres, are extremely expensive. An organisation that moves to a business park in the suburbs can greatly reduce its operating costs and pass these savings to either its customers or shareholders. Suburban locations can greatly reduce the cost to its employees by providing shorter commutes, parking, more facilities, etc. The company can still maintain a presence in a centralised area with a satellite office.

One of the most important items that must be addressed when designing a work environment is communications. Employees must be able to access communications equipment as easily as if they are in their own home office. Therefore, networks have to be designed in such a way that employees can access their own files quickly and easily from any location.

One of the best techniques is to issue laptop computers to your virtual employees and provide every office with a docking station. There must also be a way for phone communication to travel with the employee either through the use of mobile phones, local digital wireless networks, or call-forwarding systems that are managed by a central check-in point. Security must also consider the flow of virtual employees in and out of the organisation with environments built so that security-sensitive areas are kept out of the general traffic flow. Finally, employees should have a way of booking meeting rooms and checking the availability of workspace, which will require a centralised booking system capable of managing this aspect.

Occasionally, companies will place remote worksites throughout a city. This further alleviates commuting costs while providing a place for the virtual employee to go. Linking these remote sites through sophisticated communications will be critical to their success. Technology, such as linked video-conference rooms, individual video conferencing capabilities, and a high-speed wide-area networks between sites, will become necessary in building the virtual work environment. The goal should be to construct a convenient meeting place that provides fast and effective communication with other places for meetings that cannot otherwise be conducted using technologies such as the Internet.

Docking Station

A decking station is a platform that sits on top of a desk and is connected to a monitor and a network. The docking station allows a computer user an easy and fast way to connect a laptop to the corporate network by simply sliding in the laptop. The downside is that laptops are a hot commodity among thieves and leaving one in the open will surely lead to its disappearance.

The Virtual Workspace

The company must also consider the individual workspaces of the virtual employees both on- and offsite. Most virtual workspace offices utilise a sharing concept in allocating workspace. The employees will check in when they arrive at the site and be assigned a workspace, phone link, and keys. In that workspace, there should be a docking station for their laptop computer and a phone. Individual and personal items can be either brought by the employee or stored in baskets. At the end of their workday, they can check out of the office by taking all their personal belongings from the workspace and returning the keys. In this type of environment, it is important to have a set of ground rules about acceptable and non-acceptable behaviour. Territorialism must be frowned upon, over-use of the workspace must also be discouraged, and workspaces must be vacated.

Online meetings are a mainstay of any virtual work environment. Video meeting packages such as NetMeeting allow the virtual workers to actually see their co-workers. This visual communication is an important part of the virtual office because it provides offsite workers with the ability to connect with their co-workers in a manner that provides them with all the benefits that we get from face-to-face conversation. Body language and gestures often provide signals and clues as to the reception that our ideas are receiving. A phone call is a one-sided communication mechanism where we are trying to judge the response of the other person based on vocal intonation and tone. Video allows us to focus on many more clues and responses from eyes, gestures, body language, etc.

To conduct online video conferencing can be done as simply as using NetMeeting and the Internet, although more sophisticated technology is available. A word of warning, however: using ordinary phone lines linked via a modem to your computer is liable only to allow you to see jerky, poor-quality images of your conference callers.

One thing that will make the transition to the work environment easier is uniformity. If everybody has the same desk, workstation, and supplies, it will be difficult for status levels to develop, and this will in turn reduce internal politics. However, if you make a differentiation between workspaces, employees are likely to develop negative opinions of working virtually if their co-workers are perceived to be consistently getting the 'good' offices. Gaining consistency will be difficult because current buildings are not designed to be virtual offices, they are designed for corporations with executives in large corner offices, managers in the rest of the window offices, department managers and senior clerks in the inside offices, and line workers in the cubicles. Converting these spaces and achieving consistency will be very difficult given that someone is bound to get the sunny side of the building, and someone else is bound to get the office by the coffee machine.

The offsite office is just as critical as the onsite office. If the virtual employee works in another location, this factor may be beyond the control of the company and its

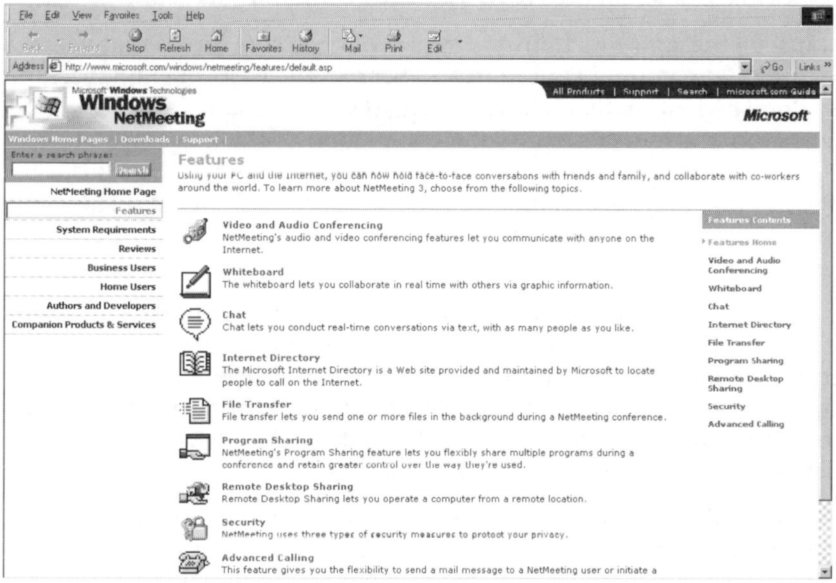

Figure 12.4
Microsoft's NetMeeting can be freely downloaded from its site – although it is included within Windows 98 and 2000

employees. If they work from their cars, again the aspect of 'offices' may not be as vital. But if they are planning to work from their homes, some effort should be invested by the corporation to assist the employees to develop a quiet workspace and timetables that permit them to complete tasks. Sending a task to an individual late at night and expecting her to complete a response by 9am is unreasonable if that individual also has the responsibility of sending his or her children to school at 8.30am. The workspace should also be comfortable and bright, not buried in a sub-basement (unless your worker happens to be a troll).

Outsourcing Staff

One definite strategy to 'virtualise' your workforce is to outsource your work to subcontractors or companies. In this scenario, tasks performed by the company are given to another company or individual to do. This is especially beneficial when the tasks are routine and simple, and the outsource company or contractor can perform the task cheaper than the company. For example, many data-entry tasks have been 'farmed out' to companies specialising in this type of work. Their staff are usually faster, more focused, and less costly than in-house staff, and they get economies of scale by doing the same tasks from multiple companies.

Which staff can be outsourced is a very difficult question. The downside of outsourcing is that the company will lose direct control over the function. Subcontractors answer only to themselves and will endeavour to do a good job, but on their own terms. You may feel that the way they conduct their business affairs is highly risky, but as long as they deliver a finished product or service on time, you will be unable to exercise any authority or control. So when it comes to deciding if an employee's tasks can be outsourced, remember to consider all the costs associated with your decision.

Two methods for outsourcing staff functions are to hire outside companies that will build some sort of interface to your organisation and bear all the costs of employees, or to hire a subcontractor. The first method allows an organisation to know with a relative degree of certainty the costs related to the completion of the outsourced tasks. The problems are that you will lose control of the work once it is sent to the other company and costs may fluctuate, depending on your outsourcing company. The second method allows you greater control over the work, but still only limited control over the employee.

Subcontracting also comes with a higher cost since the risks of employment are borne by the subcontractor. In both cases, the first step will be to define the tasks that are to be completed and a timetable for completion. The second is to identify the required skill sets needed to complete the task, and the third is to identify the costs that you are willing to bear for outsourcing. The fourth step will be to decide if it will be better to outsource the function to a company or to an individual.

In either case, you will need to search for that particular organisation or company and have your lawyers prepare any necessary contracts. It would be best to lock in a price over the terms of the agreement so that cost surprises would be minimal. Also, always check the references provided to ensure that the company has the capability to support your organisation. Finally, ensure the employee's functions have been documented, and a contingency plan built.

Outsourced Functions

There is a difference between outsourcing an individual staff function and outsourcing department functions. Entry of data into systems, application development, and accounting are all functions that can be entirely outsourced to another company. The question is whether they should be and what it will cost. Evaluating whether functions should be outsourced boils down to a couple of key decisions. The first decision is whether the function is critical to the operations of the company. If the answer is 'no', this task is a good candidate for outsourcing.

The next decision should be whether the task is a core competency. The decision that the company has to make in this scenario is whether the function performed by the staff or department requires an expertise that brings a high return to the organisation. If it is not a core competency, the tasks could be outsourced. Another deciding factor is whether the costs of running the function are greater than the outsourcing fee. In general, outsourcing should cost your company no more than if the company performed the task in-house. The outsourcers make their money by lowering the staffing costs, using more costly but more efficient systems, and by gaining greater productivity from their workforce by focusing on a particular group of tasks, such as accounting.

The benefit for the company is that it can shift high-priced managerial and business development resources from these tasks to high-return tasks, such as marketing or sales. An example is a company that designs office interiors. It may use a design software to assist in the task. It is also likely to have back-office functions such as accounting, sales, information technology, business development, and human resources. If the company evaluates these tasks, it may find that sales and business development are critical, but accounting and information technology are not core competencies. It may now evaluate outsourcing organisations to see if this type of outsourcing is financially feasible. If the company chooses to outsource the IT and the accounting, fewer resources will be required in the human resources area. This is the entire philosophy of outsourcing corporate functions, and in the world of e-commerce it opens thousands of doors for companies that can deliver non-competency services, such as accounting, over the Internet.

The Staffless Organisation

One of the newest 'holy grails' of the business world is the building of an entirely staffless organisation. In fact, it can happen if the company sets up a website on the Internet to conduct business with affiliates as a linking site only. Companies that are highly automated and involved in outsourcing those functions that are considered non-competencies may succeed in getting close to the goal of the staffless office.

The reality, however, is that a staffless organisation is not likely to grow and prosper, and is likely to succeed only with small e-commerce companies. One concept that is attainable is a company with a virtual staff. Grouping of contractors will probably become more commonplace as individuals become more dissatisfied with their lives and seek to leave established organisations for their own companies. Thousands of employees do this every year so this concept is not new. However, what is new is that these employees will decide that they can fund their own organisations in a similar manner to the one they work in for their own benefit.

Pitfalls

There are a number of serious pitfalls that await unsuspecting companies that are trying to create a virtual staff. Some employees will take advantage of the situation to the detriment of the organisation. Even if you hire people in a non-virtual environment, you will still occasionally get bad staff. However, it can be proven that the staff who choose to work virtually will almost certainly be the ones who are most responsible. To reduce the risks even further, simply virtualise those employees who have a track record for self-management and discipline.

The second problem that can arise is poor communications. If someone is located in the office next to you or just down the hall, it will be easier to communicate with him in person than if he is working offsite. Even if communications are established the virtual employee may choose to 'go dormant' or stop communicating through email or phones for a time. The problem is that poor communication can cause costly delays since tasks may be duplicated, performed incorrectly, or not performed at all.

Another problem is that the employees will need a low-noise workspace, yet most of these workspaces are not quiet at all. Kids, phones, and other factors can directly impact the performance of employees if they are unwilling to try to sequester themselves away from a noisy environment. The ability to focus on tasks will be lower, which in turn will result in work of a lower quality.

Another serious pitfall is the threat of poor security both to your data and systems and to your company culture. With people working in a fluid and unconstructed, unfenced environment there are many more targets for sabotage, at worst, and forgetfulness, at best, to occur.

Virtual employees will have limited interaction. The phrase 'you can't operate in a vacuum' is very pertinent here because virtual employees will have significantly less interaction with their co-workers. The problem with this is that if you are trying to come up with innovations, the last person you want to provide input is an individual who operates in a vacuum. For this reason, it is important to ensure that the virtual employees have the ability to communicate by using the technology, and that this factor is considered before they are made virtual.

Solutions

The first technique for eliminating these problems is to use a 'results-based' performance review and compensation strategy. The goal is to weed out the bad employees and reward those employees who are working the hardest. This task is accomplished primarily through the use of periodic performance reviews that determine the quantity of work completed by the employee and, if this is met, the timetable for this. Another thing that helps is to send managers offsite. They are usually good candidates for virtualisation and can lead the way for other employees. Their example sends a powerful message to the rest of the employees that virtualisation is both acceptable and is a favourable business task. If the managers are virtualised, they are less likely to have objections to the virtualisation of their staff.

Virtual employees should be treated with the same dignity and professionalism as regular employees. They should also be expected to return the same level of respect to the corporation. They should be made to feel welcome at the central office, and managers should go out of their way to reinforce the equality of all workers. Continuously maintaining this professionalism will lead to employees who feel obligated to complete assigned tasks.

The Least You Need To Know

➤ Define what a virtual workforce is and how it can be used in your company.

➤ Understand the benefits of a virtual workforce.

➤ Understand how to identify tasks that can be made virtual.

➤ Understand how to identify entire corporate functions that can be made virtual.

➤ Know how to build a virtual work environment in the office and how to assist your employees to do the same at home.

➤ Understand how to manage virtual employees.

183

Chapter 13

There's Gold In Them Thar Hills: Data Mining

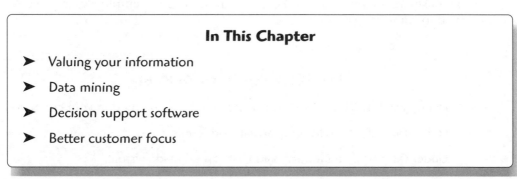

In This Chapter

➤ Valuing your information

➤ Data mining

➤ Decision support software

➤ Better customer focus

The Value Of Information

There is no doubt about it. The most valuable thing that a company will ever own is its information. Information is the single most vital input into the decision-making process, and if the decisions made are good decisions, the company will succeed.

One of the most important aspects of a company's information portfolio is the effectiveness of its ability to capture, store, and analyse this information. The output of this analysis provides a valuable tool for everyone in the company, from marketers and statisticians to traffic consultants. This valuable information has been captured by companies for many years, and is often stored in large databases; however, companies rarely capitalise on this value. As long as the data site is untouched, it provides no benefit to the organisation. It is the same thing that would occur if a mining company purchased land, built roads, imported mining equipment, and then never touched the ore in the ground.

Companies have a very valuable asset in the information they store, but it is an asset that will produce nothing unless it is 'mined'. The process of data mining simply involves the use of data-mining tools and applications to extract and report on information contained in long-term databases. We say 'long-term' because short-term or near-term information should be managed and reported on a daily basis to help run the operations of the company. An example of near-term information is current-day sales statistics. However, data mining can be combined with regular reporting and modelling tools to use both longer-term and near-term information to initiate other processes, such as coupon mailings. Long-term data mining by itself is used to spot changes in customer tastes or operational efficiency.

Data Mining Defined

Data mining is the use of software tools or applications to gather, report, and analyse operational information, such as sales, in order to instigate an action by other systems or employees that directly impacts the operation of the company.

The Data–Mining Process

The first question that should follow this definition is how is data mined? The entire process of data mining involves capturing, storing, gathering, and analysing the information of the company, and the very first step involves capturing information. Valuable information can be as simple as the name of a customer or as complex as operational performance measures such as rates of return on investments.

There are two viewpoints on this. The first is that all information has or may have some value in the future so that all information should be captured and stored. The second view concludes that information is costly to capture and store so that only strategically required information should be captured.

The second method places the organisation at risk of missing or losing some valuable data. For example, a company that sells computers may find that information about peripheral use is valuable to development, but the company may ignore other information, such as customer opinions on how they found out about the organisation. If the company then decides to release a new product through a print advertising campaign, it may find that the success of the campaign is less than it would have been if the bulk of the resources were allocated to an Internet promotional campaign. Data mining could have provided information that indicated most customers located the company through the Internet as opposed to print ads.

To Mine Data, It Must First Be Stored

However, this data would be available only if it had originally been captured and stored. The best technique for capturing data is to get the customer to enter this data directly into a capturing application such as online product-registration forms. Another technique is to have the information captured by staff during a customer account set-up process. A third option is to have the information loaded from other databases sold by other companies, including your competitors – depending on their registration with the Data Protection Act.

Some companies run contests and promotions simply as a way to get people to enter information. This happens because there is a negative attitude beginning to grow in the Internet surfing community that entering personal information is both time-consuming and invasive. This attitude is less prevalent with contest entry forms; however, individuals who enter information into these forms may not be representative of the normal population. This means that getting information that 90% of all respondents like contests may not be a good representation of the general population and may result in bad decisions.

The second piece of the data-mining puzzle is the storage of captured data. All data that is captured should be stored for future data-mining opportunities. This storage has traditionally taken the form of relational databases, and in fact most data-extraction tools are based on standard relational database formats such as Microsoft SQL. It is important that the storage mechanism is fast and efficient since extracting information is a complex process that can often take a great amount of resources. If the database chosen is inefficient in its design, the ability to get information out of it will take an excessive amount of resources.

ODBC

Open database connectivity (ODBC) is a set of standards that have been created so that software developers can build interfaces to different databases knowing that they will be universally accessible. This allows them to say that they are ODBC compliant.

Mining Databases

The key is a database structure that can store and analyse large volumes of information. Some newer databases store objects that include pieces of code that manage the information. In this case, analysing volumes of data may prove less efficient than a standard relational structure. Random customer data should be stored with some idea of how it will be extracted for mining in the future. Information that is immediately pertinent, such as sales data, can run though object code that analyses it prior to its storage. Long-term data can run through code objects that append other information that will be useful later on, such as a code that indicates the links a customer has taken from your website to an affiliate's website. Also critical to data storage are backup and recovery resources and strategies.

There is a wide array of extraction applications that will analyse the data in a database for trends. Historical data, such as the age of a consumer and their purchasing habits, is very valuable for functions

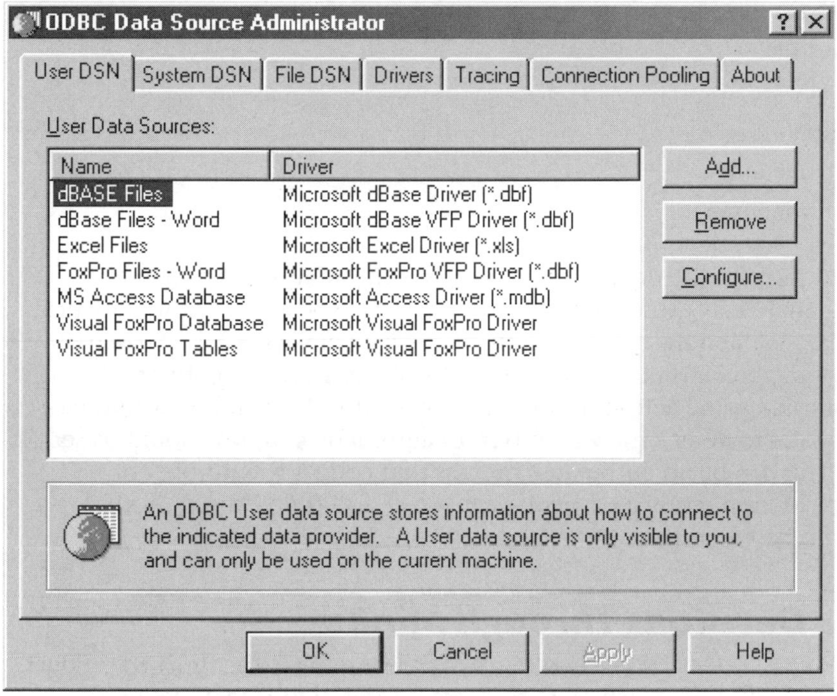

Figure 13.1
Windows users can look in their Control Panel to see the provenance of their ODBC set-up – assuming it means anything to them in the first place!

such as developing product mixes or promotions. For example, a store that has a general consumer population in its mid-thirties can analyse what those people buy. If 60% purchased a baby pacifier in the past six months, then a mailing promotion on baby supplies to those individuals may increase the overall sales of baby products in the store. Extraction tools are often closely related to the type of database being mined; however, some sophisticated extraction tools are ODBC compliant and can interface with a variety of databases.

Extracting And Analysing Data

The function of extraction software is either to search for set information that indicates a trend, such as the example above, or to allow users to search for specific types of data that match parameters they enter. In this latter extraction process, the application may locate customer information in a piece of a database, mine operational data with the same key, and statistically report on items such as sales volume by product category or money spent per trip. The goal is always to try to provide information that decision makers can use to plan new programs that, in turn, will add more revenue. It is important to note that data mining does not have to apply to sales and marketing campaigns only; it can also apply to a variety of functions and tasks such as the following:

➤ Customer service volume.
➤ Service and repairs response times.

187

➤   Customer satisfaction.

➤   Advertising results.

➤   Delivery times.

➤   Product quality.

➤   Employee satisfaction.

➤   Employee Internet usage.

Another important piece of the data-mining process is the analysis of mined information. Data analysis is usually handled by individuals who study the statistical results from the data-extraction section and then report or make decisions based on the results. However, more and more sophisticated systems are starting to provide analysis tools that cause some action to occur automatically. An example would be a tool that analyses sales to determine which type of automatic coupon should be sent to the consumer. This can be an automated process that counts the number of purchases of a type of product by a particular consumer and then causes another application to begin based on the results.

Making Better Decisions Through Mining

More Data Mining Resources

Surf hyperlink `http://www.infogoal.com/dmc/dmcdwh.htm` to get more information about data-mining resources such as data warehousing and neural nets.

The end result of data mining is the finished product, which in this case is information that identifies current and future trends or provides base information such as addresses or different ways of quantifying information. Where data mining can have a direct application to e-commerce is in the creation of communities of value. If you are a retailer with an extensive collection of stored customer purchasing behaviour patterns, you can probably use the data to design the website based on the results of a data analysis. As a retailer, you may, for example, find that your customers who surf the Internet are primarily in an age band from 18 to 35. However, you may find that the bulk of your sales are made to high-income individuals between the ages of 30 and 35. This information can then be used to either attract more of the younger component of your bulk market or to market directly to the older component through the design of the website.

How Is Data Mined?

One of the most important pieces of data mining is the software available to perform the task. Data-mining software comes in two varieties: statistical modelling software that uses advanced mathematics and theories to provide information that predicts events, and reporting software that produces reports on the number of customers in a geographic area. Companies such as IBM, Silicon Graphics, and Thinking Machines all offer software that can mine a file of data and apply statistical modelling tools to assist in the analysis.

Many of these software packages incorporate concepts such as neural networks or artificial intelligence. Neural nets are applications that mimic learning by adjusting the software parameters. Other concepts include decision trees, which use a set of predetermined decisions to predict outcomes, and a variety of other advanced mathematical concepts. The overall theory of data mining is still quite simple. The basic premise of the concept is this: input a file of data, define which extraction parameters are important, then allow the software to produce a result.

Neural Network

A neural network is a storage and application that operates very similarly to the human mind. The idea is to take a dumb computer and get it to start analysing data for trends, etc. by using advanced maths and statistical models. For example, a neural network may have historical foreign exchange rates, and it may use this data to run a mathematical model to predict the future foreign exchange rates. What makes a neural net different is that it would then analyse the outcome and adjust its level accordingly.

Decision Support Software

Some of the software noted above costs upwards of £500 000 per installation. The whole purpose is to provide the people who make decisions with the information they need to make better decisions. This type of software is called decision support software or DSS. The fundamental problem with all decision support software that predicts future occurrence is that no one person or computer can predict the future. That is where real analysis of information plays a role. For example, it is highly unlikely that decision support systems would have predicted that Amazon.com would open its virtual doors on the Internet. However, decision support systems could have reported the number of book-purchasing customers that were in a technological position to use the Internet for purchasing. Any analyst could then have figured out the rest. When analysing data, it is important to remember that machines cannot understand all the subtle interactions of the world well enough to make decisions. They can, however, provide base information to make more effective educated guesses.

It is important that decisions made through the use of data-mining techniques consider the corporate strategy. This strategy is the map for the corporate operations, and if it is not considered when other decisions are made, the company may go towards the wrong goal. For example, if a company were to receive data that 35-year-old customers were the most likely to respond to the development of a new product, but the corporate strategy was to target 30-year-olds, a decision based on the mined data would take the company away from its strategic direction. It is better to use data mining to help determine the overall strategic direction of the organisation, and then use it to fine-tune operations such as promotional campaigns.

The Benefits Of Data Mining

One of the most usable areas of mined data is the marketing department of the organisation. Customer purchasing information can be used to design new marketing and promotional campaigns to assist in the growth of the organisation. Marketing strategy is based on the identification of customer groups so that campaigns can be directed towards a certain audience. Originally, marketing companies and departments subdivided the population based on demographic principles such as income or gender. Later theories developed the concept of promoting to cross-sections of these markets such as individuals with a certain income and genders. Newer theories now discuss concepts such as 'psychographic' marketing techniques that are based on perceptions and feelings, or cross-niche marketing that is designed to develop a programme for a variety of groups with a common perception.

Using Mined Information To Target Customers

Data mining can greatly aid in these newer marketing concepts by providing information that crosses the old demographic lines and redefines groups by communities. Now companies can target a select group of consumers with products and promotions that emulate the concepts of the community. For companies that are developing an identity, this information can be extremely valuable.

Advertising And Mined Data

The world of advertising is one of images and vague concepts, and for these types of tasks, data mining has a direct role. That role has two unique characteristics. First, an analysis of mined data can indicate groupings and concepts that can be used to design advertisements. Second, more advanced data-mining software can predict potential outcomes based on past information, and this information can be used to test images or the media mix used to distribute the advertising.

An example of the first type of data mining is a technology company that mined the data in an online Internet database of the age group 18 to 23. The information indicated that the group was not purchasing mainstream software, but did have a strong interest to search for free software as well as online music information sites. Combining the free release of the sound software along with the promotion of free music on those information sites started the rapid growth of their Internet concept. The second type of data mining predicted that the growth would next occur in the immediate age groups on either side of the original group, and that further directed cross-promotion through sites such as Amazon, through the search engines and hard ads in magazines such as *Wired* would provide the greatest growth for the organisation.

Promotion And Mined Data

In the same way that data mining assists in developing and delivering advertising, it can also assist promotional campaigns which, as opposed to advertising, require significantly more planning. That planning depends on the promotional activity. Coverage in the press can often be achieved with just a good idea. However, most promotional campaigns will require an understanding of the market they are designed for. To this end, data mining can still assist the development and direction of promotional activities from traditional campaigns such as press releases and sponsorships to unconventional campaigns like live webcasts of controversial content.

The same concepts apply to the analysis of mined data for promotion as for advertising. Some mining software will assist in defining opportunities and other mining software will assist in predicting the outcome of promotional campaigns. An example of the use of mined data in the formation of a promotional campaign would be if the software were able to find a link between young males in their mid-twenties who surf to no more than four new sites per week at night and an attitude that new software will be accepted only if it has been identified by hot new sites and newsgroups. This might encourage a new sports analysis tool to be promoted on the newsgroups and by banner ads on 'cool sites'.

Banner Ads

Banner ads are those thin ads that you usually see at the top and bottom of websites. They are easy to create and easy to place, but the fees charged are based on coverage. The best coverage will occur if you can place the ad to come up for certain people. To do this, you will have to mine or capture the data to have an indication of where to place the ad.

Data mining also assists in defining targeted sales promotions. For example, an advertising or promotional campaign can be created for an existing set of customers. In this scenario, the mined data may or may not assist in the initial development. The marketing manager can then use the data-mining tools to produce a list of customers who have the highest potential to favourably respond to the advertising or promotion. This will produce a target list for the campaign and provide a higher level of return for the level of money expended. Target lists can also be used to reward loyal customers, direct sales efforts, and tailor giveaways and direct sponsorships.

Using Mined Data For Designing

Another place where data mining can provide a significant benefit is in the area of design. In this case, Internet information or customer service information can indicate design changes that are necessary. Data-mining software can assist by providing report data on factors such as consistent complaints, requested changes from customers, and enquiries by potential customers. Old data designs can also be mined for components test results and probable outcomes of design changes.

Looking Ahead: Using Statistical Modelling

Another common use of mined data are the sophisticated financial and trading programs that use historical information to apply statistical modelling concepts to identify potential risk. These results are then used by traders to place hedges that protect against these risks. The goal is to give the data miner a way to predict the future.

However, there are a number of people who do not agree with these techniques, believing that historical data has no relation to future outcome. These individuals try to predict the future by using current information. An example is currency traders who adjust their currency positions based on the latest releases of information. Data mining for this type of philosophy is more interested in producing data that predicts a trend.

Better Customer Service Through Data Mining

One of the immediate uses of data-mining software is to allow customer service staff to access customer information while they are talking to the customer. Two types of information can be provided, such as historical data about the products that customers have purchased and software predictions about what other products the customer might like. With this type of information, customer service personnel can better assist individual customers to make decisions based on information about their preferences. This type of information is becoming more prevalent on webites in order to provide suggestions to customers.

The better the information available to the customer service function, the better the service to the customer. The better the customer service, the higher the sales. But the information must be readily available, easily analysed, and presented in a format that is easy to understand. In this way, if a customer calls a call centre, the call centre system can analyse the phone number and present a page of information to the centre personnel, including:

➤ A list of items purchased.

➤ Total sales to date.

➤ Outstanding amounts.

➤ Suggested new products.

➤ Customer's contact with the service centre.

➤ Links used by the customer from the company's website.

➤ Miscellaneous personal information gathered from previous calls.

In one particular company, a customer called in about an order and mentioned that her daughter was going to college, and the customer service clerk entered the information into a personal notes area. When the customer called back the following week to place an order, the customer service clerk could see the reference to the daughter and asked how things were going. A positive and personal rapport with customers has been proven to increase the level of sales, and a key ingredient of this formula is information mined from the corporate database.

Data mining also provides management with valuable information. Managers can mine basic information, such as how long employees spend on particular functions on the network or where they surf to on the internet. They can also mine data for forecast purposes, such as the average volume of sales from customers by customer service clerks. Decreases in this measure may indicate an employee who has stopped encouraging sales. Managers can also use data mining to forecast financial performance for use in budgeting and forecasts.

Better Customer Information

Data mining greatly contributes to the information available to the customer through websites. Personalised website access provides customers with personalised information. Data-mining software can assist in loading information into a personalised web page, such as product offerings or newly released data that may be of interest to the customer. The predicting type of software can also be used as a search engine initiated by the customer. Most of the 'find other similar products' links to be found on the majority of bookshop sites are simply data mining tools that search company databases or the Internet.

The goals of providing information directly to customers are the same as the goals to provide managers with information: to assist in making better decisions and thereby encourage sales. Data-mining software can provide search capabilities for past customer information and one day may result in a personal data storage killer app where people store and analyse a variety of personal information to improve their lives.

Figure 13.2 *In common with other book stores, Alphabet Street offers 'more books like this' buttons to tempt you into buying more*

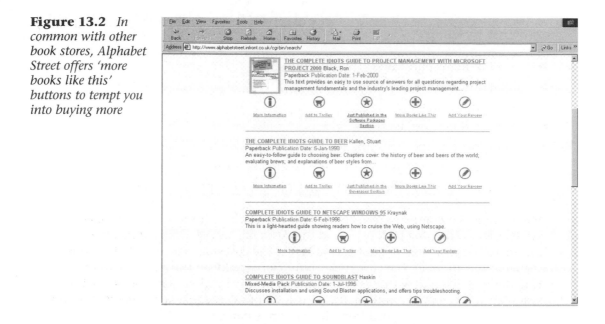

Customer–Created Data

The vast majority of data mined is entered by the organisation into vast database storage systems known as data warehouses. Mining this data produces a valuable resource for decision making, but the cost of this data capture is currently very high. e-Commerce provides the model that significantly changes that equation by getting the customer to enter the information or by having real-time integrated systems which store the data automatically.

However, customers will enter only minimal amounts of information before they find the experience distasteful. Therefore, data-capture systems must be fast and efficient with the customer's time. How the customer enters data into the system will dictate the quality of the data received. For example, if you are blocking access to your site to try to obtain customer address information through a form, you are likely to find that less and less of the data being entered is valuable. (One of the most prolific form fillers is Mr M. Mouse who lives in Florida!) However, if you run a contest where the winners are notified by post, the quality of the data will be higher.

Special Considerations For Website Design

The design of the website is also important. Certain websites provide forms with look-up lists of cities and countries to assist in data entry. This makes the task of data entry easier, and is likely to result in better entry information. Other websites use cookies, which are bits of information and code that are exchanged by browsers and stored on the customer's computer. The next time the customer enters the site, an exchange occurs between the two machines that causes the customer's profile to be accessed. This is why

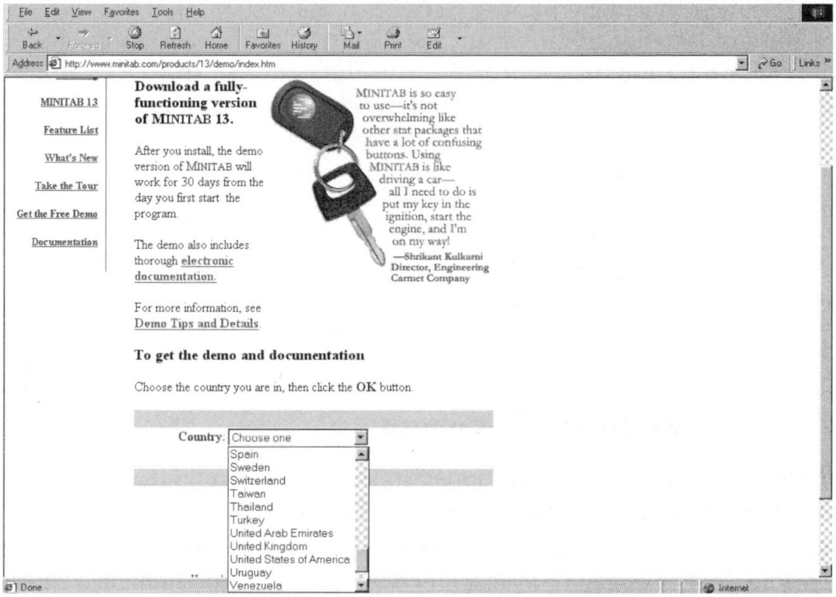

Figure 13.3 *Many forms offer drop-down selection boxes to make the form filling easier for the customer*

when you re-enter some websites, they greet you with your name (*see* Figure 13.4). Some browsers provide you with an option not to accept cookies.

Information that is entered by customers or captured by internal systems is usually stored in relational databases. As a customer enters information, a customer number can be applied to that information so that it can be easily retrieved for later use by

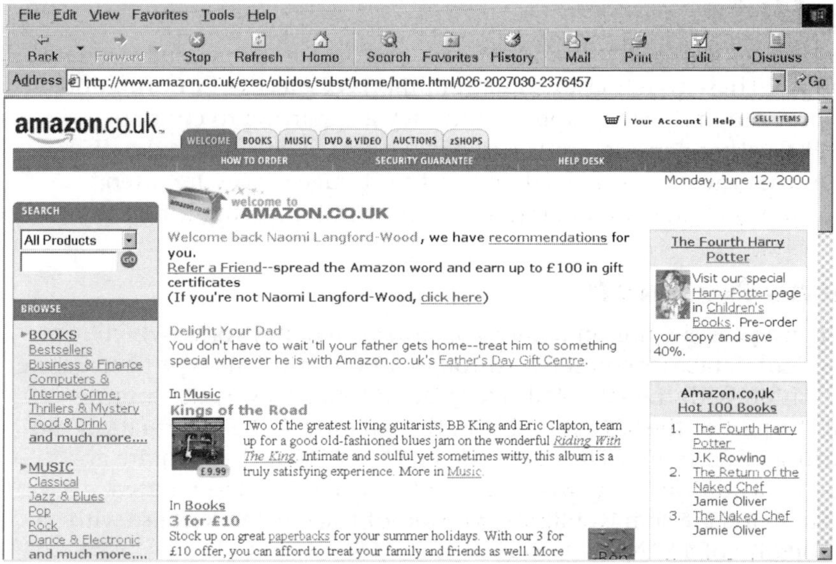

Figure 13.4 *Using cookies, websites can 'recognise' customers who have visited previously*

mining technology. The next time the customer signs onto the system, that information can be retrieved very efficiently from the database. Most websites ask the customer to create a sign-on ID and password. This gives the customer the opportunity to create a familiar log-on without having to remember a customer number.

Relational Databases

Relational databases are storage areas for information that is organised into tables. Each table pertains to a particular grouping of data, such as customer information, and is indexed with one or more keys. Keys are unique identifiers for each line in the table. For example, a customer will have a unique number that differentiates her from other customers. This customer number can be used as a key in a customer information table so that if you have a customer number, you will only get the information related to that customer. Later, when the customer calls for an order, you can use this customer number to quickly and easily complete the customer information section.

Warehousing Data

When an organisation centralises the storage of data, it is said to be putting the data into a data warehouse. These warehouses contain millions of pieces of information about customer behaviour and demographics, and they are starting to contain information about our other personal traits and behaviours. Even though the phrase 'warehouse' implies that the data is shelved, in fact the storage spaces are often nothing more than servers that contain large arrays of disks for storing information.

The Storage Area Network

Another growing concept is the notion of SANs or storage area networks, which are numerous independent databases connected through a network. This type of structure provides an organisation with the same fail-safe structure that powers the Internet, which means that if a part of the SAN goes down, the balance of the information can still be retrieved using other routes. The downside of SANs is that they require an exceptionally good data administrator who can identify where the fragmented information is. Data marts are simply a lighter version of the data warehouse with some of the functionality of a SAN.

The final step in the capturing of data is to provide a way to access the data for use in mining applications. Accessing data in data warehouses can be complicated if you do not understand the structure of the warehouse. However, accessing data in a SAN will require both an understanding of the structure of the individual data storage areas, as well as an understanding where the data storage area is on the SAN. Many larger organisations have a team of specialists who do nothing else but analyse the relationship between how the data is stored and how it is accessed. Their goal is to make the process more efficient by using software to anticipate what data will be required.

Pulling Out The Data

The standard method for pulling data from a warehouse is through a data query language such as SQL. However, there is more sophisticated software available, such as that used by Ask Jeeves, to analyse regular grammatical phrasing in questions to identify information. The question 'What is a dog?' is broken by the software into the phrases 'What is' and 'a dog'. The software then knows that it is looking primarily for 'definitional hits' on the phrase 'a dog' and it will evaluate those sites that have the highest ratio of references to the selection criteria.

If the question had been 'Where is' then the site would have ranked 'location' hits higher than definitional hits. This is an example of how this type of software mines for data in large data warehouses. The more unstructured the data storage, the easier it will be for the mining software to locate the information you are seeking. Creating a query that selects precisely the information you are seeking may be essential to internal operations, but presentation of general information, such as responses to a website search, will require less rigidity. For this reason, it is vital that businesses consider a variety of storage and mining applications from relational and object databases to query reporting tools to advanced analytical modelling programs.

Sophisticated Mining And Analytical Tools

Most data-mining software will have a mathematical or statistical modelling tool built in. These tools use complex algorithms, historical data, or both to predict events.

The easiest way to explain these tools is to take a trip to Las Vegas. Picture that you are sitting at a blackjack table with your IT expert at your side. You are holding a 10 and a 6, and you are not sure how much to bet or whether you should take another card. You turn to your IT colleague and say: 'What do you think?' He's sweating a little because they took his laptop at the door, but he turns to you and says firmly: 'Go for the next card and bet high.' You are not too sure how many free drinks he has had, but you bet high, take another card, and receive a 3. The dealer turns over a queen and proceeds to take a 2 and a 10. You win your hand and leave the table. On the way out the door you ask the IT expert how he was so sure. He responds by telling you that there were three packs in play, and he counted that 47 out of 65 cards that had already passed were valued at eight or greater, but that only 25 cards had passed by at a value of five or less. He reasoned that the odds of you receiving a five or less were quite high and worthy of

Data-Mining Software

For information on data mining, surf to `http://www.data-miners.com/`

a higher investment. The same principles apply in the sophisticated maths and statistics tools employed by more expensive data-mining software.

The idea is to use past information to predict the probability of an outcome in the future. Advanced mathematics based on population distribution theory, random simulations-based chaos theory, and a variety of other methods are included in various types of data-mining software available on the market.

To Sell Or Not To Sell – A Future View

A topic of extreme controversy on the Internet is whether companies should sell the information they have collected in data stores. These huge repositories of data have an extremely valuable collection of information about what we have purchased, what we like in terms of entertainment, what we eat for dinner, how much we spend per month, and even what our income is. However, there is growing resentment on the Internet towards companies that demand our personal information, and slowly these databases are growing full of inaccurate data as people answer the questions with any answer, as opposed to the correct one. This has caused companies that purchase information to be far more selective about whose information they are buying. It has also caused some companies to give up the concept of selling information because customers are becoming irritated, and because competitors are using the data against the company that sold it.

Yahoo! is one of the leaders in the movement towards a new model of sharing customer information. Its concept is based on the fundamental principle that customers should approve the information that they receive. That means that if a customer of Yahoo! does not want her information freely distributed, she will not provide it. If a customer authorises Yahoo! to allow certain types of promotional literature through, this information will be presented to the customer. This philosophy places the ownership of information back into the hands of the consumer, as opposed to the current philosophy that the company owns the information and can sell it to whomever it wants to for any purpose.

Consumers inherently seek information regarding new products; however, they want to choose the categories and have control of when to stop receiving this information. Many websites have tried to solve this problem by providing links to the information; however, given the volume of information available, surfers are having a more difficult time trying to locate usable information. This is where personalised websites can ease that problem by allowing the user to set parameters about what kinds of information they will receive. This in turn makes online consumers more responsive to promotions from online companies that are using this controlled technique because the customers are getting information that they have already approved. This technique also allows companies such as Yahoo! to gather more information from the customer since the adversarial environment of providing information is going to be less of a concern for these individuals.

After you have captured, stored, extracted, and analysed your customer data, then what do you do? As a business owner or manager, you have to decide what to do with the results. Decision making is truly an art, and the best business people in the world know that information is essential to good decision making, but that some level of intuition is essential for success. Many of the most successful Internet companies today would have been hard pressed to find data-mining software that indicated that they should start up on the Internet. Intuition, however, had a big role to play in decisions of people such as Bill Gates and Jeff Bezos of Amazon.

Gut instinct, intuition, insight, experience – whatever you call it, that little subjective piece of decision making can be made better with information. This is particularly true of decisions that pertain to existing ongoing operations. The business owners still need some information to fire their imagination, but the hard decisions about strategic planning and operations can be made more effective with mined data. This is also true for smaller organisations with smaller client bases. In order to grow the company, the decision makers must have the best information they can obtain from what they already have. However, don't dwell on it. More than a few large companies have gone bankrupt as a result of spending too much time studying operating results and not enough time looking into the future.

The Least You Need To Know

➤ What data mining is and how it is used.

➤ Understand how to store and capture data in a data mine.

➤ Know some of the techniques for extracting or mining data.

➤ Understand how to analyse data once it has been mined.

➤ Know how to use the output from data mining to make better decisions.

Part 3

e-Marketing

It's an entirely new world out there, and it requires a comprehensive understanding of an entirely new way to market your e-commerce company. New advertising, new promotion, and even the way you build your website all depend on your understanding of this e-commerce landscape.

In the first chapters, we will talk about how marketing on the Internet has changed the traditional marketing world and the ramifications it will have on your existing or new company. Then we'll look at Internet advertising and the opportunities to use this powerful medium to deliver your message.

You will get detailed information about the most current types of marketing models that will help drive customers to your e-business. Then we will cross over to the off-net world and explain how you can use some traditional techniques to build your e-business using media such as TV.

Finally, we will revisit the data mine and show you how to use the data to develop your marketing strategy, as well as how to get mined information from the Internet.

Knowing how to promote your company in the world of e-commerce is not the same as it used to be, and you will advance from this section with a clear idea of what you should do and what pitfalls you should avoid.

Chapter 14

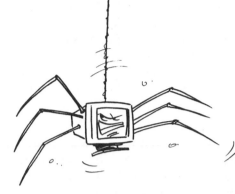

Spinning A Web – Internet Marketing

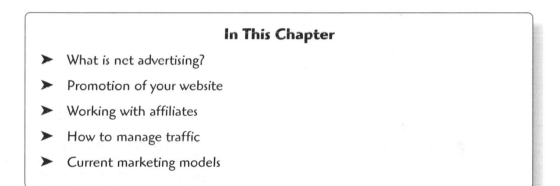

In This Chapter

➤ What is net advertising?

➤ Promotion of your website

➤ Working with affiliates

➤ How to manage traffic

➤ Current marketing models

Marketing your website on the Internet is different from marketing a product or a service. The number of people who surf the Internet, the volumes of information and Websites available, banner ads, promotion, public relations, online surveys, and new media all blend together into an ever-changing model of Internet marketing. In the old days, the choices were far simpler – you selected a target market, an image and a message together with the media outlets you were going to use.

Because the Internet changes everything, the traditional advertising and promotional mix is being melded with some new concepts about how to attract attention and a wide array of new media. Gone are the days of static images in printed magazines or audio clips on radio stations. Now you can target millions of people with audio and moving images but at a very low cost. Newer technologies go even further by offering the opportunity for users to interact with the ads.

PR and advertising firms are quick to jump on the bandwagon by offering shock content designed to make their clients' websites stand out from the crowd.

Who Are Your Customers?

Advertising and promotion cost money. That's the bottom line. The success of your e-commerce marketing programme will depend on the level of resources that you are willing to throw at it. However, more resources will not always equal more success. There is a long list of companies that spent vast amounts of money advertising only to wind up with very little to show for their efforts. Some misguided campaigns with poor imaging and a failure to understand the market have even cost some companies their lives. The most prominent of these e-commerce flops (at the time of writing) was boo.com which went to the wall in the spring of 2000.

Planning your attack on a market cannot be underestimated, but there is a great deal of intelligence that must be gathered prior to the assault, such as information about the terrain, the enemy, the tools available, and what is coming over the horizon. One of the most important pieces of the puzzle is knowing who your customers are.

Way, way back in the deep history of the Internet, five years ago, the primary users of the Internet were the high-tech gurus of new technology. University students, hackers, scientists, and large institutional information departments primarily used the Internet to send data between computers. Very early in the development of the network, form-based technologies allowed these individuals to exchange messages, and it was during these early years that people started to understand the huge potential of a world connected by computers. It was the concept of critical mass that gave life to these theories and opened the Internet to everybody.

It was entrepreneurs who captured the first major beachhead in the war to attract mid-level computer users to the Internet. Early local Internet service providers and online service providers (OSPs) such as CompuServe and AOL started the move to critical mass by making Internet access affordable to most people. Now anyone with a PC and a telephone could get on the net and start performing simple functions like surfing to text-based websites and sending email. Companies started to provide email access links to their internal email systems, which added to the growing user familiarity with the world of the Internet.

Today, the explosive growth of the Internet has created the critical mass of Metcalf's Law, and has opened unlimited opportunity for growth. It has also created the largest advertising pool in the world. Internet users number in their hundreds of millions and are likely to reach billions within the next decade. The size of the Internet audience is so large and so varied that companies have a difficult time trying to understand how to allocate their limited advertising and promotional resources. Targeting customers who are most likely to purchase your service or product will become more essential as global advertising possibilities become expensive for small and mid-sized organisations. The Cokes and Microsofts of the world will be the only players with the reach capable of justifying large expenditures on the global advertising level, while companies with fewer resources will have to be content with trying to attract the interest of market leaders to their website. They will have to be more selective about who they are going to target in order to ensure an adequate return on their advertising and promotional investment. They will essentially have to know who their customers are.

Where Are Your Customers?

After you have defined who your customers are, the next question will be where on the net are they? You can be pretty certain that specific demographic groups can be easily located on the Internet by using the expertise developed over years of marketing research. If you want to know where a group of sports-loving males in their thirties hang out, the Internet will provide you with that information. This results from the electronic nature of the net, and its ability to capture and store information about users and their transactions.

For example, a sports website, such as www.sportal.com, will have the target market defined previously, but it will also have a large number of visitors from outside this market, such as males over 40 or under 30 and now a growing contingent of women. If you place an ad on this website, you will have to pay for the impressions or the number of times your ad is shown, regardless of who views it. A better use of resources might be to advertise on a feeder website that targets your demographics by offering links to the larger site. The cost would be cheaper, and the probability of a 'good hit' would be higher.

Finding your market is critical at this point in the history of the Internet, and will become more critical as traffic builds at the major sites and the return-to-impression ratio gets lower. Other options may be more financially sound, such as paying micropayments for traffic or contact information; however, there will be the same problem of identifying your market to increase your buy ratio. The good news is that the level of statistics pertaining to network traffic is growing and more and more companies such as Yahoo! are starting to use customer-provided demographic information to build targeting packages for Net advertisers. This allows advertisers to have their banner ads shown only to specific individuals, as opposed to a random group of users. This way a company can tightly define which users they are going to target by their interests and not just by their basic demographic information. For example, when you sign up for a personal My Yahoo! customised web page, the form will ask you to choose your interests (*see* Figure 14.1). This information can then be used to deliver targeted advertising specifically designed for users with similar interests.

Another way to locate customers on the Internet is to place your ads with Internet companies that maintain transactional information on users. Some companies track user purchases by account, and this information can be a valuable marketing tool for ad placement. For example, let's say I sold fountain pumps for garden ponds. I could use the stored buying information to identify which users have recently purchased garden products and then have a banner ad shown when those users re-access the website for other shopping. There are also companies that are starting to analyse the data contained in websites for correlation opportunities. This information will provide a way to define what products or services will be required by a group of people that gather at a specific site. For instance, a group that surfs to a web location that contains negative information about Microsoft may be the perfect place to advertise roller blades if a correlation has been identified between the user groups and its tastes. Analysis of tastes and preferences are the realm of psychographic or behaviour analysis.

Figure 14.1 *When you sign up with My Yahoo!, you are asked about your personal preferences*

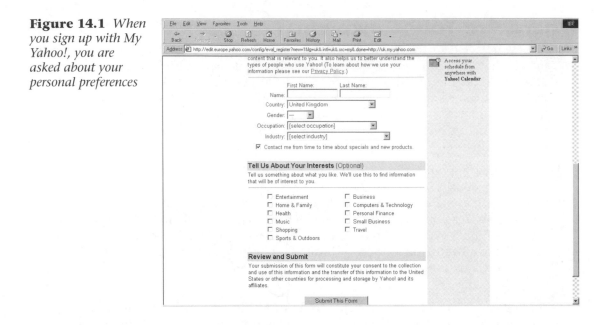

The benefit of identifying your customers on the Internet is that your resources – namely cash and marketing staff – will be more focused and will produce better results – namely profits.

Promotion On The Net

Want to get traffic really fast? How about a good scam? We are serious. One of the best ways to get traffic to your site is to pull the equivalent of a Blair Witch (*see* Figure 14.2). Create the equivalent of an Internet urban legend and then let it loose on the world and capitalise on the traffic. This has included everything from people selling vital organs on an online auction site to stars having stomach surgery live to reduce their weight. First, your most creative staff geniuses will have to concoct a story that is likely to attract visitors either to your site or to a location where your banner ad will be viewed.

Let's say I started an online auction site and then decided that I needed to draw enough traffic to create a traffic jam and thereby raise the profile of the site with a series of corresponding news releases. Let's say I put a product up for sale that would cause a stir, such as a body part. Then, as the price is bid up by a few mysterious friends, I send out worldwide news releases about our organisation's position not to interfere with our customers' strange actions. Why would I do this? It's simple – I get traffic, and if I get enough hits, I can release a second news release to identify the trouble we are having handling the volume. Now, all of a sudden, I have instantaneous press coverage just as long as the story is weird enough.

Some would argue with the ethics of creating false stories to generate traffic, and there are a number of pitfalls in this concept. However, if your team is really creative, they

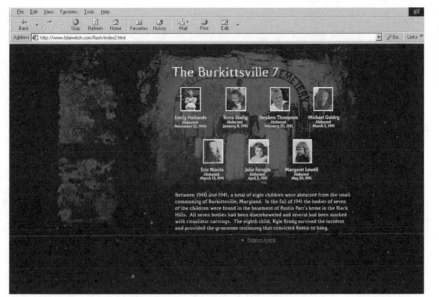

Figure 14.2 *The Blair Witch site originally gave the impression that the film was in fact a true story*

will be able to dream up concepts that are not false, yet still generate traffic and interest. The obvious benefit is that you can start to create a following or community if your team is effective at getting its message out. It is also important to remember that information sites that depend on traffic levels will have to continuously attract traffic to their site as more and more comparable or new 'cool' sites compete on the net.

One of the best promotional tools available is the newsgroup. Newsgroups are a way for individuals to discuss relevant topics such as the latest cool site, technology, or entertainment. The users of this technology are not particularly friendly to direct promotion from organisations or even corporate 'plants' that pretend they are just regular newsgroup users. These corporate plants are usually hired by large technology companies to do nothing else but argue and promote their company in the newsgroups. However, the best way to promote your company is to generate buzz from outside the newsgroup and let it filter in by itself. A little careful crafting of images and messages and some good 'ex-net' (outside the Internet) promotion and advertising will go a long way towards getting lots of buzz about your site. There was a lot of buzz about the *Blair Witch Project* movie in the newsgroups prior to its release, and this helped spread the word without the benefit of a large ex-net promotional budget.

Of course, there are a variety of other ways to promote on and off the net. You can sponsor net events such as webcasts (*see* Figure 14.3), offer give-aways and contests, or promote the site ex-net. Often, sponsoring events at trade shows, such as at the NEC, Earls Court or Olympia, can start the process of generating buzz on the Internet, especially if the product or service you are selling is unique or a killer app. Obviously, discussing your website with affiliates, suppliers, and potential customers will also help to generate a buzz.

Figure 14.3
*Webcasts are a good
way of promoting
events and can be
sponsored in their
own right*

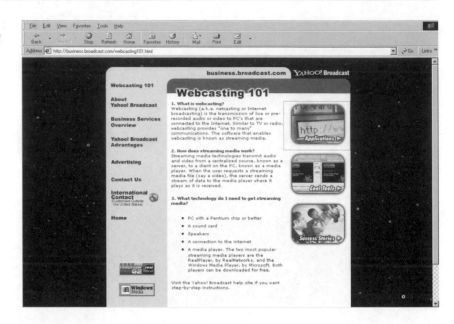

On–Net Advertising

The primary forms of 'on-net' advertising available today are banner ads. They are the long thin ads that you see at the top of most websites, and comprise an image, which is usually animated, and a linking mechanism so that if net surfers click on the ad, they are instantaneously sent to the advertiser's website. Simple animated GIFs, which are used for many of these banner ads, are multiple images that give the impression of motion when run together. These ads are usually placed by larger organisations, and are often run in a rotation, meaning that each time you access the site you may see the same ad only every third time. Sometimes, the ad placements are traded and sometimes the company running the ad pays a commission on sales or a micropayment on traffic. Most often, the ads are paid based on the number of impressions or the number of times the ad is seen. The payment is made on the basis of a cost per thousands of impressions. These prices are determined by the popularity and status of the site.

Ads, however, can sometimes be placed for free depending on the terms and conditions you can negotiate. On-net advertising can also take the form of link ads that are smaller than banner ads and often show only the logo of the website. These take up significantly less room, and are considered less intrusive than the banner ads. These ads are often used on the main web page of companies and search engines, usually to link to services or sites that pay a commission.

The greatest benefit of online advertising is the ability for advertisers who have a product or service with a wide appeal to market to a large number of people or for advertisers whose products have a narrow appeal to target ads at a more select audience. The combination of data mining from websites and the careful placement of

Figure 14.4 *Small ads on the right of the screen link to other sites*

an ad can be a very successful combination for organisations that are sophisticated enough to have clearly defined their customers. The ads themselves are also becoming more sophisticated, with the inclusion of sound and interactive functionality.

Off-Net Advertising

If a company has on-net advertising, why would it need off-net or ex-net advertising? The answer is speed. When Lastminute.com entered the e-commerce leisure war zone, it became one of a number of e-tailers. It needed fast growth in its traffic levels to start generating ad revenue and to give it the critical mass so essential to survival. The viability of the investment in Lastminute.com was dependent on fast success. This success was dependent on critical mass, and that made it essential for traffic to develop quickly. The answer was to use traditional advertising media, such as TV and print ads, as well as the sides of London buses, to generate the kinds of traffic numbers needed to position Lastminute.com as a serious contender.

The approach is to first generate a curiosity about the brand by running ads that introduce the brand name of the company and the image. Short messages and interesting imagery or dark humour are the hallmarks of an Internet hard ad campaign, and the more memorable the ad, the better. The acronym KISS, or 'keep it simple stupid', is the rule of the day in designing the first ads. The goal should be to get people to remember the brand name such as clickmango.com and thereby remember the location on the Internet. Try to avoid lofty messages with complex ideas since people will tend to find them confusing and will tune out the message. The goal is to have as many people as possible remembering the name of the website.

The Personal Approach

Advertising and promotion are an excellent way to gain attention for your organisation, but the personal face-to-face meeting is a more powerful method for raising awareness. The problem is that you cannot spend the entire travel budget on meeting your potential Internet customers (unless you are selling rare art). However, it is an excellent way to generate industry buzz through face-to-face meetings with your affiliates or partners. It also provides you with a chance to understand the strength of their business.

The process is simple. Locate the phone number for the organisation that you would like to partner with and then phone the company and ask for the person in charge of channel marketing or partnerships and affiliates. Next, discuss your new website or concept, how they might fit in with the plan, what benefit you will provide, and what you would like in return. Finally, ask for a face-to-face meeting to discuss partnering opportunities. Remember that the partnership has to provide a matching value. You can't ask Amazon to put up a banner ad in exchange for a banner ad on your site and expect them to be ecstatic. However, if you have a concept that requires the involvement of an equal partner, this approach should work.

Some companies may not have had as favourable a response if they had simply tried to establish the partnership over the phone. In the first place, seeing your partner puts a face to the concept, and provides your partner with a comfort level. Secondly, as most salesmen know, it's hard to say no to a face-to-face close; it is far easier to say we'll think about it over a phone. Of course, the downside is the cost of this approach including airfare, hotels, transport, meals, etc. You will have to make sure that the partner you are going to meet is able to provide you with real value, such as an operational advantage (e.g. e-commerce shopping site), traffic (e.g. major link site), or exposure (e.g. an online magazine – or e-zine – compiling a story).

One of the best ways to get your message out to the world is to take your application to the trade shows. CeBit in Hannover or Internet World in London attract tens of thousands of visitors annually, and can provide a lot of coverage as long as your presence at the conference is noted. This implies that you would have to create some mechanism for getting your name out since there are hundreds of other companies represented. So how do you do that? It's simple – as well as the traditional pre-show PR, you could send two teams to the show. One team should work your trade stand – perhaps with cool promotional give-aways – and the other should work the trade floor, gathering information and talking to partners. Also, consider sponsoring some of the side events that will attract attention, or even badging the carrier bags that most delegates will need to carry away their freebies.

Backing Up Marketing With A Good, Working Website

One of the most critical pieces of any Internet marketing campaign is a good, working website. Although most people seem to understand this concept, they are often in a

A Pipe Is A Pipe

The term 'pipe' is used to refer to an Internet connection. Borrowed from the telecommunications world, it was originally taken from the fibre optic installers. Now, it is used to refer to any Internet connection as in 'My pipe is down'.

rush to get to market and many different aspects are overlooked. The first is how the website functions from a visitor's perspective. Are the pieces in place that will allow the customer to fully evaluate the benefit of belonging to this online community? If you have only some of the functionality up and running, new visitors may feel the site does not offer them enough. The painful lesson here is that these first visitors are the bread and butter of any marketing campaign; they are the market leaders.

The second piece that is essential, but often overlooked, is the look and feel of the site. This goes back to all those design and image lessons you might never have learned, but that are an integral part of the graphics and advertising programmes in the art colleges. If the image doesn't match the community, the visitors you attract may not stay. Cowboy hats are not going to excite the city slickers, just as suits are not going to excite the tech world. Image counts.

Another important aspect is the technical readiness of the site or application. Nothing turns visitors off faster than a site they cannot access or a slow-loading application. Many companies have run advertisements and anticipated a specific number of hits on the site only to find that their pipe – or Internet backbone – was overloaded.

An overloaded pipe simply returns a 'cannot access the domain' message to the visitor. They will, on average, try to reload twice and then quit. Moreover, their attention spans last an average of 10 seconds, so an application that is slow to respond will cause these initial users to lose interest very quickly. Once again, they are likely leaders in their market and therefore critical to generate significant future traffic. The moral here is to ensure that you clearly understand the capabilities of your network and then schedule your promotion accordingly.

How To Choose A Good PR Firm

So, you want to market your new Internet firm, and you're a little short of resources? Well, we suggest that you use the services of a professional PR firm. Let's face it, you probably don't have anywhere near the level of contacts that they do, the experience, or the time. So, unless your available resources do not include money, it is best to let the pros do their work. What they will do is build a plan to take your organisation to the world through a mix of promotions and advertising and through the tangled world of publications both online and offline. In order to succeed, you will have to ensure that the firm you hire has the right mix of talent, experience, and cost.

First, ensure that they have the capability to understand your business and the world of the Internet. There are a wide variety of PR firms in the market and some have specialities; if they have a track record for Internet start-ups, then you've won half of the PR battle. However, some good younger firms without a track record may not only understand the Internet world better but may also have an exceptionally talented and knowledgeable staff that will produce better results. Some older firms may not understand the Internet concept but may have a better grip on the marketing image relationship and may also have an extensive contacts list. The choice of a firm depends a great deal on the correct mix of experience, size, talent, and understanding of the public relations process.

Second, ensure that they are within your budget. Going to a successful PR firm may open a lot of doors, but may also cost too much for the return. Their focus should be to start the process of generating market buzz by working to ensure that the most beneficial PR tasks are complete at the same time that the site is launched. Their cost will be a reflection of the level of impact that you require, but ensure that you decide how deep you want the PR to go. International as opposed to national, national as opposed to local, online as opposed to offline, trade as opposed to general publications, all these decisions will result in various levels of return and will have different levels of cost. Remember that Coke generated its critical mass by hiring low-cost artists to paint its logos on the sides of every old building they could find. The company still hires graffiti artists to legally paint the sides of stores.

Using Mined Customer Data

You may have to buy some data. Many organisations sell data on demographics and psychographics, mined from their own databases. In order to effectively target your advertising and promotion, you will require some indication of where the target is. This raw data provides the information that becomes the starting point for trying to decide a media mix.

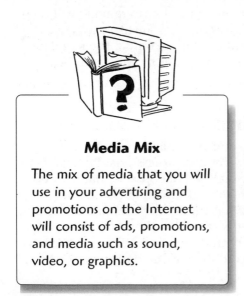

Media Mix

The mix of media that you will use in your advertising and promotions on the Internet will consist of ads, promotions, and media such as sound, video, or graphics.

A media mix is the mix of advertising and promotion that you develop based on the marketing plan of the organisation. The marketing plan should specify real hard targets such as the following information:

➤ Number of hits on the website by a certain date.
➤ The demographics of the market.
➤ The psychographics of the market.
➤ A definition of the community.
➤ How the images are to be interpreted.
➤ The actual images to be used.

➤ Locations of the target audience.

➤ Number of visits to the site per target population (e.g. an ad will be read by 20 000 of my target audience, and I expect 2000 hits), etc.

Mined data provides a valuable resource as to where the target market is located. You are likely to receive data that will indicate the demographic mix of a particular site. Placing an ad on this site should generate a relatively predictable response if your market's demographics happen to match. Some search engines can provide more detailed information pertaining to the interests of users. Delivering ads to these users will also result in higher returns on your expenditure if the 'interest' profiles match your expected market.

The data can also help to adjust your market definition if you find that volumes of a slightly different market are significantly higher. For example, let's say that your site is designed to attract grandmothers over 80 who skateboard, but on analysing mined data you find that the hits from this target market on the skateboard sites is only 10% of grandmothers who skateboard. The implication is that by changing the website to a nice floral background and including a link to a site specifically targeting grandmothers, you will generate a higher hit ratio. Mined data can help you fine-tune the images on the website and locate choice advertising sites.

Working With Affiliates

Affiliates are the organisations or websites that you will partner with to generate traffic. This relationship is usually mutually beneficial, although it is often not equal. Smaller start-ups can provide traffic through links to larger sites; however, the larger sites will be hard pressed to add a link back to the smaller site. This is because the larger sites are inundated with requests for links while the smaller sites have lots of available free space. In fact, many of the more popular websites do not provide direct links back to the smaller sites, but will sell the smaller site banner space. In return, they offer either micropayments for 'click-throughs' from the smaller sites or commissions for sales. Amazon.com has built most of its traffic through these payment techniques. This, of course, does not help to generate traffic back to the smaller site, and traffic is the name of the game.

Another type of affiliate is the cross-promotional affiliate. This is an organisation similar to yours that is offering a complementary product. Let's say that you sell toothbrushes on the Internet to dentists. You can partner with a website that provides online information to dentists to provide a link to your organisation in exchange for a commission. This payment will encourage the other website to partner your organisation. As you continue to add partners, your traffic will grow and more potential affiliates will become interested. Eventually, you may get to the size where other smaller organisations seek to become partners to your site, and you will have to evaluate the benefits of each new partnership. In general, the more partners you can add, the more benefit will accrue as a result of the critical mass theory.

The Customer–Driven Model

Because of the constraints of the Data Protection Act in the UK together with an inbuilt sense of propriety, many online organisations are not providing direct access to their customer database to outside companies. This means that they will not provide email addresses, but will provide a different type of access. Outside companies can advertise on the website to specific types of customers based on criteria that the customer has provided, such as their interests. Other companies ask customers if they would be interested in receiving information from partners. In this scenario, these partner companies would then send email information to the online customer. These are called customer-driven models because the customer or visitor to the website provides the approval to receive this information. Without this expressed approval, no information is sent. In the case of the online banner ads, the entry of 'interest' information simply allows the online company to offer a more directed delivery method to its advertisers.

Traffic Jams

Traffic is simply the number of visitors who go to your website. The goal of advertising and promotion is to attract these visitors to your site. If you are too effective at your promotion you may cause a traffic jam. A traffic jam occurs when your advertising or promotion is run to an audience who all try to access your site at the same time. If you have a single connection to the Internet and a single web server, the result may be that your customers cannot get through. When this Internet busy signal occurs, a message pops up in the user's browser which indicates that the connection cannot be made. Most ISPs provide demographic applications that will track the number of hits to your website, where they came from, when they were visited, volume of traffic, etc.

When an ISP connects to the Internet, it often uses T1 lines or direct fibre optic links that carry a large number of calls. A traffic jam occurs when everyone tries to access your website at the same time after an ad has been run. It is therefore vital that you discuss with your ISP the capability of its network to handle the volumes of traffic to your website that you anticipate and plan with it for your marketing campaign so that it is not overwhelmed. Occasionally, you will be required to change providers to one which is capable of handling the traffic.

The second aspect that can cause traffic jams is the capacity of your server. Companies that have their own T1 lines have the added worry of ensuring that their servers are capable of handling numerous simultaneous hits. Options include using the ISP's server and hotelling or installing your own server in the ISP's location. A big consideration in this regard is the power of your server to manage the hits.

The e-Marketing Plan

Business development is the term usually reserved for the development of a business. This often includes marketing, planning, and strategy. Developing a business plan for your e-commerce company should follow the basic principles of planning, including the following:

➤ Planning the company concept and image.

➤ Developing a strategic or business plan, including establishing goals for the organisation and milestones for completion.

➤ Developing a marketing strategy that identifies the target customer and media/ promotion mix.

➤ Obtaining the necessary funding to complete the company and building the applications or website that you will distribute.

➤ Ensuring your technology is ready, complete, and capable of handling the traffic.

➤ Identifying your partners and establishing agreements.

➤ Preparing your public relations campaign for your launch.

➤ Ensuring that your organisation is up and running, including traditional areas such as back-office functionality, manufacturing, and logistics.

The Least You Need To Know

➤ Who your customers are.

➤ How to promote your business on the net.

➤ What to consider when building an advertising programme.

➤ Why face-to-face promotion is important.

➤ The basis of an affiliate relationship and how it affects your plans.

➤ How to build an e-marketing plan.

215

Chapter 15

Internet Advertising

In This Chapter

➤ Finding the ad customers

➤ The pros and cons of banner ads

➤ The future of rich media

➤ Animation

➤ Push technologies

➤ Linking

➤ Cross-promotion

Advertising On The Net Is A Whole New Game

Internet advertising is rapidly becoming a subset of the larger world of commercial advertising simply because many of the concepts, principles and media used in traditional advertising do not apply to the new world of the Internet. Of course, some of the basic principles of image and strategy still apply, but creating Internet ads requires a different focus or understanding of the mechanics of the net. Advertisers who are familiar with producing print and video ads now have to develop banner ads consisting of short messages, cramped images, and motion, similar to the limitations imposed by teletext, or SMS messaging on mobile phones. There are links to affiliates' sites, micropayments, cross-promotional ads, rich media, push technologies, sound bites, and a growing global perspective. This is different enough from the traditional advertising disciplines that art colleges and universities are starting to add Internet advertising courses to the curriculum.

But all of these technologies are still based on a fundamental design principle that it is more efficient to target a select group for your product than to target the entire world. Your 'target', however, may appear to be as broad as the whole world – for example, people who want fast access to information or to purchase a book, which seems to include most of the Internet population. Unfortunately, if you have a limited advertising budget, you will have to select where to place your ad to get the biggest bang for your buck.

Another fundamental principle is that the design of your ads and website will have to use images that are consistent with the message of your site. The difficulty will be in imaging a message designed to build a 'community of value' (*see* Chapter 6). You will also have to understand the dynamics of your market – the rules have changed, and the freedom of expression and individuality that is part of the Internet will have to be considered when you design new ads.

Where Are The Ad Customers?

The Internet population numbers in the hundreds of millions and the ability to tap into that market through a website is incredible. If you sell books, the population of book readers is vast. If you sell shares, the pool of investors is immense. If you sell surgical-grade steel, your customers may be a little tougher to find. You can sell books and CDs just about anywhere in the world, and if you place an ad somewhere, there is a good chance that it will hit some part of its market. But if the surgical steel manufacturer tries that strategy, he may spend hundreds of pounds for an ad and get a zero response rate. These people will have to be more selective about where they place their ads, searching possibly on websites related to surgical and hospital supplies. They also have to decide whether their market is on net. Finally, they will have to decide whether they will get enough response to warrant the ad, or whether they are better off to change the focus of their effort. Perhaps putting an ad on a punk site will encourage direct sales from the body-piercing community.

The key to not pouring money down the Internet advertising drain will be to identify where your market is located in the vast expanse of cyberspace. The best way to do that is to study information about websites published by companies and e-zines, as well as the traffic levels associated with these sites from tracking companies such as Media Metrix.

You can also obtain demographic information or targeting statistics from websites themselves. The next step is to identify which sites have the most relevance to your market. How many of your customers will visit the site out of the total number of visitors? How many of them will see the rotation of your ad? How many will click through to your website? And – ultimately – how many will purchase something?

This last item has caused Internet companies to start moving away from a 'micropayment for click' model to a 'micropayment for solid contact information'

Traffic Stats

You can get an excellent selection of statistics at `http://cyberatlas.internet .com`

model. This ensures that click-throughs actually benefit the company before a payment is made by ensuring that micropayments occur only for customers who leave valid contact information. Another technique is to pay commissions on sales.

Creative organisations will find their customers in the most unusual places. Women searching for information about the Viagra impotence pill at viagra.com, men searching for lingerie at victoriassecret.com, politicians looking for one-liners at jokes.com. Often the market you are trying to reach is based on a psychographic division, such as people who think UFOs exist and that the government is covering it up. For these types of breakdowns, you will have to study other sources of information until the volume of stored Internet information about individual users grows enough to provide this level of detail. The best way to understand where the customers are who fit unusual psychographic profiles is to read information about the users who surf specific sites or to read the newsgroups that relate to the specific profile you are looking for and research any mentioned websites. The whole benefit of knowing where the customers are is to ensure that every pound spent on ads generates the highest return.

Banner Ads

Banner ads are the long thin ads at the tops and bottoms of most websites. Called banner ads because of their banner-like shape, these ads were originally made of a special interlaced graphic interchange format. Anyone can create a GIF by using one of a number of graphics programs, such as Paintshop Pro or the Corel suite of graphics products.

A GIF animator is a special software package which allows users to copy a series of GIF images into a program and save them as a single image that rotates through the series. By making slight alterations to the GIFs in the series, you will create the effect of animation or movement.

The second important piece of a banner ad is the ability for the user to click on the ad to go to the advertiser's website. This doesn't require any special software because your website software will be able to create a hyperlink from the GIF. However, you can also create banner ads using programming languages such as Java and JavaScript. Java also allows you to include applets or small pieces of code that can perform tasks in a browser to provide the same effect as an animated GIF.

More recently many websites have started to use the Flash Shockwave format for their banner ads which use vector graphics – which by their nature are very much smaller than bitmapped (or raster) graphics and so download much faster.

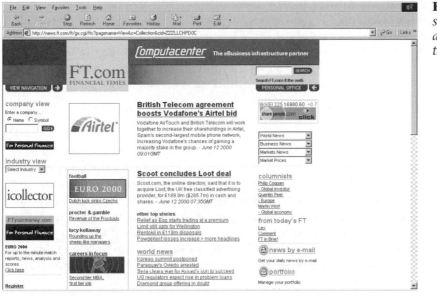

Figure 15.1 *Many sites feature banner ads at the top of their home pages*

The problem with banners is that they provide a limited amount of space to work in. If you include an animated image to catch a surfer's attention, there is almost no space for a message. So the message that you deliver will have to be concise, clear, short, and creative – just as in any headline format.

The other issue that your advertising team will have to be aware of is that surfers are becoming immune to certain types of messages. Win Win Win, Make Loadsamoney, Lowest Prices are all messages that are starting to lose their impact with net surfers. They are being replaced with outlandish headlines that are improbable to say the least, but whose sole purpose is to get you on to the site. Other sites use interesting animated images and colours to catch your eye. Working in a tiny space concentrates the mind and requires a different design philosophy of quick impact in a short time frame.

Rich Media

Rich media is another term for the latest type of banner ads. They are designed using software such as Java and have the added capability that the software provides some form of interaction with the Internet user. Surfers to these sites can interact with the banner ad to open drop-down lists, perform actions with the mouse inside the ad, or select buttons. One example is a banner ad that shows a plane and a series of smoke lines, like you would find in a wind tunnel drifting over the plane in an animation. If you place the mouse over the plane and hold down the button, you can drag the plane inside the banner, and the smoke lines will adjust accordingly. This level of interactive banner ad is becoming more commonplace on the Internet, and it is forcing organisations that use the old-style animated GIF to retool their existing banner ads.

Rich media ads are also beginning to deliver sound bites. In this case, a particular snippet of sound is saved in a file, and when the user clicks on the ad, the sound file plays. Again the messages are very short for efficiency reasons, and will have to be carefully crafted to present the correct image. Another type of rich media banner ad allows you to expand the banner size to present more information. One downside is that these types of ads can be incompatible with certain browsers and platforms.

Animation

The intent of animation is to catch the eye of net surfers so that they are intrigued enough to follow the link. The limitation of banner ads means that the image changes will have to occur in a small space, and this has caused some companies to start returning to a non-animated approach to advertising. This serves a twofold purpose: first, certain demographic populations do not care for animation and often find it annoying and confusing; second, loading and running an animated GIF can slow down the website. If you have a lot of information to load, this can be a significant problem. However, in general, the benefits outweigh the costs, and some animation will still be a significant part of most web pages.

The image that is contained in an animated GIF requires different design principles from those of a standard two-dimensional advertising image. First, there will be numerous graphics in a single animated GIF. Each image must be designed to portray the specific marketing image of the company, and then the total animation image must be reviewed to ensure this same consistent image is ultimately portrayed. This is different from designing a standard, one-dimensional print ad simply because other factors – such as what the animation portrays, what the speed and message of the animation should be, what style of animation should be chosen, and how the users feel about the choices made – are all essential elements that will have to be carefully studied.

Flash Technology

Flash technology by Macromedia provides a variety of new animation applications for websites and can be found at www.macromedia.com

Rich media presents even more problems with designing sound bites, evaluating how users will interact with the software, how this impact will affect the image being delivered, and what can be done to improve the overall delivery of the ad. It also creates problems related to the type of rich media mix that should be used whether it is an application, sound, video, or animation.

Push Technologies

Push technologies relate primarily to information that is pushed to your web page, as opposed to your computer going to get the information from the web. The primary application driving this type of technology is the webcast in which a stream of data

– often video or audio files – is sent to numerous users and represents the more recent innovation to the static push technologies used by PointCast in which a file is sent periodically. This provides users with real-time information similar to the way in which a television network operates. The advantage for the advertiser is that these technologies are starting to deliver a rich media format including sound and video.

Push technologies require the user to sign up for the service, and this provides a registered viewer base to the advertiser, which can then be used to target messages. However, to use this technology will require webcasting software and an ISP that can host your webcast server. Another downside is that the 'push' aspect of these technologies takes a lot of bandwidth to deliver a stream of content. In corporate networks this, combined with the pushing of too much information, has proved to be such a problem that there is a swing against using push, which has been a serious detriment to push-based web companies.

Pop-Up Windows

An offshoot of push technology is the loading of special web pages or multiple web pages. These are essentially nothing more than linked pages that load six or seven other pages when you open the first page. Primarily used to drive up traffic stats, these multi-page loads are annoying to the visitors who enter one of these sites. This technology is, however, being used more effectively by some websites to load a single pop-up window to access new software downloads. The careful use of the pop-up screen can provide an excellent delivery mechanism to make announcements. The problem is that people will find it annoying if the information provided is not of some

Figure 15.3 *Some canny site developers deliver pop-up windows containing sales messages when you log onto their pages*

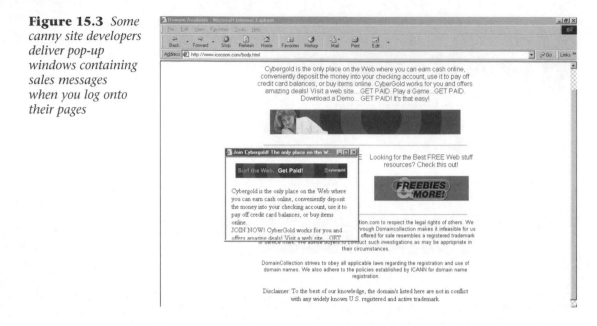

interest to them. Upgrading a browser plug-in is an acceptable use of a pop-up window, but providing a link to another site is not. Pop-up windows are easily programmed into a website using JavaScript already available on the Internet.

Linking To Other Sites

Linking to another site is an effective way to both sell and buy advertising. These smaller link boxes provide the same functionality as the banner ads. When a GIF or other type of image is loaded on a web page, a hyperlink is added so that if the user clicks inside the boundaries of the image, he will be sent to the linked website. For companies that sell space on their web pages, this linking provides ads, micropayments, or commission revenue. For the advertiser, it provides a direct link that can generate traffic.

Affiliate linking is usually an agreement between two organisations to link to each other's websites for mutual benefit. The second type of link is related to adding a non-affiliated organisation on your web page. These links are often encouraged, but rarely paid for. In this case, the web page owner adds the link in order to attract visitors to his site with or without the knowledge of the linked page. This could include links to share quote pages, news services, etc.

The process of getting others to link to your site can be as simple as offering the link graphics free for downloading, or it can be as complex as an agreement to establish a formal linking relationship. However, the one thing that must be present for both companies is a value for the applications that are being offered. If your website does not provide any value to the other site, then the chances of obtaining a link are unlikely.

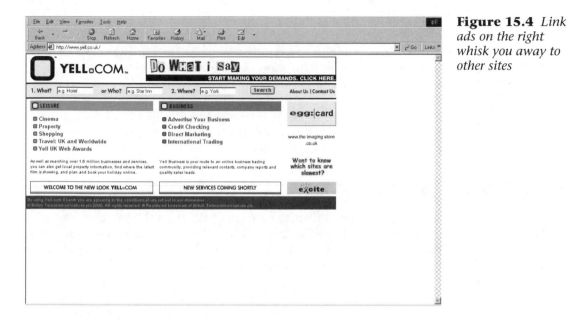

Figure 15.4 *Link ads on the right whisk you away to other sites*

Amazon was a site that did not provide a significant value to other sites because it did not provide main page links. Although the traffic at Amazon was growing, it was difficult for web masters to understand the value of a link to a site that sold books. Amazon solved this problem by creating a value through the payment of commissions for links to the site. Now the web masters could see a value in adding a link to their sites. The AltaVista search engine didn't face the same problems because it provided a valuable service, which was a way to search the Internet for information. It was easier for web masters to justify adding this type of link because it provided a real value.

Cross-Promotional Ads

The traditional advertising world has long understood the benefits of cross-promotion. Co-operative advertising, where two companies with a similar vested interest link their promotional activities to get the same coverage for less money, is becoming more common. This same concept is becoming more prevalent on the Internet as companies link together to reach the volumes needed to attain critical mass. Sometimes, these associations occur between companies that sell compatible products, but often they occur between companies that are direct competitors. For example, a company that manufactures chip sets may form an association with a company that manufactures communications devices to create a new technology or device. They may form a mutual partnership under a single banner and image that can then be advertised on the Internet. This way, both manufacturers can effectively sell their products while splitting the cost of advertising.

Some companies form advertising partnerships even though they compete directly. A simple example of this is the search engines that frequently show up in browser search pages all listed together. Although they compete directly with a search engine such as Hotbot, the Hotbot search page lists them anyway. This is a similar concept to the idea of placing stores in a mall and advertising the mall. Centralising stores in one location will not only save each store money on its advertising budget, it will draw people to the location to reduce the time that shoppers spend driving around. The same concept applies on the Internet. Saving time by locating a series of choices in one location is the future lifeblood of the Internet. Amazon doesn't sell a few books; it sells thousands from competing publishers. Often, the best way to add value to your site is to save net surfers time by combining similar sites into a single location.

The Website As An Advertisement

Let's not forget the most important advertisement that will be on the Internet – your website. It is the place where visitors will travel to learn about your company, products, or applications. It must be carefully crafted using images that are designed specifically for the Internet. There are a number of issues that must be considered when constructing your web page as an advertisement. First, the imagery must be appealing to the majority of your target market. Dark web pages are less attractive to women than men, too many moving animations make the page difficult to look at, unprofessional designs fail to instil confidence, and too much information is cluttered and confusing. In fact, designing a web page incorporates an entirely different design philosophy from that used in print advertising.

The second concern in building a web page is the speed of the page in loading and operation. Visitors to websites on average have an extremely short attention span, and web pages that load slowly are often abandoned in favour of other sites. It is critical that the technical aspects of web pages, such as the depth of the colour in the graphic, the speed with which an application loads, or the order in which the page loads are all carefully considered before the page is ever designed or built. In addition, the way the page works should be tested from different locations and using different browsers to ensure that the page is functioning correctly. The speed of access will also depend on many factors that may be outside your control, such as the level of Internet traffic.

The content of information and flow through the website are key elements in the design of websites. Flow is concerned with where information is located on the site and the structure of that information. In general all information should be able to be found within three mouse clicks from first entering the site. The content is also important to ensure that the proper message is relayed to your customers. Websites that are highly technical in nature will produce little in the way of sales to the general public. The content of a website should never be designed as if you had created a print brochure online but should instead offer easily navigable hyperlinks to bring your visitors to the information they require quickly and easily. Naturally it should reflect the tastes and images of your customers' world and all content should be carefully proofread.

Special Offers

A number of businesses on the Internet make special offers to attract traffic to their websites. The most common are contests that offer visitors the chance to win a prize. Online coupons are also becoming more popular as a means of enticing customers to particular websites. Other offers include:

➤ Free games.

➤ Free software.

➤ Free products.

➤ Free information.

➤ Free help.

➤ Free email.

➤ Free websites.

➤ Free advertising.

➤ Free graphics.

➤ Free e-books.

➤ Free e-zines.

➤ Free music.

➤ Free messages.

Are you starting to see a pattern? Yes, free, and the content of some of the offerings is excellent. The choice of quality freeware available on the Internet is outstanding – animated graphics, free books, e-zines, and information on almost every subject are available by using the search engines. There is also a plethora of free email and web accounts for the taking.

The idea of distributing information or applications for a fee is rapidly disappearing as more and more e-commerce companies try to build critical mass through the provisioning of free stuff. It is highly unlikely that a company would succeed today on the Internet by trying to charge a fee for access unless the information was extremely valuable and, here's the key, not available anywhere else. The problem with believing too much in this last concept is that right now there are hundreds of thousands of individuals bringing their free content to the net each year, and eventually no information will be sacred.

The best defence is to get there first and make a name for your website and its own free content.

Banner Surveys

Banner surveys are a market information-gathering tool available to anyone. Companies offer support and services for the creation of these custom banner ads that draw in Internet users often through the use of give-aways or contests. The survey's links are then distributed through the placement of banner ads, and the data is collected and reported. This is one way to gather information about a population with very little effort; however, selecting a specific population (Internet users) who are gathered at a particular location (a website) and enticing them with an offer (contest) will undoubtedly skew the results of any survey.

Nevertheless, depending on the placement of the ad and the questions in the survey, the information should, in general, provide helpful insight into the market.

The Micropayment

A micropayment is a very small fee paid for each visitor who is sent to your site from another website. The payment is usually tracked by a third party and when a specific amount has accumulated, the fee is paid to the website that sent the traffic.
This payment mechanism provides a way for you to encourage other companies to add your links into their website. As customers visit the other website and click the link, the click-through to your website will be recorded. When enough visitor click-throughs have been accumulated, a payment will be made to the company that sent the traffic.

The problem with payments based on click-throughs is that some web masters have found ways to defraud the system. The extensive use of pop-up technology to create the appearance of large traffic volume is one area of concern. Surfing to a website that loads numerous pop-up windows records a click-through for each of those pop-up windows. This way one visitor can generate instant traffic click-throughs to as many websites as there are pop-up windows. Another technique involves hiring rings of users to continuously surf through linked websites to generate click-through data. Companies have since moved away from the click-through model by only paying affiliate partners for the click-through traffic or by moving to different payment models, such as commission on sales or contacts, or traffic trades where one company trades links to another company.

The Future Of Internet Advertising

No one can predict quite how the future of Internet advertising will pan out, especially with the advent of high-speed delivery mechanisms such as ADSL (asynchronous digital subscriber line) technology and satellite, both of which allow a user to receive other types of media, such as sound bites or interactive functionality faster. In the very near future streaming audio and video could be sent to each visitor to a website. Imagine going to a web page and being greeted with a true video message that is clear and fast. The technology exists to send and load both video and sound files, but its use has not been widespread so far – partially due to bandwidth constraints.

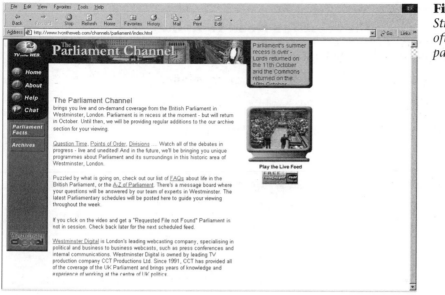

Figure 15.5
Streaming video can often bring a web page to life

Personalised Ads

As data mining and content delivery become more sophisticated, ads that are customised and delivered to Internet users will become the standard on the Internet. These ads will use data-mining techniques to deliver to those particular users ads that are custom designed for them, including using personal information, such as the user's name in the content, or designing images based on personal psychographic profiles. Users will surf to websites and be greeted with personal webskins, or customised websites, that match their personal profile. They may, for instance, include darker graphics for men or lighter graphics for women. Messages will incorporate the visitor's name and purchasing behaviour and will give the impression that the website is actually interacting with the user. All choices and selections will be logged for future mining. All of this technology is available now and is already in use on the Internet.

Advertising on the Internet may incorporate many of the design principles that have been identified over the years through print, radio, and television advertising. But they provide only the foundation to this latest medium that will incorporate new delivery mechanisms such as direct customer interaction. This entirely new world will require organisations, designers, marketers, programmers, artists, and sales staff to rethink the way they use the technology of the Internet to advertise. A new understanding of advertising image, colour, content, message, strategy, and execution is starting to develop, and the success of your e-commerce programme will depend on your level of knowledge in this regard.

> ## The Least You Need To Know
>
> ➤ How to locate ad customers.
>
> ➤ How and when to include animation on your website.
>
> ➤ How linking and click-throughs work.
>
> ➤ What the future direction of Internet advertising is.
>
> ➤ How micropayments work.

Chapter 16

Internet Marketing Models

In This Chapter

➤ Affiliate marketing

➤ Free knowledge model

➤ Creative buzz model

➤ External drive-in model

➤ Repetitive one-hit-wonder model

➤ User group model

Affiliate Marketing

An affiliate is a business you want to partner in order to gain a benefit for your own business. This benefit can be traffic sent to your website, or it can be less obvious, such as the bringing together of similar organisations into an association to form a critical mass. Companies like Amazon could not exist without the publishers, and a shopping site would have difficulty without its online shopping affiliates. Affiliates are a standard method of doing business on the Internet, and although your e-commerce company will survive without affiliates, it will do much better with them.

In traditional business, the concept of affiliates came with a mountain of legal documents trying to protect the interests of both parties. These associations were just as essential as today's e-commerce affiliations, but the level of investment and counter-

Figure 16.1
Amazon provides its affiliates with an agreement which lists the terms of the partnership

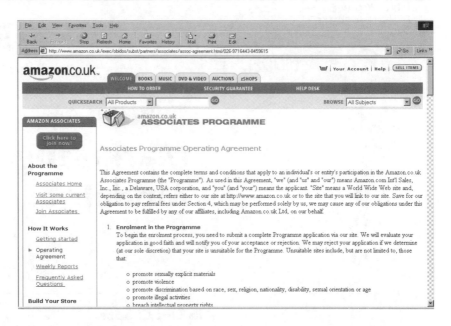

party risk tied to today's e-businesses is far lower. For this reason, many e-commerce affiliate agreements are less complex documents that do not require extensive negotiation or the involvement of teams of lawyers. To become an affiliate with Amazon.com requires you to complete a form and review an agreement that clearly specifies the terms of the affiliation (*see* Figure 16.1). By the time everything is up and running the whole process will have been completed within 15 minutes. This, of course, places a great deal of trust on Amazon to live up to its commitments contained in the agreement.

The Click-Through

It is in Amazon's best interest to ensure that the affiliate programme functions within the terms of the agreement. If the e-commerce community were to find out that click-throughs were not being compensated, Amazon could be embroiled in lawsuits that would keep it mired in battles for the next few years. Who would know that they hadn't lived up to the agreement? You, that's who. First, any click-through to Amazon can easily be recorded from your site by using standard demographic data. Second, companies can use a third-party click-through tracking service to ensure the integrity of the agreement. Finally, even if you have been ripped off, it is unlikely that you have lost much as long as you haven't been recording click-through traffic as a receivable and borrowed heavily against it. The nature of the Internet involves an unprecedented level of trust between organisations, and any company that is unwilling to move fast in favour of extensive legal agreements will be left in the dust.

Strength In Numbers

Why even have affiliates? Well, you can go it alone; there is no reason why you can't. Many successful websites started with a good idea and had no support from the online world. But that has significantly changed in recent years. Smart companies realise that they are far stronger by affiliating with partner companies that offer compatible products than they are by themselves. The Metcalf theory of critical mass is more relevant today than ever before because of the level of competition that exists on the Internet. Affiliate marketing models provide benefits to both parties, and although some organisations are being inundated with offers to partner, they will in general be receptive to partnering in order to attain Melcalf's critical mass.

How Critical Are Your Affiliates?

Developing an online affiliate programme is an essential part of any online business that wants to grow significantly. Most e-commerce start-ups dedicate a great deal of time, effort, and resources trying to establish an affiliate programme. In general, they first approach organisations that are critical to their company's development and to the operation of the online application. In traditional businesses, establishing your suppliers is an essential element to starting up. In an e-commerce web company, the affiliate may not be supplying critical parts for your manufacturing process, but it may still provide a critical piece of your building traffic pattern, and therefore deserves just as much attention as you would give to a major supplier of parts.

The next level of affiliate that you will add to your marketing programme will be those online organisations that are not considered critical to the early development and growth of your e-commerce company, but are essential to your long-term growth. These companies may be organisations that will carry a link to your application as an additional service to their own online community.

The third level of affiliate will be those organisations that will generate traffic by linking directly to your site purely for the benefit of their community. These affiliations are usually registered through an online form when micropayments or commissions are involved or simply by encouragement through a 'benefits of affiliation' web page. Never underestimate the value of this type of programme. Amazon owes its size to these types of affiliations and the informal process that was used to sign up these companies. Of course, the more informal the affiliation, the more likely it is to cause problems, so a couple of

Cybercash

Some organisations are creating online banks to facilitate the flow of commissions and micropayments from affiliates.

Cybercash is one organisation at the forefront of Internet payment technologies used by online banks. Surf to
http://www.cybercash.com

issues should be resolved prior to creating or joining an informal affiliate programme. First, the affiliate agreement should be clear, concise, and enforceable in a court. Ambiguity should be avoided at all costs. Also, a dispute resolution mechanism should be outlined. Second, your organisation should not consider any income or traffic flows for the purpose of raising capital until those flows can be ensured.

Partnering with affiliates is a key component of any e-commerce marketing program, and provides the most effective way to grow your traffic. Although there are some security and legal issues, in general, affiliate relationships will be beneficial to both parties and should be encouraged as much as possible. Maintaining these relationships will be an important piece of any ongoing growth.

Free Content Model

Content is crucial to any website and any e-company. A print news organisation that now wants to deliver its news over the Internet is supplying content. But content doesn't just include information; for example, your website may include gaming software in which the content is an application. Content is anything that is put on your website for access by others. It is extremely valuable to the organisation, and almost every company would be unwilling to give that content away for free. Right?

Content Accessed By Mobile Data Users (Japan)

In April 2000:

➤ 55% Entertainment

➤ 14% News and information

➤ 11% Ticketing/lifestyle

➤ 6% Financial services

➤ 5% Local information

➤ 5% Dictionary and tools

➤ 3% Travel

➤ 1% Restaurants

Source: www.emc.com

Wrong. The Internet is a world that was built on the free flow of information and the hoarding of information is doomed to fail (*see* Chapter 6).

Hoarding information, by trying to keep it to yourself or by charging a fee for access, is likely to be a short-term, narrow view that is doomed to fail. It is doomed because your advanced expertise that is contained in your top secret knowledge database has already been gathered from the Internet by the 'techno kid' down the street, and he is ready to release it to the world in his new free information database.

This was the case for online brokerages that thought their analysis should be shared only with paying customers. Along came E*Trade and the traditional brokerage world was unprepared for the onslaught. Most information that is available currently in the world will eventually make it to the Internet for free at some point in the future. Given this scenario, it is far better to provide your information for free than to force users to pay a fee to subscribe. If the quality of the information is exceptional, your users will come to rely on it, and will revisit your site. This now

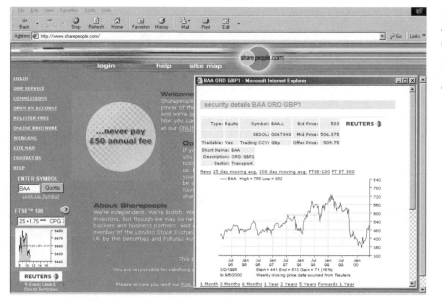

Figure 16.2
Sharepeople.com is an online brokerage that offers share information to its customers

provides you with the opportunity to expand your information offering and grow your Internet-based organisation.

Top Five Selling Products

Books are the biggest sellers on the Internet – no surprise there – and the market for CDs is substantial too. In the summer of 2000 biggest sellers looked like this:

➤ 47% Books

➤ 25% CDs

➤ 12% Videos

➤ 9% Electrical equipment

➤ 7% Flowers

Source: www.ipoints.co.uk

Content can be divided into the following types:

➤ Time-critical information with a short shelf life.

➤ That which is difficult to obtain from anywhere else.

➤ General with a long shelf life.

➤ That which is widely available.

If you think about it, the first two categories are the only ones you can consider charging for since with the last two visitors can invariably find the information they want elsewhere.

Free Applications

Applications are even more difficult to distribute for free. Companies and individuals invest a great deal of money and personal capital to develop an application. To release it on the Internet for free would seem to be a ludicrous waste of resources, or is it?

Macromedia provides downloadable player software for free from its website. Its technology allows visitors to the website to play games created using Flash or Shockwave software. So what is the point of investing so much time in development if the software is going to be released for free? Traffic is the answer. By releasing the software for free, you will generate traffic to your game-playing website, and this will provide a number of benefits. The first benefit is advertising revenue for banner ads, the second is income from the sale of the development software needed to create similar games, the third is the ability to advertise your e-commerce products such as Shockwave's new Shockmachine game system, and lastly it encourages more users to visit, which can make your software the standard of the market. We all know what being a standard can do for your company every time we fire up Windows. Apart from that, Macromedia is giving away only the player software rather than the developer software for which it charges a premium.

However, to generate large volumes of interest, the kind necessary to create critical mass and make your e-business the standard, will often require more than just great information. In order for your concept to get enough traffic to become a standard, it will require some level of support from affiliates or partners, or some level of advertising and promotion. This isn't necessary if your expertise is not transferable to the web. For example, a surgeon can't very well do surgery over the net, but can attract visitors to her practice through free information offerings on her website as well as undertaking some consultations. But is it necessary for her to generate huge volumes of traffic? No, she will need only a specific type of individual located in her home market. In this scenario, affiliate marketing models are not appropriate for the site.

How To Generate Revenue

If your e-business is designed to generate revenue from online sales, then the greater the number of visitors to your site, the greater the potential for revenue from sales.

However, this is not the only way to generate revenue based on traffic. The most common form is advertising through the use of banner or link ads. Like most advertising programmes, the more visitors to the website, the more revenue can be charged for the ad. Click-throughs that generate payments as a result of visitors who use a link are another form of revenue. The more visitors to your site, the greater the chance they will use a link that pays a click-through or commission.

Revenue that is generated as a result of comparable product offers, like the Shockwave example, is another form of revenue. After critical mass is attained and your application is the standard, there will be numerous opportunities to capitalise on it. The billions of dollars of wealth Microsoft created occurred because DOS became the standard operating system, and the step to Windows was its licence to print money.

Being the choice of millions of online users is the goal behind the free content marketing model. This model is also the most prevalent in the world since it is used by almost everyone who has a website. Almost everyone who builds a website starts out by adding free content to the site that they think will be beneficial to web surfers. It can be as simple as a recipe for waffles or as complex as an application that performs some useful function.

Creative Buzz Model

Often, web organisations do not have the ability, resources, or compatible benefits necessary to grow through the use of affiliates. An organisation such as a movie production house might have interesting information available on its website but provide little in the way of benefits to another website (with the exception of a movie link website). An affiliate-linking model would probably produce limited benefit for the volume created. The content provided by this movie site may not only be interesting, but there is a delivery mechanism technology for things such as video. However, since the content has a relatively narrow range of interest, just supplying it for free will not guarantee good coverage.

In this case, it may be better to try to generate traffic by creating a buzz. A buzz is the conversation that occurs between people about a particular topic, for example, your website. Creating buzz in the correct manner can generate an extensive amount of traffic, and if your company continues to create buzz, the website will grow. This concept is used extensively by Hollywood stars and their PR firms to ensure the star is kept in the press spotlight. Keeping the stars in the spotlight encourages their popularity and that leads to continued roles in movies. Creating a buzz about your website and then periodically generating new buzz will drive traffic to your site on an ongoing basis, just like the stars keeping their names in the press.

How To Generate Buzz

Buzz is generated in a variety of ways – face-to-face meetings, phone conversations, advertising, promotion, trade shows, media announcements, sponsorships, etc. Getting people to remember the name of your e-business is the first step.

Figure 16.3 *By the time Bras Direct closed down it had a huge following and still draws visitors, to whom it offers useful links to other sites which could fit the bill*

It solves all kinds of problems if your market can remember your name. Amazon is easy, Virgin is easy, but long and ungainly names might cause some problems.

So how is buzz generated? You can generate it by talking about your website to other people. Before you do talk, however, set up a quick website just for people to go to. Even if it is not functional, having a place to go that has some basic information about what the business is and what it will contain will make it easy for you to say 'visit my site' and start generating a buzz. It can take quite a while to generate a significant level of buzz, and it will depend on your resources and your tactics.

Some companies generate buzz by using an affiliate model to start the process. Face-to-face meetings with partners and suppliers are a good starting point, but may not generate the chatter necessary to grow significantly if your application is not interesting enough. The real win will come when the buzz crosses over from the industry side to the general population side of the market. If you create buzz inside an industry about an application, it will generate a lot less traffic to the site initially than if you can create buzz with the general population. Let's face it, a bunch of technical gurus getting excited about a cool website isn't the same as 100 million users wanting to know more about a new application.

Shock Promotion

Some companies go to great expense and great lengths to create a buzz by using shock promotions that gain attention – for example, live births on a webcast, hosting an extreme sports demonstration, even using quirky ads during the Cup Final. In creating these unusual sponsorships or promotions, it is vital to ensure that the name of the website is prominently displayed. If give-aways are handed out, make sure they are associated with the website. An example might be giving out free hot chocolate at an outdoor game in reusable cups with the website name on the side. The main goal of these promotions should be to generate the buzz needed to attract visitors to the site and not necessarily huge volumes of traffic. If the curiosity of market leaders is captured during these events, they will generate the buzz that will eventually lead to the traffic.

Industry or affiliate buzz is an essential element to getting a good response from the media. A good response from the media is the way that the general public starts to hear about new websites. It is this 'general public' buzz that leads to larger and long-term traffic flows. However, the press is inundated with press releases from a variety of companies, and each day thousands of new start-ups send out information hoping for a spot on one of the news distribution channels.

Generating Industry Buzz

One of the best ways to have your information noted and recognised by media organisations is to ensure the organisation is already familiar with your company. One of the best ways to do this is to generate industry buzz that crosses their desks or to partner with an organisation that counts. For example, if we form an alliance with a small start-up and send out a press release on company-headed paper, it is likely to get binned. If, however, we form an association with Worldpay and release details of the partnership under the Worldpay banner, the media will not only be more receptive to the information, it will also take note of our name.

Generating buzz is a process of creating chatter first at the industry level, then through the media level, and into the general population. The benefits are that industry buzz opens the door to the media, which creates buzz in the general population. This is what translates into growing traffic volumes. It will help to stage some spectacular sponsorships or in-your-face promotions to further push the buzz. Also, you will have to continually create and issue information to keep the chatter alive. The results from this model should be a steady and growing traffic level. All of this, of course, is standard PR practice.

External Drive-in Model

Traffic is the name of the game, and sometimes it is easier to go directly to the general public and 'drive em in'. Using this model, e-companies will go directly to the market to promote their websites, with the goal being to create instantaneous traffic.

Advertising is usually the fastest way to generate traffic, and the number one place to put an ad has to be a major sports event, such as Wimbledon or the Cup Final. Millions of viewers will see the ads, and these can easily generate significant traffic if these are remembered. The problem, of course, is the cost.

If your website is not up to handling the traffic load, and is not capable of capturing the attention of a bunch of football fans, then the money you spend will be wasted.

On the other hand, if you are Walker's Crisps and you're running a contest to win tickets to next year's Cup Final and for some reason want to generate traffic, show the website with a picture of Gary Lineker and Gazza and you could get lots of traffic from those same fans. That's called direct traffic generation, and is what an e-business does when it goes right to the source of traffic. However, if your product offering has a narrow interest, spending millions on a Cup Final ad may not pay for itself. One of the best direct-to-source promotional campaigns has involved advertising hoardings that were chosen on major traffic routes leading into some high-tech office buildings. Black with white lettering and a website address was all that was on the billboard. After a week of running the ads, the number of hits to the site from the target audience – those high-tech employees – more than justified the expense of the billboards.

Sponsorships

Another way to drive in traffic directly to your website is through sponsorships of events that attract your audience. Pets.com could easily sponsor dog and cat shows around the country or major events such as Crufts. If it places its web name throughout the events, it would be likely to generate significant direct hits on its sales website. Other sponsorship ideas include having teams of people handing out dog treats in parks that simply have the website domain name imprinted on them. Promotional ideas have ranged from shining massive lights on large monuments to threatening to place a large floating billboard permanently in the sky. Success is always measured in hits, and traffic will translate into revenue either now or in the future.

Figure 16.4 *Pet sites could generate traffic by sponsoring pet events such as Crufts*

Repetitive One-Hit-Wonder Model

What is a repetitive, one-hit wonder model? It's a way of generating repeat, large volume traffic through a website by changing the content. This is essentially the model behind some of the most popular offbeat websites today, and is fundamentally what underlies most of the news sites. We read the newspaper to get information about the world around us. We rarely buy newspapers to get old news or stock information we could get elsewhere. In fact, we buy newspapers to get information about those odd events that just happened, the newsworthy events. We turn the TV on and are glued to *Sky News* not because we needed information about nappy rash but because of the weird event that is unfolding. Disasters, politics, war, and the weird event of the day all make their way into the newspapers, and the circulation volumes drift with the story. The repetitive nature of these news stories is what keeps people buying and providing a steady circulation. If the story never changed, the traffic would decrease. This is the fundamental principle behind the repetitive, one-hit-wonder model.

e-Commerce companies that are trying to attract visitors to their websites can implement this model to change their content frequently to keep visitors interested. When flooding hits the south of England, the Met Office website is deluged with hits on its pages; when a tech business makes a big announcement, Bloomberg gets the hits; and when the markets drop, FT.com gets the traffic. One-hit wonders are all those little stories that drive up the traffic – for example, people getting live surgery, webcasts of rock concerts, and breaking news stories.

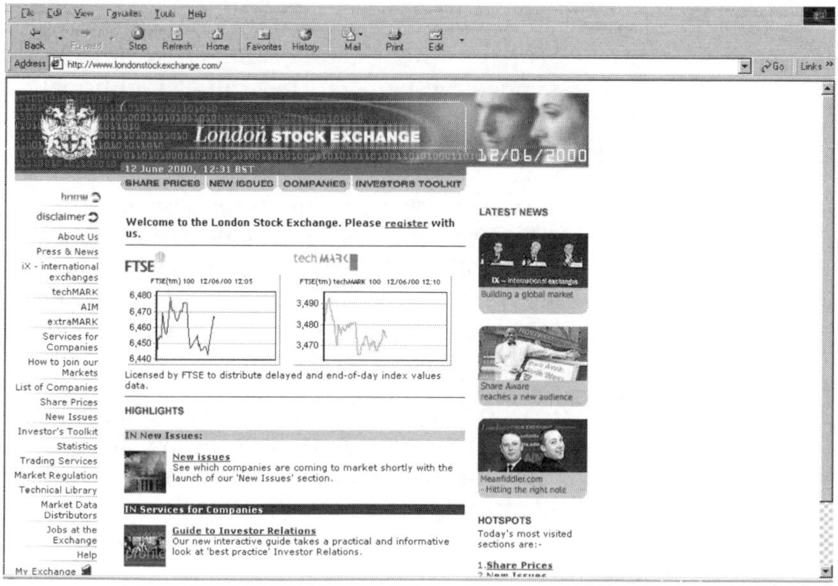

Figure 16.5 *The London Stock Exchange's website is a useful place to find information on the stock market*

Examples Of The Repetitive One-Hit Wonder

Repetitive one-hit wonders occur all the time in the world, and some e-commerce companies have taken full advantage of this to generate traffic.

So how is this even remotely about your e-commerce company? Simple. Even regular e-commerce companies can create direct traffic by frequently changing content. Just because your site sells something doesn't mean it can't capture those one-hit-wonder benefits. By recreating yourself or your company occasionally, you will keep the content of your site fresh, and your visitors will continue to return, especially if the one-hit wonders that you are using are relevant to your group. For example, let's say that you want to start an online travel agency with all the usual trappings, holiday planning, travel information, ticketing, hotels, cars, etc. Now let's say that you also want to generate traffic. You can start offering other services that will be compatible with your existing product but will enhance it on a regular basis. Travel advice, travel destination weather, special last-minute offers, chat, email and a wide variety of other information can all be provided at a relatively low cost or no cost with banner ads. I, as a traveller, might become very used to travelling to your website, and if the information is good, I might even make it my browser default page. Now that's traffic building. As long as the information is fresh and contains those one-hit-wonder items, visitors will return to your site seeking more information and may bring their friends as well.

User Group Model

The last model we will talk about is the user group model. In Chapter 6 we discussed 12 rules for building a killer app, and one of those rules discussed the concept of building a community of value. This is essentially a website or e-commerce company that is built around a community of like-minded individuals. They can be traditional demographic groups or a group that simply has the same opinions about a subject, shares an interest, or belongs together out of some sense of inner self-worth.

Some of the other models are more relevant to this particular model because free content is essential to gathering individuals into a community of value. Other ways to attract a community of value include adding affiliates to create interest, generating a buzz in the community, and providing the community with one-hit wonders. The real issue will be whether or not the online community already exists, or is being created by the website.

Online communities do exist, but often they do not have a way to express themselves as a community. Large groupings, such as women or sport fans, have always clearly existed and have always had outlets for their collective soul, but some groups have just recently started to have a unified voice and meeting place. The Internet has provided the perfect medium for these groups, and new e-commerce companies are creating these online community environments every day.

Niching

The 'ties that bind' are quite easy to locate in today's early development of online communities. But as the main divisions start to get taken up, new companies will have to find different ways to redefine these groups. This technique is called cross-niching.

Cross-niching involves defining a population of people by either demographics or psychographics. The next step is to identify niches within these broad groups that you will initially target. Finally, these niches can be expanded by either promoting to new niches or by redefining the groupings. For example, let's say that I'm a divorce lawyer, and that I want to start a website for divorcées. I can redefine the female population that may visit my site by narrowing it to include women who have been or are divorced. I can further narrow the target, if I choose, into categories, such as women who are dissatisfied with their divorce and those who are satisfied with their divorce. We can use one of these niches to target women who are dissatisfied with their divorce and then expand the definition to include men and women who are dissatisfied with their divorce. Now I can start up my website and create an online environment with helpful advice, online forums, chat rooms, and links to other affiliates.

Keeping Your Audience

The goal in trying to keep your audience is to ensure that the images and messages are consistent with your market. Occasionally, you may want to tweak the mix in order to expand the market by cross-niching, but caution must be exercised because the wrong image can alienate your audience and cause your traffic to decline.

The greatest advantage to building a community of value is the ability to tailor your image and messages specifically for this group. It also allows you to pinpoint their location, both on-net and ex-net, for promotional, advertising, and partnering opportunities. Allocating resources to encourage these users to try your web offering will yield a far greater return on your investment, and will generate traffic that has a greater chance of growth, as long as your content and environment are what the market is looking for.

As an e-commerce company, you should tailor your offering or design your company to cater to your target market. The easiest way to stay focused on this task is to build and maintain a community of value. Building this community by using a user group marketing model will help you not only maintain traffic but grow the traffic as more and more of the market becomes aware of your site.

None of the above marketing models will work better than the next, and in some scenarios, combinations of them all will be the best option. Your choice of model will depend extensively on your business plan and your markets. It will also depend on your resources and your milestones for implementation. Carefully evaluate all of these options and the others that are out in the Internet marketing world before you start down the long path of Internet marketing.

The Least You Need To Know

➤ How to build an affiliate programme.

➤ Why your content should be free.

➤ How to drive in the traffic.

➤ How to create buzz.

➤ What's a one-hit wonder?

➤ What is a community of value?

Chapter 17

Off-Line Marketing For Online Businesses

In This Chapter

➤ The benefits of face-to-face marketing

➤ Using promotions to build traffic

➤ How to spin great stories about your company

➤ How to use public relations effectively

➤ Keeping investors informed through investor relations

How Important Is External Marketing And Promotion?

There are well over 10 million websites, of which more than 10% are estimated to be business websites. With that level of competition, who needs to market? Anyone who wants to survive on the net, that's who. In the last few chapters we discussed how to market your organisation on the Internet and, in some cases, off the net. This off-net or 'ex-net' marketing is a very important component of any e-commerce marketing campaign. Face-to-face meetings, promotions, public relations, and investor relations are all essential elements of any good organisation. They are the key methods by which owners and executives communicate with the world, and meeting people is a vital piece of the e-commerce puzzle. However, like all good communication, you have to have something to say. You can talk about the weather, you can discuss sports scores, but we all tend to gravitate to the person telling the great story over in the corner of the room. That's your e-commerce assignment: tell a great story to as many people as want to listen.

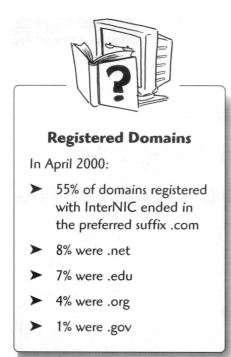

Registered Domains

In April 2000:

➤ 55% of domains registered with InterNIC ended in the preferred suffix .com

➤ 8% were .net

➤ 7% were .edu

➤ 4% were .org

➤ 1% were .gov

Spinning A Great Story

What makes a great story? It is characters, plot development, climax, and style. Any writer will tell you that the responses they get after they have written a story will be that some people hate it, and some people love it. And to make things more complicated, the 'some' of the people you were certain would hate it actually loved it, while your strongest supporters may tell you to go back to the writing table. However, no matter how you write a story, not everyone will like it and not everyone will hate it.

Writing combines a wide array of potential styles, flows, images, subtleties, and impressions. It may flow logically, or it may flow erratically towards its completion. It may be concise, or it may be detailed. No one story is correct, and this is what the true art of creating a business story is all about.

Your Vision Of Your Company

Your e-commerce story should be about your vision for your organisation. A tale that begins, progresses in the middle, and even ends. It starts with an introduction and quickly progresses to an evaluation of where and who you are, your company's resources and strengths. It should move to identifying where you want to be, with a clear direction and flow. It should include milestones, benefits, and goals. It should progress to a climax of potential and establish a precision target, such as income, as its goal.

What Makes A Good Story?

Good stories are like fine wines, they start out smooth and end flawlessly. They have little or no downside, or the downside is dwarfed by the upside. If Amazon had walked into your office four years ago, you might not have given them the time of day, but if you had listened carefully to their story, you would have realised the potential. A world market of six billion people served from centralised distribution points. Even the harshest test criteria could not ignore the fact that just a small portion of this market equalled gigantic profits. So why do these companies lose money? That's the art of the story. When you invest in Amazon, you invest in a new way of doing business that intuitively sounds low cost but in fact sets the standard so high that the margins have to be non-existent at the start. The company will eventually attain profitability, but right now, building critical mass costs money.

Most of the good e-commerce stories follow a familiar pattern. A company offers an application that is needed widely, and distributes it for free or at a loss on the Internet.

Some examples of great stories are the following:

➤ Real audio for sending streaming audio and video.

➤ PointCast for streaming content.

➤ MP3 for digital audio.

➤ Yahoo! as a search engine.

➤ AOL as a community.

➤ Shockwave for online games.

➤ Java for web language.

➤ NetMeeting for Internet telephony with video.

➤ Linux for an alternative operating system.

➤ Amazon for online shopping.

➤ Tesco Direct for online groceries.

These stories were relatively clear and concise. All they had to say was that their application performed a function that had great potential over the Internet. Almost anyone who has spent any amount of time surfing the Internet knows the great potential of these applications simply by trying them. But the same can be true even if you do not have a bunch of hot-shot app builders in your office to build you the next killer app. A lot of Amazon's success had nothing to do with a specific application, but more with building a community and critical mass for its website. Of course, it is now on the defensive as established players such as Waterstones.co.uk or start-ups come gunning for a share of the pie (*see* Figure 17.1). But it was originally unhampered because it was the first to market or at least the first to capture huge critical mass.

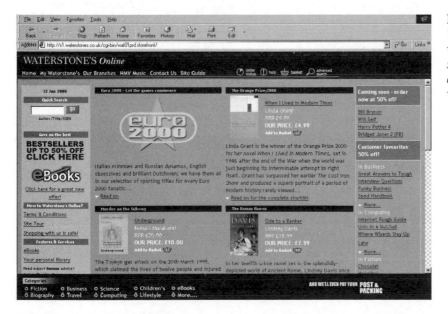

Figure 17.1
Waterstones is a well-known high street name which competes directly with Amazon.

Increases In Traffic – Top 5 Sites

In the 12 months between March 1999 and March 2000:

➤ Yahoo! sites

➤ Microsoft sites

➤ AOL Network

➤ Excite@home

➤ Lycos

Source: `http://cyberatlas.internet.com`

Good Content Equals Good Websites

Even new content distribution companies can make a splash in the Internet world. You don't have to have a killer app – just a killer concept, which if it succeeds like Amazon will become a killer app in the eyes of the world. The key to growth will be making the content unique enough to attract traffic, and that usually will require a couple of twists to the formula story. You may decide to deliver content to users through an online cooking website and tie it into a shopping database for kitchen wares. Although it may not be a killer app, the size of the cooking market is enormous and as long as you have unlimited recipes and cooking information on your site, you will attract lots of attention and with enough traffic, sizable sales. Spinning a story about your idea for an e-commerce company is easy but takes some time and patience to get it right. However, the rewards of customers, investors, partners, and even your competitors will be worth all your effort.

Figure 17.2
Cucina Direct is benefiting from the huge demand for cooking sites

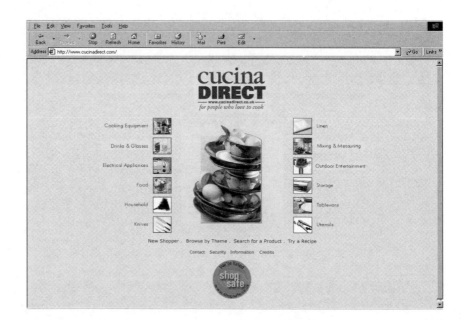

Face-To-Face Meetings

Don't we all just love going on road shows? Living life like a snail with your house on your back and a family who don't recognise you when you return? Just keep in mind that it's only for a relatively short time. The power of the face-to-face meeting is an important thing. It's very hard for an organisation or a group of investors to get a feel for your company if they can't meet you. This doesn't mean you have to go pounding on every door selling the company since that would be grossly inefficient or wasteful. What we suggest is that you call the channel manager in those companies that you need to affiliate with in order to be successful and use a bit of soft persuasion to set up a face-to-face meeting. Remember that whenever you meet your potential affiliates, always have a clear understanding of how your website or application will benefit their company. Don't hard sell because you are supposed to be getting partners.

The Road Show – Presentations

The road show is an integral part of any organisation's attempt to get its message out whether it is to potential investors, potential affiliates, the media, or customers. The advantage of a road show is that it significantly reduces the costs of travel and generates industry and investment buzz all within a narrow time frame. As you set up your organisation and start to visit affiliates, you will need to raise some capital to get the job done. It's a bit of a catch 22: you can't travel without cash, it's difficult to get in the investment door without some buzz, you need to visit affiliates to generate buzz, you will need to travel to visit affiliates, and around it goes. Breaking the cycle with the use of seed capital allows you to split the balance of the funding between investor road shows and affiliate road shows.

There are some simple tips to make the road-show task easier:

➤ Don't get too keyed up about the whole programme. Relax and have fun. You will be more welcomed by these groups if you are professional and don't use hard-sell tactics.

➤ Remember that they need good investments as much as you need money, and there are a lot of dogs on the road-show circuit.

➤ It often helps if you can add a hired gun who has experience in this field. Some of the most arrogant and obnoxious individuals can make your company a success on the road-show circuit. What counts is their enthusiasm, soft salesmanship, and the most important thing in a sales call – their ability to close the deal.

➤ Be prepared to tell the story in varying lengths from 15 minutes to three hours. It is important that you get across the main points in all presentations – the concept, the potential for the concept (either revenue or traffic forecasts), the benefit to the person or company you are presenting to, and the close.

➤ It is very important that you do not take their rejections personally. Remember that not everyone will get excited about your concept, and some people who say 'no' will either come back or pass your name along to someone else.

At the end of your road show you should get some feedback from affiliates and investors. Be open-minded and flexible; they may appear to be totally clueless about your idea, but they may bring some other element or piece of information to the table that may be essential. That information could be another competitor, a better piece of software or service for you to use, a twist on your concept that you had never thought about, or business wisdom that is worth its weight in gold. Of course, most people won't have a clue, so smile politely, answer their questions, shake their hands, and leave. There is always another day, another investor, another affiliate, another partner, and another plane to catch. Most individuals you talk to will have at least one valuable piece of information to provide, and don't be shy about asking questions. Remember that people love nothing more than talking about what they've done and who they are. It gives us all a chance to brag.

You should always be wary of dubious individuals, investors who want total control, affiliates who want money, and partners who want too much. Never give away the shop, and never sign on the bottom line unless you are comfortable with the individual you are dealing with. There are a lot of con artists and crooks lurking around Internet start-ups.

You should ensure that you do follow-up calls with those people who are wavering, if for nothing else than to give them the opportunity to say no and at a minimum to reinforce your company name in their minds. If you believe in your concept, so will others, and there is both a vast pool of money for investment and more new affiliate businesses opening on the net each day. Always remember that your pool of resources will be limited so you will have to target your face-to-face contacts wisely. Major affiliates and major investors should be the primary focus at the start and never, ever turn down good media coverage.

Promotion

Promotion is a real art. Anyone can do it, but few do it really well. The art of promotion is a tangled mess of face-to-face meetings, carefully crafted stories and images, creative campaigns, and targeted delivery. The point of your first promotion should be to get the story out there. Spending thousands of pounds on a stand at the latest internet exhibition in the middle of hundreds of other exhibitors is probably not a good first step. Having your company van blown up accidentally by the police on the six o'clock news is getting there.

Having the Prime Minister answer questions in Parliament about why he is surfing to your pornography distribution website is the ticket you are looking for. Promotion is quirky and twisted on the Internet, but it doesn't have to be. Sponsoring the last-place team at Brands Hatch might not cost that much given their track record, but if it promotes your website, that would probably generate some significant press, especially if they go on to win.

Promotion should reflect the beliefs of your target audience. You should not try to change them but rather try to attract them to your website or application. You may be able to attract them for things like curiosity, genuine interest, fake disgust, or out of sheer boredom. Of course, you can hire a PR firm to create and execute a great promotion, but most companies will have limited resources for this task. A better use of the money would be to pay them for media distribution and interest gathering prior to an event built and executed by your own staff. An example might be a company that chooses to sponsor a promotional event and fundraiser by hanging a gigantic banner from a huge building for three days during a conference. In this instance, the PR money would be better spent on getting the PR firm to use its contacts to host a media party during the event inclusive of graft.

Delivering The Company Message In Promotions

All promotions should deliver the message of the company and its story. Some promotions are designed to attract traffic or interest, and in these cases promoting the name of the company will be the main goal – for example, hanging banners with only the company name on them. However, in the early promotional stages, the main goal should be to promote both the company and the story. Sending a banner unfurling hundreds of feet down the side of a building is interesting, but following it up with a speech at a conference or a special party will provide you with an excellent opportunity to get your message out.

Remember that new cool things or NCTs attract attention. Your staff should work to find that 'new cool thing' that will get your message out there. Coffee mugs and key rings just won't cut the mustard in today's world, but a digital watch, or something else which is regarded as 'cool', might.

What's In It For Your Audience?

Everyone is looking for a benefit. That's a good thing to keep in mind as you promote your story. In fact, you can practice this beforehand by asking, what if the Microsoft reps drop by? What's the benefit to them? Or what if AOL asks what you are doing? Again, the response should indicate what's in it for them. Benefits are everybody's sweetener. They can be traffic, advertising, promotion, partnering, commissions, micropayments, compatible offerings, or even competition. They are the grease that drives the Internet's e-commerce wheels, and they open the doors. Make sure that you clearly understand the deliverable benefits for each person or group to whom you will talk.

Public Relations

Public relations are a vital part of any e-commerce promotion, and are an ongoing part of any company's operations. Usually, the owners of small businesses will perform this function, as opposed to larger organisations that have individuals hired for the task. Different companies view public relations from different perspectives, and there is nothing to say that one structure is better than another.

There are, however, some basic principles that should be followed, especially for Internet start-ups. First, ensure that your website is functioning, even if only to provide some minimal information about the company. Nothing is more annoying than receiving a web address that doesn't work. This also applies to having back-office staff who answer the phone when the principals are away. Too many start-ups send the primary staff out on the road without an adequate communications backup in the office. This could result in investor reps whom you talked to on the road calling your company for more information but not receiving any. In addition, the people who do answer the phone should have a professional manner and the capacity to forward a call to you on your mobile phone. These are basic functions that are almost universally ignored by even the most intelligent Internet start-ups.

What Do PR Firms Do?

The main function of a public relations firm is to get your name and story out to the world, primarily through the media. They can book interviews, schedule speeches, plan conference attendance, issue press releases, call the press directly, host events, plan promotions, liaise with your advertising agency, create a media mix, and even develop a marketing plan with you. Their goal is to get you as much favourable coverage as possible, and in some instances, as much unfavourable coverage as possible. Whether you have the resources to hire these services will depend on your success at raising capital. If you are successful and your concept is sound, a good PR firm will take you to the market with a much better result.

There are a number of simple things that you can do if you do not have the resources for a big PR firm. For example, you can create a mailing list of the e-mail addresses for

Figure 17.3
Topspin is one of many PR and marketing firms to have realised the potential of having a web presence

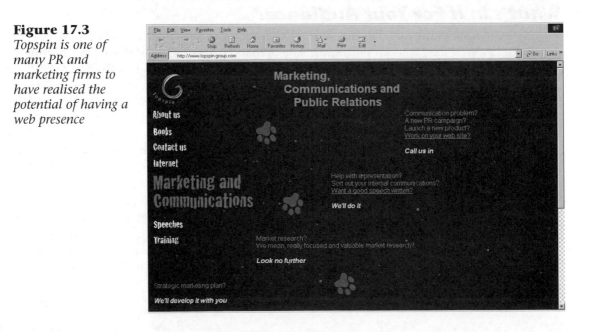

the online news and technical services and find their requirements for submissions. Call these organisations beforehand and talk to one of the tech reporters about your story. Use this contact name as the reference for the press release. Issue an online press release to the media companies that you are targeting that clearly describes your company, you, and the concept. Don't wait for the phone to ring; follow up with the reporter and ask for her opinion on the story. Most opinions will be negative, but don't let that discourage you since you are not calling for anything but to keep the company name in their heads. Offer them your name as a contact and follow up with an e-mail or letter.

Using Public Relations During A Road Show

A road show is a relatively easy thing to plan, but a complex thing to execute. You will invariably run out of time and resources so careful planning will be essential to your survival. Never schedule meetings close together unless you think you can make them. Since a critical function of public relations is to handle any queries related to the organisation or its concept, train someone who will stay behind and perform the task professionally while you are on the road. If you do not have the staff, forward your calls and emails to your mobile; however, this may not always be the best approach if you are in a meeting with an important affiliate or investor. In this case, at least one onsite staff member is probably a reasonable investment.

The Big PR Event

PR firms also design and execute public relations events that can require a significant level of resources and can often be pulled off more efficiently by someone who has experience. However, it is not necessary that this be the case. You can plan and execute your own PR events, and some companies have individuals to do just this task.

e-Commerce concepts come in very handy during the execution of public relations functions. Websites can and should be used to provide the public with information. Call centre and telephone systems can easily manage incoming calls, and customers, investors and affiliates can email the company for information.

Investor Relations

Public relations pertains to the entire world of people who may contact you for various reasons. Investor relations is a subset of public relations, but with a particular financial undercurrent. In fact, understanding finance and stock markets is so vital that investor relations groups are usually part of the finance or treasury department of large organisations. Their ability to talk about the forecast earnings per share and how it will be affected by specific events makes their area of expertise rather important.

You can perform investor relations without a strong financial background, but we don't recommend it. Understanding your financial statements is an integral part of this task, and unless you can discuss return on investment, gearing, leverage and exit strategies and a whole lot more besides, we suggest you add a good financial director to lead your executive team.

Most of the initial calls regarding investor relations will pertain to the story that is being told about your company. This implies that the individual picking up the investor relations phone line must be fluent in the company story you are telling to the world, and he must be confident and competent enough to deliver it to callers. The last thing you want is a second-level investor who is looking to silently bankroll a small e-business like yours hanging up the phone in disgust when she can't get information about forecast gross margins from 'Olivia', your wonder programmer. You must have individuals in the investor relations department who will instill a high degree of confidence and professionalism in the investor who is calling.

Publishing Financial Information

Using your e-commerce expertise, you should now be able to see how you can use the power of your website to publish financial information. Most online companies recognise the importance of investors and give them a separate home on their websites. These investor relations areas should contain the following information:

➤ A short version of the company story.

➤ A detailed version of the story.

➤ The corporate business plan.

➤ Analysis of the markets.

➤ Information about unique company strengths.

➤ Inside information about key employees.

➤ Risk mitigation factors such as insurance.

➤ Financial information.

➤ Share price.

➤ A variety of other pieces of information.

Ensure that when you release data to the public on a website you are not breaking any rules of the stock exchange where your shares are listed.

Releasing Financial Information Online

Another way to use e-commerce technology is to release data to the financial media through email. Most financial news services can receive company announcements through the Internet, making the distribution of information extremely easy. Using the right software you can produce entire multimedia packages, complete with video clips and sound bites. In fact, all potential investors should have the opportunity to receive online investor information packages through downloads from your website.

The package can include a short video message from the founders, as well as a brief sound and slide presentation that explains the company story and provides general information about the company and documents on financial performance and press releases. You should also offer the option to have these packages mailed to individuals at their request.

The goal of investor relations is to provide the information that the investor requires to make a decision to purchase your shares. They also attempt to mitigate any negative information pertaining to the financial performance of the company and work closely with the public relations department in providing co-ordinated external communications. Investor relations are a fundamental piece of any public or private company that has a significant number of shareholders. Performing the task well will result in favourable buzz about the shares and assist the company in attaining a stable growing share value.

The Least You Need To Know

➤ Why face-to-face promotion is important.

➤ How to make and promote a great story.

➤ How to put on a road show or presentation.

➤ How to effect great promotions and why they are important.

➤ How to manage public relations on your own or with a PR firm.

➤ How e-commerce can assist you with public relations.

The Marketing Goldrush: Data Mining

The Old Days Of Mining

Remember those rooms with the raised floors and special ventilation systems that everyone had years ago for their mainframes? They were the storage areas of millions of pieces of accounting information and after month-end reporting was complete, a tape was made and put into storage, never again to see the light of day – unless there was a crisis.

Today, things are significantly different. Information is stored in data warehouses or distributed over a storage area network, and both architectures have the capacity to store trillions of pieces of information. These new data architectures combined with new applications allow us to extract this information instantaneously and perform complex analysis used in e-commerce decision making.

In the old days of computing, they used to have to reload the tapes every time someone wanted information, and then a programmer would have to create a special program to extract and report on the information. Data mining really didn't take hold until customer information started being stored in a way that users could look at it easily. By accessing customer account information, a marketer could sometimes tell what a customer's personal likes and dislikes were and what they might be ready to purchase, but only if the customer had an established account. Plus, general trends could be identified from the generic sales data that were stored in the accounting system. It wasn't until the mass installation of laser-enabled, point-of-sale terminals and bar-coded customer shopping cards that retail companies really started to capture extensive databases of customer shopping preferences.

POS

Point-of-sale (POS) systems are the laser readers and cash registers that you see in almost every retail location. By scanning a customer card, the laser will store such information as the product purchased, the time of day, the location of the store, and the method of payment. This data can then be used to analyse such things as which customers are most likely to buy a particular product based on the buying trends of other customers who have purchased that same product. The analysis is used to create promotional campaigns or to direct advertising efforts.

Retail stores gather an extensive wealth of information and combine it with personal data to run a variety of analyses. For example, they try to determine what products you have purchased, which ones you are likely to purchase in the future, what you have recently stopped purchasing, your average expenditure per trip, the location of where you shop, etc. All this information is extremely valuable to marketing analysts. They can develop mailings to encourage you to buy specific products that you may need, create in-store advertising for the market demographic that shops at a specific location, etc. The depth of the information is amazing. By running award program systems on a desktop, an analyst can tell when you will be likely to leave your house to shop, how long it will take, and how much you will spend. They can also tell that you don't like broccoli, have children and like Madonna. A bit scary, isn't it?

Capturing Data

Point-of-sale systems, combined with customer loyalty cards, are an excellent way to capture information about a customer. Automated supply chain systems also perform the same function. When a customer sets up an account at your online company, he is, in essence, building the foundation of your data mine or a way for your analysts to track information on transactions back to that customer. Unlike a regular mine in which the ore is haphazardly scattered and mixed with other minerals, your data mine should be carefully crafted to store information for later retrieval. When storing information in a data mine, you will have to consider where the information is coming from, how that information is to be extracted in the future, and what type of analysis is to be performed on the data once it is extracted.

The real success of capturing data and putting it somewhere for future reference will depend a great deal on how you identify and store the information. If you tag information incorrectly, it won't necessarily mean that you will not be able to extract it at some point and run an analysis; it may just be a more difficult process. The phrase 'more difficult process' should always be read as 'costs more money and takes more time'. Remember from the previous chapters on e-commerce automation that the goal of your business should be to streamline operations as much as possible. Storing information is no exception. If you tag every piece of information you store, you will be saving and managing a lot of tags. If you group like information and tag it, your storage and retrieval process will be much more efficient.

Sit back and think of all the information you could capture about a transaction and then think about what type of information you would like to get out of the analysis. For instance, you may find that each customer's purchase can provide a valuable volume of information. From that information, you would like to see a report that shows the type of product purchased so that you could group all the information by product and then narrow the search by age in order to produce a mailing list. For this task, you will need a way to differentiate customers and items purchased (two static codes), and each customer will need to have his or her age stored (no code required). You can run this same process over and over again to identify all the flows of information that you require and the reporting needed. The result will be a storage map that will guide the developers building your information systems.

Back in the last century, accounting systems were custom developed for each organisation or purchased off the shelf and pushed and crammed into an organisation. Currently, systems come with some simple customisation tools that easily allow you to perform this customisation without a staff of high-priced talent. Of course, if you have the resources, the big systems are what you need to really add power to your world. Most older systems followed traditional accounting structures that forced organisations to align their internal operations along sales divisions or some other form of accounting measure. The problem was that organisations wanted to align their operations in other ways, such as by product category or customer group. The ability to gather operational data from these various divisions proved difficult, and often resulted in different pieces of accounting or operational systems for different areas.

Today, organisations are built for e-commerce, and the flexibility required to succeed in this world implies that the accounting and operational systems must now flex to meet the organisation. The problem is that very few do so. Often, the underlying architecture of today's software has firm roots in the structures of the past. In choosing any solution, the first question out of your mouth to the vendor should be, 'How do I change it?' If the answer is 'No problem' or 'You can make any changes you want', then you have a system you can at least work with. If the answer is 'Why do you want to change anything?', find a new vendor. In Chapter 8 we discussed real-time systems, and in Chapter 9 we talked about the automated supply chain. These concepts should form the basic foundation of any e-commerce operations system, and should incorporate the most current technologies available.

The storage of information that is captured by your operational systems can be done in a number of ways. Relational databases are the standard method for capturing and storing information. A relational database is simply a series of tables, each with one or more indexes or keys. Think of it as a spreadsheet with multiple pages. The more indexes in the database, the faster the data can be extracted, but the longer it will take to load.

Free Tools

Seagate software provides some free data analysis tools on its website. Surf to www.seagate.com and follow the Seagate Software link.

OK, so now you have chosen a database and had Libby the wonder kid build a hot

Figure 18.1
Sybase supplies the software that is used by many leading internet companies

application that captures every piece of information flowing through your company and stores it in some manner that allows you to know where it is. The next step is to get the information and analyse it. Almost every database engine has a query and reporting capability built into it. You can also use third-party reporting tools.

Leveraging Your Data Mine For Marketing Information

You should now be able to use tools such as Seagate's Crystal Reports to dig into your data mine and start pulling useful data. For example, you should be able to access information by using your static and dynamic codes and their associated information to run reports on particular data (such as the area of the country that made the most and the fewest purchases of a particular product or the number of member hits on your website by gender). How would this information be obtained? Very simply and quickly, assuming that we have applied our identification codes correctly. For example, keeping customer information in accounts or user IDs allows us to link back to specific stored data about gender that we may have stored with these codes.

Getting information from individuals, however, is becoming increasingly difficult as people are becoming more and more annoyed with the time they have to spend entering the information. This is even more evident when they receive nothing in return. For example, despite the Data Protection Act, some companies literally demand demographic information from their customers and then turn around and wholesale it to anyone who knocks at the door with a cheque. There is a growing discontent and resentment among surfers who are beginning to question whether they need to enter the information. In most cases where there is no benefit, they are entering bogus or false information. Using some innovative techniques, companies are attempting to turn the tide of resentment.

Companies both on and off the Internet have long understood that one of the best ways to get information from consumers is to gather it by offering something in return. Contests and give-aways are the best way to gather demographic information. For example, a grocery store that has a contest can ask and usually receive an answer to questions such as age, gender, and income range. Higher response levels can be obtained by avoiding personal health and financial data and by using generic ranges as a choice instead of an exact number. Gathering data can also be performed when special services are used, accounts are set up, or an online help centre is accessed. In these instances, users perceive they are going to receive some benefit from providing the information so they will be more open to providing it.

Many organisations, especially in the USA, gather data and then quickly resell it to others. If we follow the model of the killer app, this information may even be distributed for free one day. Until then, your company will have to decide if it will sell the information to third parties or not – again dependent on the terms of your registration under the Data Protection Act. The benefit is revenue, especially if you

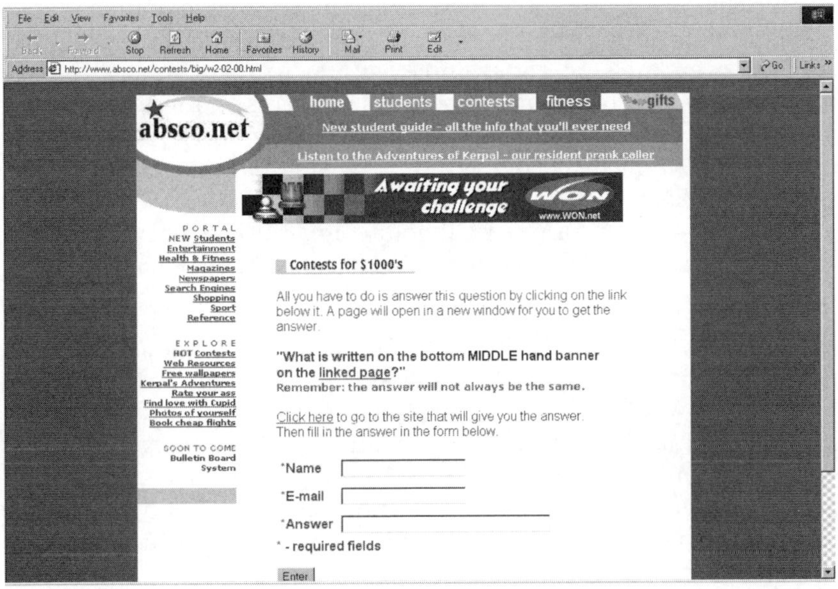

Figure 18.2
Contests on the Internet are two a penny

have a large membership. The disadvantage is that a spammer can infuriate your customers. A second option is to collect the data and distribute it only to your affiliates or partners. Once again, however, they could sell it to any email bulk-mailing company they want.

The most promising data-mining model that we have seen is to distribute the information only in a generic form to your partners or third parties. This way, they are buying your analysis but will have to do individual promotion through your website. This method benefits you by allowing you to control whether the application is something that you want to supply. For example, you could supply a demographic breakdown of click-throughs to your partners without names, addresses, or email IDs. Your partners could decide that they want to run a promotion to your community, based on the mined information. You could evaluate the offering on behalf of your community to decide if you would like to offer it. The benefits can be ranked, and a delivery mechanism chosen such as a direct link, a banner ad, or an information notice. In some cases, you may not want to accept the offer at all. For example, if you were a family-oriented site, and the offer was a link to a pornography site, you could decline the affiliation.

Niche Marketing Using The Mine

Niche marketing is the concept of taking a large demographic or psychographic profile and breaking it into smaller units called niches by using multiple divisions.
For example, a larger demographic that you may choose to promote to, such as males between the age of 30 and 35, can be broken into successively smaller groups, such as

those within that group that like sports and drive a lorry. The advantage of niche marketing is that you can promote to a portion of your competitor's market, sometimes without them even knowing. For example, let's say you and your competitors sell the same products but your competitor's market is youngsters between 13 and 18 and yours is 18 to 30-year-olds. If you run an ad to target their demographics, you will invite immediate competition. The alternative is for your company to run an ad targeted at your 18 to 20-year-old subgroup that promotes and uses images that the 16 to 18-year-olds aspire to. If your competition isn't swift, and we know they aren't, you will successfully bleed their market before they have a clue about what has hit them.

Cross-niching is even more successful. The above example is called cross-niching, and is the process where promotions are targeted by using images that apply to two distinct demographics or niches. The whole concept of demographics was created to allow companies to more efficiently and effectively target their promotional budgets. However, with the cost of promotion falling to almost nothing thanks to e-commerce and the Internet, the concept of niching and cross-niching will become more essential in the new millennium. The biggest use of data stored in e-commerce businesses will be for marketing new products and services.

Advanced Maths And The Neural Networks

Advanced mathematical and statistical tools are incorporated into data-mining tools so that past information is used to mathematically predict events. This type of analysis is used extensively in the world of finance, derivatives, and options to predict prices of things such as currencies or the price of oil. In a regular data mine, they are used to predict such things as buying behaviour. A simple application of this technique would be to look at the historical buying behaviour of customers who have recently purchased a new product. If the majority of them exhibit a specific behaviour, such as they had just recently purchased another compatible product, then these advanced models should be able to identify this behaviour based on the data in the mine. Then the database can give you a list of your customers who are most likely to purchase the new product. Now you can target those customers in a special promotion for the new product.

A neural network is an extension of this concept. A neural network mines data in data warehouses or SANs and analyses the data using many of the same mathematical and statistical concepts. The difference is that a neural network measures its guesses and attempts to learn from its mistakes. In most cases, it uses the equivalent of a very advanced averaging formula and adjusts the formula to account for the degree by which it missed its original guess. In this way the software appears to be learning from its mistakes. Neural networks are great for predicting behaviours that tend to follow something of a consistent pattern, such as load volume in a processing centre, in order to plan staffing levels. The problem with software that predicts trends is that computers lack intuition and gut instinct. They probably would have told Jeff Bezos that he should sell books in a store.

Do you need all this advanced stuff? No. You can get by without it. But, in the future, if it is implemented properly, you can probably use it to great advantage. For the time being, you should keep it in mind when you are loading data into the mine. If you see certain historical data that can be used to predict actions, that is likely to be the best place to start advanced data mining when you choose to do so.

What To Look For In The Data

Now you have captured the data in some form of database and located the tools to extract and report it. What are you looking for? You are looking for information that you can use to find opportunities with your customers, make better use of your vendors, make your internal operation more efficient and effective, etc. Information that is properly identified and filed can be easily extracted and analysed by your team.

Remember that historical information is just that – historical. However, it helps to have a map that shows the ground you have already covered so that you might be prepared for what to expect ahead. The map can't tell you how the landscape has changed, but it can give you a pretty good idea of what should be there. Customer demographic and psychographic information coupled with purchased items' information can indicate the colour, preferences and size for existing customers. This is valuable information to have when ordering stock of new products. For example, if your vendors' mined data indicates that a particular sweater is purchased primarily by women 20 to 30 years old and 50% of your 20 to 30-year-old female customers prefer red in a size 12, you may bulk up the orders of this sweater in this particular colour. If you use advanced data-mining techniques, it may help you to predict a movement towards a new colour or size based on trends within your own market (for example, your market leaders are starting to buy a different colour so tone down the order numbers of red sweaters by 5%).

Vendor information can be coupled with item sales' trends to indicate falling turnover rates by customer group. For example, let's say that you ran the sales numbers for the past 12 months on a particular product by age group. What if it showed that sales for 20 to 25-year-olds had started to drop? You can use this type of data to ask the vendor for a new promotional effort, or you can use the information to clear out inventory and reduce ordering quantities. Advanced analysis might indicate the same subtle percentage adjustments were occurring in the younger demographic in front of the 20 to 25-year-old demographic and inventory orders should be further adjusted downwards by 10%.

Both of these examples assume that you actually carry an inventory, but if you can provide information like this to vendors, they may be willing to carry the inventory for you through a direct connection to their own systems. The advantage to the vendors is that they can fine-tune their own inventories thanks to your advanced information analysis effort. The advantage to your company is that you may not need to carry any inventory or may need to carry only a very small inventory. Eliminating the need to finance an inventory is an immense cash saver for the company since an inventory that is purchased usually never returns the investment until the business is sold or closed, for example, you pay for the inventory and when it is sold have to re-buy it. Inventory has to be the lousiest investment in any business.

There are hundreds of ways to use internal historical data to assist in decision making as long as you remember that it is historical data and that your focus should always be on the future, not what has happened. Some trends to look for in your data mine include the following:

➤ Sales by age group by product.

➤ Sales by psychographic division (i.e. interests) by product.

➤ Item turnover by age group.

➤ Response to promotion by psychographic division (i.e. favourite music or 20% of country listeners responded).

➤ Average order completion time by vendor.

➤ Forecast item purchases by age and gender.

➤ Reduction in production inventory after new, 'just in time' ordering is implemented.

Data is by far one of the most valuable resources available to the firm. So much so that blue-chip executives have been overheard to say they would give up all the traditional manufacturing infrastructure if they could keep the data. Even American Airlines once said it would give up the aeroplanes as long as it could keep the Sabre reservation system (*see* Figure 18.3). However, data, like ore, is not very valuable in a mine. It is far

Figure 18.3 *The Sabre web page*

more valuable after it has been extracted, separated from the junk, and turned into a final product. That's the goal of data mining – to take your data and turn it into a shiny piece of gold. There really is gold in them thar hills of data.

The Least You Need To Know

➤ How to store data in a data mine.

➤ What the difference is between relational and object databases.

➤ How to extract the data.

➤ How to analyse the data.

➤ What specific data you are looking for.

➤ How to effect niche marketing.

Part 4
e-Strategies: Managing The e-Company

In this section, we will start to discuss how all of the information in the previous sections hangs together. e-Commerce is complex and requires a new way of thinking about business so we will try to highlight some of the things that you will have to consider about setting up and running an e-business.

First, we will look at planning your resources for your new business, including outsourcing considerations and developing a web presence. Then the management of your knowledge assets will be covered. Your corporate knowledge base is one of the most essential ingredients of any e-business, and managing them for this new high-tech world will be critical to success.

Leveraging your e-commerce assets is the process of making more out of less. Your resources are limited, and leveraging these resources to get customers by using affiliates and partners is an excellent way to bring growth to your company.

At the end of this section, you will have the necessary pieces to build and manage a successful e-business.

e-Commerce Resource Planning

In This Chapter

➤ What is resource planning?

➤ Choosing an e-commerce strategy

➤ e-Commerce is not for the faint-hearted

➤ Outsourcing today

➤ Outsourcing tomorrow

What Is Resource Planning?

Resources are anything that an organisation needs and uses to complete its operations. Resources include capital, cash, employees, raw materials, inventories, technology, market intelligence, and anything else that goes into producing goods or services. The primary push behind e-commerce was both a need to capitalise on the fundamental changes in communications because of the Internet and the need to capitalise on the realisation that with the assistance of technology, businesses could much better manage all their resources. Enterprise resource planning was a key paradigm in the last half of the 1990s and had some of the largest players explaining how their software was the only one that could provide true ERP. This quickly vanished into the paradigm of e-commerce. So, rather than just jump on the latest buzzword bandwagon, let's look at what these concepts were really all about at the sharp end.

Businesses in the early 1990s were running flat out in the world of technology trying to keep pace with the problems noted by Moore and Metcalf. Their internal operational systems had to be replaced to take advantage of the newer technologies and to pass the Y2K testing hoopla. In the process of upgrading software, companies abandoned the large internal development areas in favour of 'off-the-shelf' solutions that would magically be upgraded by the giant software companies. The savings were immense and allowed companies to focus IT resources on networking and the emerging technologies of the Internet.

At the top of their wish list to the vendors of these operational systems was a request to integrate the various pieces of software so that, for instance, manufacturing systems would talk to the nominal or general ledger and human resource systems would communicate with the project planning software.

This complete integration of operating systems was called enterprise resource planning because it was based on the concept of providing systems that would better plan and utilise the resources of the organisation through integration. The goal was originally to automate the supply chain process in manufacturing environments, but it quickly spread to the entire organisation. Now ERP has been rolled into the wider concept of e-commerce, and the big ERP developers, such as SAP, have shifted their focus to remain at the forefront of the latest paradigm.

Tracking Resources

In order to add value, down in the bowels of the development labs the app wizards set to work on redesigning the way operational software interacted. Now companies could install a piece of software that could track everything from raw inventory to how much time an employee had spent on a project. In the mid-1990s, software companies were still trying to complete the missing pieces of their ERP developments when along came the Internet.

Companies such as Germany's SAP or American-based Oracle are rapidly redefining themselves for the world of the Internet and e-commerce. As the subtitle on an Oracle web page clearly indicates, the Internet 'Changes Everything' (*see* Figure 19.1). Now those systems have to be retooled to communicate over the Internet and even run applications over the Internet. The problem is that the foundations of these systems were never built to even consider the way a business would work in the world of e-commerce. Virtual companies with virtual employees who communicate over vast networks and need instantaneous access to information are still an area under immense construction, as far as the software companies are concerned, and just when you thought it was complicated enough, throw into the mix the fact that standards are constantly changing. Will Windows continue to dominate or will it implode, leaving the way clear for Linux or another operating system? Will the public Internet continue to grow or will privatisation and the relentless desire to patent everything that moves kill the growth? Will XML and WML and the growing complexity of technology outpace the skill sets of the workforce that have to use it?

It is literally a war. Companies have to manage runaway technology budgets, keep pace with rapid change that is altering the entire way they do business, stay ahead of the

Figure 19.1 *Words of wisdom from the Oracle*

competition, and still manage to conduct business. They need to better control the way they manage their limited resources, and one wrong move could cost millions of pounds. So companies attack the world of technology by gaining beachheads in the battle with Java development staff and HTML coders. The goal is to try to map out a strategy to move inland.

Choosing An e-Commerce Strategy

Choosing an e-commerce strategy involves making tough decisions, but some have already been made for you. The Internet and distributed computing environments or networking models are already here and the chances are that you are either using them or need to. Every organisation can benefit by putting a logo on the Internet if only to give the location to its real business. Evaluating the cost of an Internet site isn't much of a task given that the cost of a single business phone line is easily identifiable. The fact that you can put a web page up on the Internet for free should make the decision to create a web presence quite easy. Of course, the vast majority of businesses will hire web designers to create the page and ISPs to host the site. After all, how many businesses design a professional-looking logo or their headed stationery?

So what is going to be your e-commerce strategy? What will be the main goal or mission, what will be the smaller goals along the path, and what will be the schedule to completion? The answers will depend on the nature of your business. You will probably have to have some sort of presence on the web, and you will probably have to upgrade your technology, not because you want to but because your suppliers and customers will demand it.

You could grow vegetables in your garden or allotment and sell them at a farmers' market without any need for technology, but eventually you'll need to use some form of technology to do your banking or else face the higher costs that come with the old ways of doing business. So, some decisions are already being made for you. In most cases, what the standards are for your industry will not be impacted by the decisions you make. The big question is, how then do you allocate your limited resources to use these standards to your advantage?

Choosing The Best Technology For Your Strategy

The choice of technology will have to fit your vision of what you want your e-business to be. If your business will remain traditional but with an outlet to the Internet and an integrated operational system, then your traditional business strategy may suffice. For example, you may own a shipping company and have as your goal to do business as you have always done, only with the addition of an information website and a new internal system.

However, if you want to accept shipping orders over the Internet and manage your logistics better, the development of your technology or even partnering with an Internet shipping killer app will require that you rethink your strategy and how you allocate your resources. You may need to set up regional shipping hubs and collection outposts, or you may change from a local shipper into a state-wide shipper by adding affiliates to the hub network. These strategies may or may not be vastly different from your current strategy.

There are a number of steps that you can follow in deciding what strategy is best for your company. Start by defining what you are going to do or what your concept will be. For example, you may decide that you will develop a website that will offer the use of an online software program for free. Define what benefit you will receive from the application, such as revenue, traffic to your traditional business, greater operating efficiency, or critical mass. Then set a long-range target for your business, such as to continue current growth rates, to become a leader in your market, to be a global boutique, to become a standard, etc. Now you can start to define what the foundation of your organisation will be.

Spending Carefully

Investing in technology is a tricky business and is becoming more so every day. Organisations can spend thousands to upgrade systems only to find that they are out of date the following year and unusable in five. Making the correct choices will require research either by you or from a third party. Some companies choose to outsource the technology to organisations that are more capable or have better resources. For instance, you can say that you will create a website of 'how to' information and rather than create the entire site, including the posting of information, you add a link to information sites. This will still require you to have resources for website construction and management and promotional costs for the site, but it is an example where you have outsourced the content and technology to other sites. If the standards of the Internet change, those sites will have to bear the burden of upgrading their technology, and you will only have to deal with your website. This same technique can also be used for hard technology assets such as internal systems. The choice will be to decide if you are going to take on the burden of technology, or if you are going to outsource it.

Human resources are the most costly of all your resources, but they provide the greatest opportunity for a return. For example, just imagine the return on your stock if you had hired Jeff Bezos to run your bookstore, or if you had hired Bill Gates as a partner in your fledgling software company way back when. Which employees you hire and how you utilise their talent is one of the most critical resource management issues you will ever face. The answer is directly affected by what you choose to do as a company and how you choose to use the technology. Linking to an information site is not a very complex process and may not even require any staff. Building an information network or e-commerce retail site will take considerably more people.

Resources Hard And Soft

Hard resources such as stock, investments, plant, and buildings are an integral part of any strategy. So are soft resources such as intelligence, skill sets, information, and marketing ability. If the strategy is the map to achieving your goals, both hard resources and soft resources provide the fuel to get you to your goal. Put your foot down on the accelerator too hard, and you might not make it to your goal before you run out of fuel, but be too cautious and you might miss the goal altogether. Managing these resources is what business is truly about. Whether it's taking your tomatoes to market or building cars around the globe, the choice of how to invest in resources, how to efficiently utilise them, and how to direct them to achieve your goals is what you as a business owner will have to decide. Deciding how to use hard and soft resources in an e-commerce strategy is no different from any other business strategy, but in some situations getting rid of or not needing hard resources is the end result.

Building an online retailer does not mean that you have to own any hard resources. Constructing an online community of value may require only a website. On the other hand, you may want to expand your tomato distribution efforts to include lorries, plant, salsa factories, and juice retailers. The major difference between traditional business strategies and e-commerce strategies is that the choice of, and the implementation of, resources will depend heavily on the e-business plan, technology, and human resource strategies of the organisation.

e-Commerce Is Not For The Faint-Hearted

Got a heart condition? We're not sure we would recommend e-commerce as a hobby. Imagine learning a new technology only to find out that it's obsolete before you finish the class, or how about partnering a small company that supplies vital information to your website only to find out that Disney has bought it and the service is no longer free. Welcome to the hurricane-powered ocean of the Internet where a business that is up one year can be wiped out the next and where traffic patterns can change overnight with the next big wave.

Parts of e-commerce are manageable, such as internal automation. For example, overhauling your technical structure in three-year increments makes the process a whole lot smoother than getting the latest upgrade installed as soon as it is released. Also, partnering established organisations provides a certain level of comfort even if you do miss a couple of trends and opportunities that you would have had with the smaller companies.

Investing In Change

Technology changes extremely rapidly and putting all your eggs in one technology basket is risky. On the other hand, avoiding change is even riskier. You will have to strike a balance between studying and investing in new technology and holding development steady while your operation has a chance to run. Ongoing research and development into technology is probably the best investment that an organisation can make as long as the expenditures don't get out of control or take too many resources away from the task of making money. In addition, smaller organisations may not be able to justify the resources required to participate.

For example, if your systems person has spare time during the day to learn Java, this may be an effective investment, particularly if you would like to provide some web-based functionality to your customers such as a mortgage calculator or game. On the other hand, if your function is to sell items and you are contracting out your website and e-commerce functionality, the expenditure on Java research may be inappropriate and wasteful. However, allocating your technology resources should always include some type of technology strategy of which ongoing research and development are a part.

Another way to limit your exposure to changes in technology is to outsource the function entirely. Some companies outsource their computers and networking functions. This places the burden of training and IT resource management on the outsourcing firm. It is their responsibility to train their staff and upgrade the leased machines periodically. The problem is that the costs of these arrangements are usually much higher than if you performed the process yourself, especially for smaller companies. Also, relying on other organisations comes with its own inherent risks (*see* Chapter 5 on The Virtual Company).

Making Your Company Stand Out From The Crowd

What if you build a site and no one comes? Public relations can be an expensive task, as are promotion and advertising and the ability not to blend in with the millions of other websites, which can be a challenge. In fact, some search engines are charging to separate business sites from personal sites. Although this runs counter to the concepts and rules of the Internet, these companies may just succeed if they narrow the access and get rid of the junk.

However, currently most of what they have is sales junk. Of course, in true Internet fashion, someone is bound to come out with a free app that can get the best of both worlds. 'Limited linking' sites that only provide links and limited searches to valuable information or 'controlled content' sites are the wave of the future. These online companies will succeed as people try to get better information without extensive searching or advertising.

What if you build a site and the wrong people come? Imagine that you open a little coffee shop in a new trendy mall. You sell speciality coffees and some gifts and put out a few cool magazines for people to read. One day you arrive at your shop only to find that a bookshop has opened a mega bookstore on the opposite side of the mall, and put in a coffee shop. The same thing can happen to an e-commerce company on the Internet. The big boys may like your killer app so much that they'll reproduce it, add a lot more offerings, and promote directly to your customers. Pretty soon, thanks to their unlimited bank accounts, they'll be going for a stock exchange listing, and you'll be trying to find another new killer app. The other threat is that a multitude of other companies open web portals just like yours, thereby confusing the community.

Branding

The best thing you can do is to define a brand image for yourself that the big boys can't copy without a huge copyright infringement lawsuit. The goal should be to build something that their money just can't buy. It could be an image or a community, but try to build on something that you have that the big companies can't get for any amount of money. Then you can position yourself right beside their Internet front door and pick off their best customers. Nothing infuriates a big company like a smaller one that can pick off the cream of their market. It has long been a tradition for restaurants to open up right next door to the most popular restaurant in town in order to get instant traffic and recognition. The same thing can be done by linking to a collection of different shopping sites and selling advertising space on your main web page.

Automating Your Company

The automation of your business is another area that can keep you up at night, especially if you are converting from a traditional operation to an automated operation such as a supply chain or a back office. Employee resentment and fear, contractors and resellers that leave your business with limited support or high-priced consultants' bills, existing technology that has to be replaced or upgraded, or implementations that go ahead without any understanding of the dynamics of the business are all factors that can directly impact your business. However, change is a manageable process, and doesn't have to include massive risk. Here are a series of steps to follow to implement new systems:

➤ Identify the direction that you would like all of your technology to take (technology strategy).

➤ Understand and document what you do, right down to step-by-step instructions.

➤ Work with your software vendors to identify the solutions that are best for your business.

➤ Decide how much you can afford to spend and make sure that you have someone dedicated to managing the project from start to finish.

➤ Develop a plan to implement the system(s) and what changes are required.

➤ Train your employees.

➤ Make any required changes to operations.

➤ Implement the system.

➤ Test the system.

The goals for implementing and integrating technology into the organisation should be the same as any strategy. Identify where you are (what you do), where you want to go (technology strategy), and the path to get there (project management). The better you do these tasks, the better the result will be with less disruption to your existing operations. If you can, it is sometimes better to implement pieces of systems, as opposed to entire wholesale system overhauls. For example, you can start by implementing a network, then add a server, a back-office system, proxy, etc. Or you can gut the company and retool entirely, or open a brand new location with new systems and slowly migrate your existing operations.

The world of e-commerce is fast-paced and full of risks and rewards. Keeping on top of all the changes is a full-time job. Learning and using the technology is even more than a full-time job. Picking and choosing your battles and tools carefully will help you survive the stress of playing in the world of e-commerce. It is definitely not a place for the faint-hearted.

Outsourcing Today

Outsourcing today has taken on a whole new meaning, thanks to the incredible growth of the Internet. Today, virtual corporations with virtual staff no longer need to risk investment in infrastructures such as offices and technology. With enough operating cash flow you could marshal the resources required to build an e-company without doing anything. For example, you could hire a web designer to build a portal to the Internet that your contract channel manager could then fill with links to affiliate sites. Your online site management company would control the technology to run your website, and your PR firm could manage your customer and investor communications through an e-centre. Finally, your online accounting firm could process your e-bank deposits and accounting and email your financial statements to your virtual CEO working from his home office. He could analyse the information and report to you at lunch.

Of course, you probably won't be able to lounge by the pool while the millions roll in – or maybe you will, depending on how good your e-business is. The reality of the situation is that you will have to work very hard to create the brand image that can

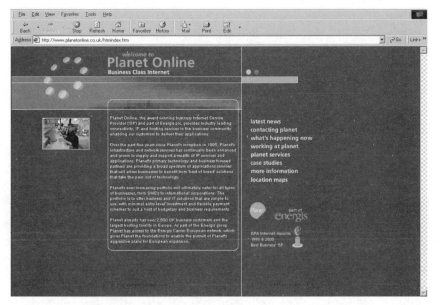

Figure 19.2 *Planet Online is one of the 200-plus ISPs in the UK alone to offer companies a web presence*

carry a virtual organisation. So for now, unless you are already independently wealthy, you will have to perform many or all of the operational tasks needed to launch your company, including promotion, back office, and systems. However, as you grow, your most critical decision will be to decide what functions you want to outsource and how you will do this. Simply outsourcing the accounting of a mid-sized organisation is a major undertaking. The advantage will be that so many online services will be opened in the next ten years that the idea of successfully running a truly virtual organisation is not just a pipe dream. It can be done today.

Outsourcing Tomorrow

Outsourcing in the near future will be a unique experience. Massive organisations will have small executive offices and almost every service will be farmed out. Even as employees with very specialised skill sets start to market themselves to the online world, they will be establishing home offices for their speciality with Internet-capable communications for work with their clients.

The ability to select the organisational operations that you need from a smorgasbord of online functions will be the wave of the future, and will significantly redefine the way all organisations do business. Starting to prepare for this world today can save you an immense expenditure of resources later on when your corporate ship, the *Titanic II*, has to make a quick turn in the technology ocean. You can prepare by doing the following tasks:

➤ Study the new technologies even if at a high level.

➤ Set aside time to review the online technology e-zines.

➤ Surf a bit each week.

➤ Start using technology that is proven (such as email).

➤ Attend seminars and conventions.

➤ Start talking to potential partners.

➤ Hire young talent and give them some e-toys to play with.

➤ Develop a web presence.

➤ Map your current internal operations.

➤ Think about how you will capitalise on an increased ability to communicate with an entire world and how you might make your voice heard above the millions of others.

Get A Web Presence

We think that the key to ongoing corporate growth is to develop a web presence and start marketing it in your own world. A simple web page and domain name are not very difficult to do. Get an ISP contract for an Internet service, one that can host a website, and surf to a registration service such as register.com (*see* Figure 19.3). Then start typing names until you locate the domain you want. You should check out any trademarks and registered company names and verify that you can use the name for your purpose. Start thinking about image, function, and content that you could provide on your site and how you can gather a community of value. Build the site, have someone build it for you, or use one of the online services. This will start the process of becoming an e-commerce company.

Allocating your resources, whether they are cash, employees, technology, or plant and equipment, is a difficult task and is the true essence of being in business. Choosing the

Figure 19.3 *You can both search for, and register, your domain name at register.com*

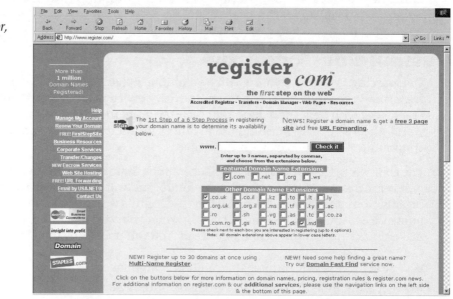

correct strategy will help you efficiently perform the allocation process. Capitalising on those resources is what will make your e-business a success. The world of resource planning and utilisation is changing right down to its core, and the way we do business will never be the same. The Internet and e-commerce systems have forever changed all organisations and those that choose the correct mix of change and risk will ultimately be rewarded for their vision. Unfortunately, many businesses that do not understand change will fail, as will many online businesses that do not understand the dynamics of sailing the Internet oceans.

The Least You Need To Know

➤ How to use e-commerce to plan your resources.

➤ How online resources are available for your company.

➤ How to choose an e-commerce strategy.

➤ Why e-commerce can be risky.

➤ How to outsource the needs of your business today and tomorrow.

Knowledge Management

The Rapid Speed Of Technological Change

Trying to clock the speed of technological change is like trying to figure out how high is up. We know it's fast, so fast in fact that by the time you finally load a software package, it's time to upgrade. Keeping pace with technology used to be easier because there were not so many standards to learn. There were only a few operating systems, only a few flavours of office suites, only a few networking systems, and only a few graphics packages. Then came the Internet and a whole variety of new standards. Now your operations require that you not only know about operating systems and networks, but also how to connect to the Internet, implement real-time operational systems, build an intranet, HTML, XML, Java, JavaScript, CGI, e-commerce systems, streaming content, and so on. Given that you can successfully find and keep the staff you need to manage a specific program, trying to find people with enough experience in all these standards as well as your company's operations will be almost impossible. Your staff and your content make up your knowledge resources and managing them in a world of fast-changing technology will be immensely difficult.

The problem is that to gain the depth of skills necessary to program Java is not that difficult, to install and administer an NT network is hardly rocket science, and to create and operate an Internet portal is quite easily manageable. You may even find someone who has lots of experience in all three technologies. However, the ability to pull them together and manage them to the benefit of the company is a skill set that is very rare. It is well said that there are those who understand what they do not manage, and those who manage what they do not understand. It may require an understanding of fundamental programming, mathematics, systems analysis, finance, systems engineering, electrical engineering, operations, logistics, design, marketing, database administration, network administration, Internet website construction, and a variety of other technologies both existing and emerging.

Understanding Technology

You can, of course, hire specialised organisations to perform these functions. However, to effectively manage this resource, you must first understand what it is that you are outsourcing. The more you understand the technology, the better you will be at using it to successfully grow the company. Too often the senior managers don't understand the fundamental principles behind the newest technologies presented in all those professional-looking reports from underlings. It's always a 'must have,' and it invariably costs far more than it should. This problem arises from the fact that people are political by nature, and decision makers rarely have enough technological depth to make an informed decision. When you hire staff you should not be looking exclusively for specialists who will present their narrow view of the world, as is the case with most technology organisations' HR practices. Instead, you should seek to mix a couple of generalists into the pot to provide an 'out of the box' or 'forest as opposed to trees' perspective. Our point is simple: you have to understand technology just as you would understand mining in a mining company, shares in a brokerage, or logistics in a delivery company. Technology has become such a fundamental part of our business world that it has crossed from being a tool to being the very foundation of our e-businesses. If you do not understand it, you will make poor decisions about it, regardless of how many top-notch technical specialists or consultants you have on staff.

Keeping Pace With Technological Change

The ability to keep pace with changes in technology does not imply that as CEO you should dedicate the majority of your time to learning the intricacies of Java. However, unless you understand the principles of what Java is, how it works, why it was developed, what the competing technologies are, how it would benefit your organisation, what it will cost in resources, and what return can be expected, you will be making decisions that are meaningless gambles. In larger organisations, the management of your knowledge resources may be as simple as encouraging your staff to communicate their knowledge on a company intranet or to present their findings at a weekly corporate team meeting. The problem is that the majority of people, like organisations, protect their expertise as if it were a personal fortress, rarely willing to bring their peers up to their knowledge level and invite competition. This is directly impacted by the corporate culture and environment. If the leaders of the company encourage and reward sharing, then the knowledge will spread among workers. Hoarding information both internally and externally should be discouraged and replaced with assurances that positions will be secure and internal politics outlawed.

Figure 20.2 *With even free intranets on offer, no company has an excuse for not getting to grips with internet technology*

Knowledge Resources

Your employees are only one piece of your knowledge resource. Another significant piece is the knowledge resources of the entire organisation. As staff come and go, the company gains from gathering and storing expertise in its systems and operations. This is primarily a function of the way knowledge and expertise is passed from person to person. If this free flow of information is not performed in the organisation, the knowledge asset attributable to the organisation will not grow.

For example, let's say that you hired a Linux expert to obtain a Linux distribution and test its capabilities for the company. That individual can spend months becoming the firm's expert in Linux, but unless he or she shares this expertise with others in the organisation, either through collaboration or reporting, the organisational knowledge base will not grow in this particular area. Many would argue that to spend resources such as assigning two people to study a technology is inefficient and in some cases this is true. As a business owner or manager, you will have to define how much information should be shared and how much should be kept at the individual level.

Knowledge is the most critical asset of any organisation, and by investing in and expanding the knowledge base of the corporation, you will earn a return on your investment. This return will be in the form of your ability to perform your operations more effectively and more efficiently than your competition. This is especially true in e-commerce, since the complexity of the multiple systems will require an extensive and varied knowledge base. Your company will have to obtain not only this expertise, but also the expertise to make all these diverse systems work together to the benefit of your organisation.

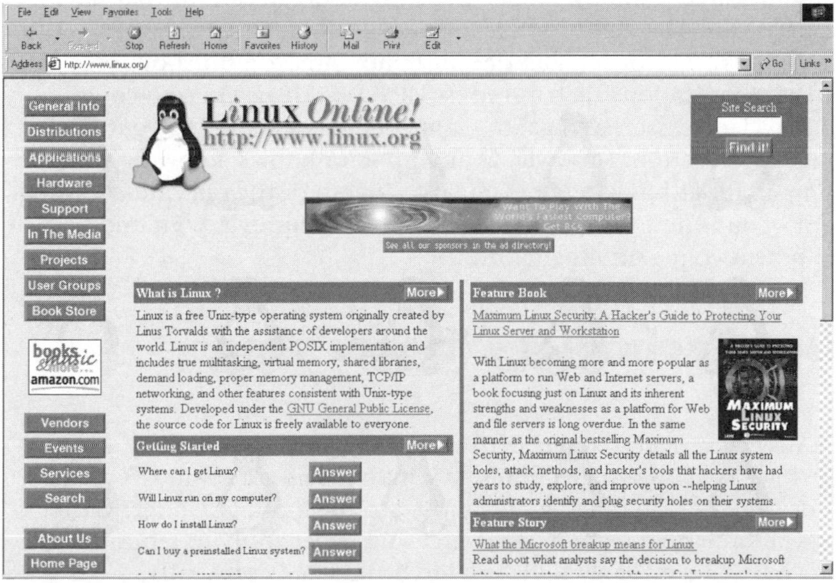

Figure 20.3 *Linux is a free computer operating system – a classic example of the open-source business model*

Figure 20.4 *Red Hat makes money by supporting the free operating system Linux*

Building A Portfolio Of Knowledge Assets

What about a virtual business? Virtual companies that operate without hard assets, such as employees and equipment, still require the knowledge of e-commerce so that their organisations can be designed and built to take advantage of these technologies. Could you outsource this knowledge as well? Yes, with enough cash anything is possible – even having your virtual knowledge resources recorded. However, a person could achieve exactly the same result by simply investing in organisations that have an extensive knowledge base and the ability to use it. Some examples are Sun Microsystems for Java, Microsoft for NT, Red Hat for Linux, Amazon for shopping, and associated support organisations such as FedEx, UPS, WorldPay, etc. You could build a portfolio of knowledge assets and get the same benefits as building your own complete e-commerce organisation. However, as any investor knows, knowing what you invest in is as important as knowing how much to invest, or the old card-counting theory of investment – counting cards at the black jack table improves your odds significantly and improves your gambling return.

The Two Classes: Technology 'Haves' And 'Have-Nots'

There is definitely a new class distinction occurring in society: the technology 'haves' and the technology 'have-nots'. Young techno-savvy individuals are about to enter a world where even their own capabilities will be pushed to the limit. No longer can individuals leave education with a technology degree and expect only to return for the occasional refresher course. Technology skills need to be updated constantly.

For example, spending the day administering a network has to be followed up with a couple of hours at home on technology study just to keep up. This has caused a noticeable rift between the technology 'haves' and 'have-nots'. The 'haves' own one or two computers personally and have one or more at work. They, on average, have two Internet connections, one at work and one at home, two email IDs, and a personal web space allocated to them by their ISP. They will have at least attempted to load a web page, be involved in technology at work, will be thinking about networking their home, and will surf the net regularly for both work and pleasure.

The 'have-nots', however, do not necessarily come from a different socio-economic background, although there is a direct correlation between an individual's technical capabilities and the ability to purchase a computer and obtain an Internet account. The majority of those people in low-income groups who do not have direct access to the technology are starting to fall behind those with the ability to purchase personal computers and Internet connections. Even within the same socio-economic group as the technological 'haves' is a large group that is not technologically competent enough to keep pace. Children from technologically advanced parents have a greater statistical head start over those whose parents are not technologically advanced. This is because these parents understand the power and benefit of technology, and are surrounding their kids with it. That, of course, takes money, and since not everyone can afford the latest version of Windows, they start to fall behind.

The Growing Shortage Of Technological Workers

Although this differentiation has been viewed as nothing more than a curious anomaly in our expanding economy, this division is growing greater as the speed of technology accelerates. It has a direct impact on our lives since as the technology becomes more complicated, technology organisations will try to attract talent that understands both how to create and use the technology and how it relates to their new e-business. The shortage of this particular skill set and the demand that will be created in the next few years will drive up the price of this type of talent, making a new class of technology worker that is significantly higher paid than the general population. Already e-commerce contracting rates for top site builders with HTML, Java, and e-commerce have risen enormously and include share options too. Companies have rewarded these techno employees generously because of the huge returns they are capable of producing and the limited talent pool that has this capability.

At those rates, there are a lot more people driving new 4-wheel drives and sports cars. Meanwhile, the line employees at the plant are lucky if they haven't had their wages cut over the past 10 years. This is a vast division that is likely to grow as more and more technology workers update their skill sets, and the demand for technology workers drives up the wages. The problem is that this division is a cycle because higher wages start putting pressure on the rest of the economy, and the race to beat the competition drives software companies to make advances in technology for such areas as faster streaming content and delivery of video. Technology workers with the capital to upgrade systems will stay ahead of this wave in technological change, and the 'have-nots' will fall even further behind. Governments are aware of these impending skill shortages and have started programmes to train the youth of their respective countries in the advancing technologies. However, in most cases, the government workers designing the programmes and the teachers who are teaching our children are members of the 'have-not' knowledge population.

There Is Opportunity In Technology

So what does this have to do with e-commerce? Opportunity – lots and lots of opportunities to help the technological 'have-not' companies and individuals keep pace. Online training and services assist organisations and individuals to become competent in technology. Of course, this doesn't mean that everyone will start building websites, but it does mean that people with skill sets that are not technology based can still capitalise on e-commerce technology by using the online educational services or online e-business services. Now you can take generalised information, such as that contained in this book, find additional online resources to fill in the gaps, then start to build your e-commerce company or adapt your existing company without having to hire expensive e-commerce specialists. Of course, if you want to jump way up the technology learning curve, spending capital resources to gain knowledge onsite may be your best investment.

The Rising Backlash Against Change

You can't see it. It isn't getting press coverage. It's more of a rumbling, or more correctly, a grumbling of discontent. It's discontent that companies and individuals have to spend so much in resources just to keep pace with the change of technology. Companies that finally figured out how to share files over a Windows network and eventually grew to use NT are now faced with the changes presented in Windows 2000. Licences, incompatibility, high prices, and the need to upgrade or put in patches and fixes every few months is probably driving the economy to newer heights as workers move towards the technology sector and away from traditional service and manufacturing sectors. But resources have their limits, and the completion of upgrading for Y2K has led to the push to rationalise capital expenditures on technology infrastructure. Luckily, this push is still falling on deaf ears as business owners and boards of directors realise the fundamental changes that are shaking all industries thanks to the Internet.

Some business leaders are starting to question why a move from Office97 to Office 2000 is essential to their organisation, or why NT 4 will not suffice for the next few years. This type of attitude is new and unusual in a world where the frantic pace of change has caused companies to abandon their entire IT departments in favour of IT outsourcing. When Microsoft released its Office 2000 software, the rush from businesses to upgrade was decidedly lower than the movement to Windows98. Of course, the difference in price was significant, plus there was a concerted need to keep operating systems consistent with the new machines that were purchased and loaded with Windows98. But many people question the benefits from the minimal additional features in Office 2000. The same is true of the faster and faster chips being released. Many organisations that moved from 486s to 333s with each change as soon as it was out have started to draw the line in moving to +700 MHz chips by forcing IT departments to justify the costs. This resistance is likely to continue.

Do We Really Need To Go Faster?

Individuals are also starting to question the need for speed. Gaming is one of the biggest users of PC power, but with the +400MHz chips and 56kbps modems, most users are content with the functionality of their machines. Couple this with the human tendency to avoid change, and you have a recipe for slowing the growth of technological development. Technology will always grow and change, but the pace will slow slightly as software companies find a divergence in their user groups and pressure to make all upgrades compatible. This can be seen in the Office 2000 software that has backward as well as forward compatibility (a file created in one version can be seen in the other, although specialised functions may not work). This will also be more prevalent as the technology 'haves' push harder for improvements while the vast majority of new users, the 'have-nots but changing', need to keep the pace of change within reach. Complicating the issue will be companies such as Amazon that will forever set the benchmark exceptionally high.

Hold On To Your Seat

A seat is another term used to describe an installation of software. If I have a network that has five active computers or clients and I install MS Office 2000 on all of them, I will need to pay Uncle Bill for a five-seat licence; otherwise, the software police will introduce me to Bill's extensive legal team.

This does present outstanding opportunities to the net-savvy people to create the support mechanisms that will help bridge this widening gap between the two groups. Online information and online help, technology change management, application service providers, and better technology strategies are just some of the areas that will grow rapidly in the first few years of the millennium. These companies can help stem the rising backlash against too rapid a level of technological change, but they will be unable to stop it. As new applications are released on the Internet for free, more and more individuals will turn from the traditional 'buy because it's new' mentality to one of 'Do I need it right now or can I get by with what I have for a few years?' decision making. The advantage is that companies that are wiser about accepting change will become the norm, and this could have a significant dampening effect on technology vendors.

Convergence To The Rescue

There are a couple of very bright lights on the horizon that could change this impending scenario. The first is convergence. When someone builds a piece of software, they can create it in such a way that other software manufacturers can easily share data or use the functionality of the application. This sharing and interrelating is called convergence. For example, if you build an application such as an online order-taking system and then make it compatible with some sort of standard such as ODBC (Open Data Base Connectivity) or JDBC (Java Data Base Connectivity), you will be able to use other software such as a particular database that is also compatible with the same standard. This means that purchasing a particular software product should not require the purchasing of a whole host of other software from the same manufacturer just to gain the compatible functionality you require. For example, an MS Word document can easily be posted to your website or intranet by saving it as HTML. This means that MS Word is compatible with HTML, and you don't have to run out and buy a separate software package solely for converting the Word document into HTML. That's convergence.

As more and more software and application companies seek their own piece of the e-commerce world, you will find greater and greater variety available. As long as the software is convergent around a specific standard, you will not be required to learn two different individual software programs or separate applications. You will have to learn only the one you are using and convert it to the standard. This level of convergence between software and application is likely to grow as the pressure from companies and individuals becomes more intense due to falling upgrade sales and lower purchases of new software.

Convergence And e-Commerce

Convergence is also vital to the new world of e-commerce. Functions such as automated supply chains will require that all operational software communicates with each other. One way for this to happen is for everyone to have the same software. That, however, would provide a monopoly to a software company that would further reduce competition and force up prices. The best situation is for the market to define non-proprietary standards and then allow any and all competitors to use these standards as the basis for their development. The Internet was designed on such standards and as long as no single company owns the standards, the market will grow and prosper. The minute one company owns the standards of a market, and it locks down distribution in favour of profit, growth stagnates, and the market becomes divergent.

Imagine how different the Internet would be if Microsoft owned the rights to HTML and XML. One very good example that shows the difference between open and closed standards is the battle that erupted between the VHS and Beta video standards. The result, as we know, was the success of the VHS format that was open to the world of electronic manufacturing while the Beta standard was closed and proprietary and is now used almost exclusively by professional broadcasters and recording houses.

Convergence around standards has always produced growth in the past, and it can be argued that standards are a true maker of market efficiency. The Internet luckily is one large open standard, as are Linux and Java. This embedding of a proprietary property as a standard succeeds only because the companies are able to create critical mass through free distribution. During the birth of the PC, it was Bill Gates who captured the standard for operating systems, first with wide distribution of DOS and then with a comparable agreement to distribute Windows. Microsoft's goal has always been to get more copies of its software into the hands of users, thereby creating critical mass, and now that everyone else knows the trick and has less capital invested in infrastructure, software such as Linux and Java are poised to become the new standards. The key to their success will be convergence with the standards of the Internet and with each other.

Ease-Of-Use Standards

The complexity of software is growing each day and with fundamental changes to the operating systems, it is getting more difficult for the average user to figure out the technical details of installation and troubleshooting. More and more software manufacturers are making the process of installation easier by working with hardware manufacturers and other software vendors to make easy installations the norm. This creating of 'easy to install and use' systems is becoming more of a standard as customers want to spend less time on installation and maintenance and more time operating the software. Working seamlessly with other systems is also becoming a requirement as customers demand compatibility.

Ease of use lowers the cost to customers in training, installation, maintenance, knowledge transfer, and the costs of making incompatible software communicate. It also allows the organisation to focus resources on those tasks that are value added. The difficulty was always that software manufacturers were focused on the production of the application and its compatibility with Windows. Compatibility with other peripheral devices was not always high on the priority list. Therefore, customers usually had to answer what appeared to be a series of skill-testing questions about their peripheral devices in order to successfully install the software. Installation of drivers, choice of IRQs, and varying standards such as ISA and PCI made it difficult for a technical novice to interpret what was required.

Even today, trying to locate drivers for the installation of a new device such as a DVD player can be challenging to some. Some software manufacturers, especially game software builders, have added installation routines that are not only easy to use and comprehensive but also entertaining. Plug in the device, put the CD in the drive, select 'install', and that's it. The software detects the configuration of the machine and installs itself without interaction from the user.

Ease Of Use And The Internet

This concept of 'ease of use' is also extending to the Internet. Manufacturers are using the standards inherent in the Internet to install plug-ins to browsers that provide the

Figure 20.5 *Java servlets are mini applications that can process data sent across the Internet from HTML forms*

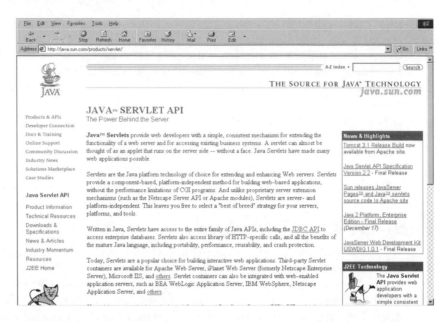

functionality necessary to use a new website with little or no intervention by the user except to start the process. New technologies already in use allow the user to create a 'tunnel' to the web server and run applications on the e-business website without extensive downloads or installations. This process is similar to the distributed network environments in offices, but will require some solutions regarding bandwidth and other Internet-related issues.

Bandwidth

You can think of bandwidth as the amount of space on a road. If the road is full, you might have to wait to get on or go slowly once you are on. The question of bandwidth and the Internet relates to how much traffic the backbone or infrastructure can manage. It will get better as more bandwidth capacity is added and newer technologies make more efficient use of existing bandwidth.
New functions such as streaming video or servlet architecture will take up large amounts of bandwidth, and must be addressed before we are all stuck in a big Internet traffic jam.

As the technology becomes more and more complex, the pressure to take away some of the technical aspects related to software and hardware installation and administration is beginning to disappear. The evolution of plug and play to new USB (universal serial bus) architecture and even the 'easy-to-use' standards of the Internet are helping reduce the technological knowledge gap among individuals. But for e-commerce companies, ownership of this knowledge is still a fundamental part of being able to build a successful online business. This means that companies that intend to move with the technology must gain the depth of knowledge to understand this new world, while individuals will have an easier time as new online information sources coupled with easier-to-implement technologies take hold. One of the greatest benefits of going to Windows from DOS was the ease with which files could be deleted, moved, and copied, all in an easy-to-understand graphic world. Of course, Apple and Acorn users had known this all along!

New Knowledge Models

Knowledge of technology is becoming more and more vital in this increasingly complex world. The information needed to attain this high degree of knowledge is becoming easier to obtain thanks to the Internet and the dissemination of information. However, companies that have a resource of information about their products or services are facing increased competition from other websites and conversely, users are having a more difficult time in trying to locate useful information. The new knowledge model takes the concept of online education for the masses to new levels. Now anyone with a computer and an Internet connection, even one at a public library, can become technologically knowledgeable in the most intricate details of a software product.

Content providers are embracing the new distribution techniques such as e-books and online tutorials to provide users around the world with access to clear and concise information. The hoarding of information is being dismantled throughout the online world thanks to these new models in much the same way that people who had access to books became well read and knowledgeable.

Technology is not the only thing you need. The hottest Java programmer in the world isn't nearly as valuable as an experienced Java programmer and database specialist combined. This is simply because knowledge is a lot like critical mass: the more you have, the more you will obtain benefits from the total volume and depth of this knowledge. People have long since known that a depth of knowledge or how much and how varied your education is has benefits to your life.

Concentrating all your knowledge in one specific area is not as beneficial as studying a variety of disciplines with a concentration in one area. For example, business managers who have technical expertise tend to succeed more than business managers who have only business management expertise. The well-rounded individual is usually a more valuable resource to an organisation because of his or her ability to think 'outside the box'. A concentration of knowledge in areas such as technology is good, but employees should also be able to understand accounting, operations, politics, philosophy, maths

... and life. The Internet is already starting to create these individuals as more and more information becomes available in customised learning communities.

So, knowledge is a key ingredient of anything we do and e-businesses are being presented with a once-in-a-lifetime opportunity to grow their business by helping others. The key ingredient of building a community of value is providing value. A community of sales information with no discernible benefit to the surfer is not a community at all; it's a website. A website that provides a benefit to the users, such as knowledge content, starts the process of creating a community of value. Unobtrusively adding sales content to the site is the way your company grows.

The Least You Need To Know

➤ What are your knowledge resources?

➤ How to manage your knowledge resources.

➤ What is causing the technology knowledge gap?

➤ How can this gap be reduced?

➤ How to distinguish new opportunities for online content.

Chapter 21

Customers: Leveraging Your e-Commerce Assets

In This Chapter

➤ Reducing transaction costs

➤ Increasing your supplier reach

➤ Leveraging your partnerships

➤ Leveraging your systems

➤ Leveraging your traffic

Reducing Transaction Costs

You could go to the library and use an Internet connection to create a free web page, get a couple of online partners, add a couple of links to your website, spread a few rumours in the newsgroups about a new website, and away you go. An instant e-business free of charge. What are your transaction costs? Zero is the correct answer unless you count the bank account you may need to cash commission cheques, and there is even a way around this. For the guys manufacturing the product, the costs to the loading bay will probably not change significantly, unless they have added e-commerce functionality. However, beyond the loading bay, the manufacturer's costs associated with sales and marketing will have dropped to represent only those costs related to the website. This is the greatest benefit of e-commerce – the ability to lower your transaction costs to zero.

Although not all companies can achieve this level of cost reduction, most companies can gain significant benefits from using pieces of the e-commerce philosophy. Automating all or part of your supply chain, creating a web presence to reduce calls to your office, or building an online store to capture order information are just some of the things an organisation can do to start reducing the costs of operations. The trick is to use the low cost of communications that is available from the Internet to lower your transactional costs. These cost reductions can come in the form of reductions in staffing levels, or more appropriately the redirection of staff to value-added services, or the reduction in the growth rate of staffing levels as a result of expansion. Other forms of transactional cost reductions are in the hard costs of operations, such as supplies of paper, pens, office space, computers, benefits, parking, cleaning, and phones. Using the Internet can help reduce, eliminate, or redirect all or most of the capital spent on these costs.

Using Technology To Lower Transaction Costs

The goal of reducing your transaction costs can also be achieved by using technology to implement a combination of systems that create the virtual organisation that best meets your business requirements. Leveraging off your existing assets can provide your organisation with a specific advantage over your competition, but only if you are willing to change the way you view your suppliers and competitors.

Do you remember the example of the American Airlines CEO who stated he would rather give up the planes than the Sabre reservation system? He understood the great value of being a standard in the market as opposed to the small individual pieces that operate the market. It was more beneficial to sell all the travellers their tickets than it was to actually transport them to their destinations. The business was run by an IT infrastructure that was a sunk cost with a very low operating overhead compared with running an airline. Yet the small profit generated from these information-based operations was worth far more because the cost per transaction was exceptionally low, and the volume of transactions was exceptionally high.

Of course, the Internet has changed the dynamics of the online ticketing world, and many larger organisations have created online travel agencies. Now customers and travel suppliers can connect directly over the Internet without having to pay fees in the middle (*see* Figure 21.1).

Lowering Your Marketing And Sales Expenses

The true underlying rule remains – faster, wider, and cheaper electronic communications systems lead to a significant reduction in transaction costs. Obviously, one of the biggest reductions comes in the form of lower marketing and sales expenses. The old traditional operating infrastructures required a significant amount of resources to grow organisations to a global scale. Just to reach the world's population with sales and distribution channels was such an incredibly large task that even organisations such as General Motors or

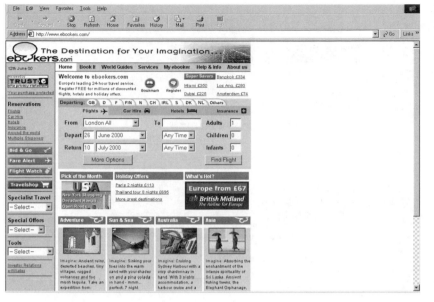

Figure 21.1
E-bookers.com offers visitors the ability to book holidays online

McDonald's needed the investment of others in a franchise distribution network designed to create critical mass.

The car manufacturers even took this principle back down the supply chain by contracting parts and inputs to small companies. It's almost to the point where anyone can build a car simply by ordering all the parts and having them placed together at the automobile assembly company of his choice. But that would require an excellent communications model where the masses could easily produce their own cars online and communicate these wishes to the car company. We all thought that would never happen – but it could … in theory. It would give a whole new meaning to the phrase 'pick-a-part'.

Now let's say that you could order a car over the Internet and then have it delivered to your door. No salesmen, no pre-dealer inspection, just shipping charges. Naturally, if you had still to pay the same for the car as you do now, but without all the hassles, haggling, and the comparative shopping, how much would that add to the profit of the car company, especially if they had outsourced the assembly process back to the low-cost smaller supplier? The answer is the profitability of these companies would grow considerably. (Luckily, however, the British consumer has finally realised that compared with their European cousins, cars have been overpriced in the UK for some considerable time; and a number of websites have sprung up giving discounts of 30% and more on previous high street prices.) The other option would be for the small vehicle assembler to bypass the car companies altogether and build finished cars for anyone who walked through the front door of the website. Of course, they would have to establish a favourable brand image, which is a very difficult task.

Figure 21.2
fish4cars.com was one of the first UK websites to recognise the potential of cutting out the middle men in the overpriced UK car market

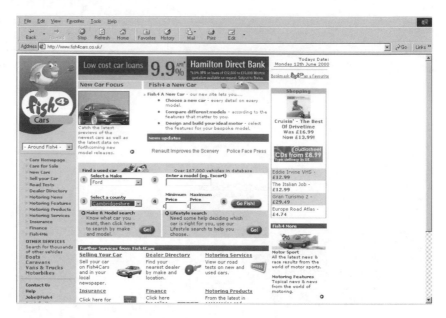

Competition And The Internet

The cost of raw materials and the expense of turning the raw material into a finished product used to be so great that only companies with deep pockets could compete against each other. Companies that could lock up the distribution channels or overpower the tastes of the market with extensive promotion of their own brands further tightened their grip on an exclusive marketplace. In the future, this scenario may still be evident, and there are threats of just this sort of thing happening to the Internet as companies have discovered that branding and other business criteria apply equally to the Internet as to pre-Internet businesses. For now, however, anyone can start a web company for almost no money (and in some cases no money at all) and start the process of building brand awareness for his brand of product.

At this point in the history of technology, there will never be a better time to open an e-business or capture all the advantages of e-commerce and still be able to compete effectively with the biggest companies in the world. If you don't think that Microsoft, currently the world's most successful technology corporation, isn't just a little worried about the idea of every techno geek thinking that he

Competition

27% of European companies with e-business strategies fear that their biggest competition comes from their peer group, not dot coms. In contrast, 43% of US firms believe this to be so.

PricewaterhouseCoopers

is the next Linus Torvalds (the creator of Linux), then think again. It is seriously concerned that the knowledge contained in books such as this one will filter out to the common man and if just a handful of those people make it to the top like Jeff Bezos and Amazon, or Linus Torvalds and Linux, the competition would be unbearable for Microsoft. Of course, that could change when your killer app hits the e-commerce world – and there is still a lot of room for improvement in the current product roll-out by the big guys. However, when you do go to the net, remember that the sophistication of some of the hot software on the drawing boards of the new techno generation is undeniably awesome.

Control Of The Internet

The one thing that could change all this is if one or a handful of the big corporations managed to wrestle control of the Internet away from the multitude of companies it currently needs to make it a success. Microsoft could have continued to grow if it had gained the upper hand in content so that access to the Internet was essentially regulated. However, at the time of writing, as the debate rumbles on in the US on the anti-trust matters of Microsoft, it could lose its dominant position. The Time Warner/AOL proposed merger will likewise stand or fall on the thoughts of an American judge, although in content terms they would be way ahead of Microsoft. When you consider that Time Warner has all the music content from EMI, its own stable of films and publications, the user base of AOL, and the browser capabilities of Netscape, should we be shedding a tear for Bill Gates who has received such adverse publicity?

Saving Users Precious Time

So what does all this mean? There is a growing opportunity to narrow down the search for good information while still allowing the free exchange of all information. The goal is to turn back the tide that is costing users their leisure time by providing quality information while keeping the opportunity for a free information market. If you can succeed in providing this to your community, you may succeed in beating the big guys at their own game. Of course, managing information can be a costly venture if you are trying to run your own search engine and superlinking site.

A better solution is to partner with existing organisations that can provide you with quality information or online services. By giving customers exactly what they want, the best product available, or the greatest variety,

Sticky

If your site is sticky, your customers not only come back, they also stick around. That means that they will look at other pages on your website or use your site to access other websites. Your e-commerce goal is to have a sticky site.

you will beat the big guys who only offer the content from those providers willing to pay. In other words, provide a section for edited, top-quality information and a section of open and free information, and you will succeed in creating a sticky site.

Can you supply all the information yourself? Probably not, and why would you want to duplicate all the other knowledge sites that are out there when you can access most of them free of charge? In general, the rule is that the more partners you have, the better your offering will be to your community, and the more they will stay with your site and not stray elsewhere.

e-Commerce Partnering: Supplier Reach

Any business starts life with capital and invests in procuring the supplies it needs to produce a product or service. For example, a mining company purchases or leases the land that has the ore underneath it and then buys everything from mining equipment to pencils for the office. Eventually, hundreds or even thousands of suppliers can supply these inputs. A football team invests money in joining a league and hiring the talent of the players and coaches as inputs, as well as pencils for the office. An e-commerce company also has to invest in technology to build a web presence, but a web presence may be all that is required. No pencils are needed.

How do you successfully build a business without inputs? You build it solely as an outlet for the supplier of the only input you need – content. At any point in time, you can start to move backwards through the supply chain to provide content or even go so far as to manufacture the products that are sold on your site. This is one of the great equalisers of the Internet – anyone can join the e-business world at any point along the supply chain, from suppliers of base inputs to creators of an online community. The key to the entire process is partnering.

Evaluating Partners

We have discussed extensively the importance of partnering for the e-business and even how to go about partnering. We haven't yet discussed how to evaluate your potential partners or what the partners gain from a relationship with you. Your e-partners may not be as critical as they are in a traditional business environment. For example, if you manufacture a product and you have one shipper who handles your unusual products and for some reason this supplier cannot get your product to market, your business will suffer financially. If the same thing occurs on the Internet, you will simply change online shipping companies. As long as there are ample suppliers of the product that you carry, you should face a relatively low risk from suppliers who are defaulting, thanks to the ever-increasing reach of your supply lines.

The Internet also allows both manufacturers and online suppliers to extend their supply lines globally with very little effort. A plant in China that manufacturers a component for your product can now sell directly to you through its website and ship using an international courier. The importers and distributors would be wiped from the equation, given that the details of the logistics, such as customs clearance, are likely to be managed by an online customs brokerage. This allows for a truly global supply reach for manufacturers or retailers who want to offer more variety to their online community or reduced costs.

Supply Reach For Gathering Content

The concept of 'supply reach' also holds true for information or knowledge. The ability to gather content supply from anywhere in the world is extremely evident, thanks once again to the global reach of the Internet. Writers, authors, companies, communities, or anyone can supply content on the Internet. e-Commerce businesses can obtain the content for minimal up-front payments in exchange for royalties back to the authors. As long as the content is linked or can be supplied online, the reach of the supply line for the business can be global.

Choosing A Content Supplier

When choosing a supply partner, as opposed to a traffic or distribution partner, you should look for a couple of specific things. You should partner with organisations that have a clear concept of what they do and what they want to be. Vague linking sites and questionable product offerings mean that your potential partner might not understand e-commerce well enough to survive. They should also be professional. This does not mean that they are in good office space in the right business area of town and wear suits. They can be two kids in their basement as long as they have the drive and desire to see the project through to the end. They should at least be aware of the concept of doing business on the Internet and have a clear plan as to how they are going to provide you with content.

The content that your supplier will provide should be professional and of the highest quality. We are not talking Shakespeare. The information does, however, have to be clear, concise, and well written for the target audience. If it is written above or below the level of the audience, they will either lose interest or lose trust in the information. You should also feel intuitively that your partner organisation is actually going to stay in business. However, don't get too hung up on this because there are lots of content providers on the net.

e-Commerce Partnering: Affiliate Partnerships

Affiliate partnerships are those where both companies gain an advantage by partnering. These types of partnerships can provide a range of benefits to both parties. Affiliate partnerships tend to be stronger because it is in the best interests of both partners to work for the common good including, but not limited to, survival. It has always been a fundamental human tenet that you partner well in order to survive well. Communities could more efficiently gather and produce the food that was required to live, and they could join together in times of crisis to defeat enemies or save the village from disaster. The same holds true for the Internet – the combining of groups into affiliated partnerships adds mass and bulk to the participating organisations, making them far less vulnerable to large corporate predators, although not entirely immune. They still operate independently within their own operations, but collectively as a whole, affiliates benefit each other.

Communication Among Affiliates

We discussed the importance of affiliates and the way to go about contacting affiliates in previous chapters. The communication between your affiliated partners and your business must be clear and concise. You must spell out responsibilities of both parties and the deliverables. For example, if your site depends on their content, they should be willing to ensure that your community will have access 24×7 (24 hours a day, seven days a week), and they should clearly stipulate their failure expectations and disaster recovery capabilities. They should clearly indicate what, if any, payments will be made, the method of paying those amounts, and a schedule of payments. Finally, they should indicate how payments are to be tracked and verified. If it is a mutual exchange of traffic, they should stipulate what is to happen if the balance of 'traffic generation' shifts too much to one partner.

Whether you use lawyers to draft the document, use standard partnering agreements, or just trust the company is purely your decision. However, legitimate companies will understand the necessity of fair agreements and will satisfy your requests. Remember that if the benefits are marginal, agreements may not be necessary because there is little to protect.

Managing Affiliate Relationships

Your affiliate relationships are important, and they should be protected and managed. Usually, specific individuals are assigned the task of establishing partnerships. They spend a great deal of time phoning and travelling to partnering companies to obtain specific information regarding the partnership, including negotiating agreements and establishing milestones and deliverables. They maintain contact with the partners, ensuring that deliverables and milestones are attained. They monitor such things as performance, payments, and traffic measurement. They also manage co-operative promotional programmes that divide the cost of advertising, promotion, or public relations. A healthy relationship with your partners not only helps both businesses function more effectively, it also helps both businesses grow.

The greatest benefit of partnering is that you can build a virtual corporation for very little capital expenditure. This is essentially leveraging your assets and your ideas by utilising partnerships to get those pieces of your organisation that you require. Traditional businesses use leverage by raising capital to purchase assets and then use those assets as collateral to raise more funds. For example, if you raise capital to lease a retail location and purchase stock, you can then pledge the stock as collateral to raise funding for operations and advertising. In the virtual company, you raise capital to

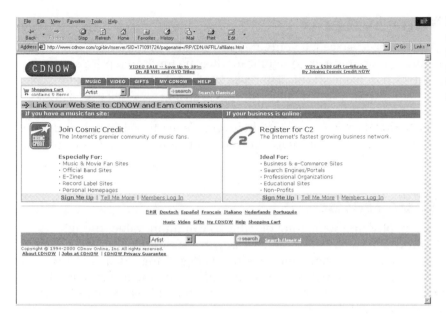

Figure 21.3
cdnow.com is one of many sites to openly court affiliates in order to boost its sales.

build a killer app and use it to generate traffic. The traffic may be the result of partnering, or it may be passed on for revenue generation by click-throughs or commissions. The revenue and partnerships can then be leveraged to raise capital that can be turned into advertising and promotion to increase traffic levels.

Amazon.com

Amazon started with a shopping website to sell books. It used this application to pay commissions for sales generated by click-through traffic. With this model, it was able to attract thousands of websites to become partners by placing a link to the Amazon web page on its website. The result was a significant jump in traffic to Amazon. It was then able to extrapolate or forecast traffic growth rates for the website. These potential growth rates attracted the attention of the investment world for the IPO. The result was significant funding for investment in systems and promotion or an $11 billion leverage against a simple website.

Leveraging Your Systems

Internal systems can also be leveraged. If yours are incompatible or need to be upgraded, the investment required to do this may be significant. Raising funds to replace systems can often provide a return in reduced costs. However, in general, the return will be relatively low compared with investment opportunities available for value-added areas such as promotion. A system that costs thousands of pounds can often be outsourced to a partner, but the operational costs and risks in these arrangements will be higher than if you had purchased the system. The advantage, however, is that the capital can be used to grow your business either traditionally or online.

Leveraging Your Traffic

Leveraging is the act of pledging something of value to gain more value through investment of the proceeds. We are pretty generic in this definition because leveraging does not have to apply only to money. You can also leverage things such as traffic. Pledging traffic essentially means that you agree to send your traffic to a specific site in exchange for something you can invest or an actual investment itself. Something to invest is more traffic or actual funding.

An investment can be the use of an application or use of advertising or promotion. More visitors will generate more revenue, and higher revenue and traffic can be used to raise capital for investment in advertising and promotion. It's like a snowball rolling down a hill – it will gather more snow, and as it does, it will grow.

The Least You Need To Know

➤ How to reduce your transactions costs.

➤ How to gain supplier reach.

➤ How to leverage your affiliate partnerships.

➤ How to leverage your systems.

➤ How to leverage your traffic.

Chapter 22

Land Mines Lurking On The Net

In This Chapter

➤ Diminishing hits

➤ Lawyers alive and well on the net

➤ Overvaluation of Internet stocks

➤ Commercialism

➤ Privatisation

➤ Divergent standards

Diminishing Hits

There are a lot of people who have never had Internet access, but with the price of PCs and the cost of connecting to the Internet falling, there will be high growth rates in the total volume of Internet traffic in the coming years. Over the next few years, there will be increases in the numbers of people who make purchases over the Internet. However, there will also be millions of new places for them to go.

Let's say the Internet was composed of one million users and one website. If the entire online population surfed, you could expect most, or all of them, to belong to the community of that one single site. If a second site was opened, the number of people who would 'belong' to your community could be expected to fall by 50%, assuming that the two websites offered essentially the same value and the inertia quotient was

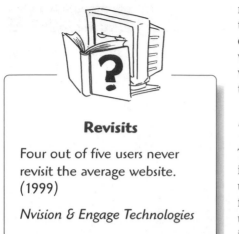

Revisits

Four out of five users never revisit the average website. (1999)

Nvision & Engage Technologies

not taken into consideration. Some experts estimate the current ratio to be approximately 10 users for every website. Of course, the vast majority of websites get very few hits, and a small handful of websites take the lion's share of visitors; and visitors tend to visit many different sites.

The Thrill Is Going

The problem, as we noted in previous chapters, is that users will tire of the thrill of the Internet and usage will eventually taper off as the Internet moves from a technological tool to a utility. How many of us actually pick up a phone and use it just because it's a phone? We use it because we have to talk to someone at a distance. If the Internet was to generate the same level of intense interest, like just after you buy a new car, the level of usage would be starting to have a significant impact on the level of time spent on entertainment such as the TV.

Anyone who has surfed the Internet for leisure has noticed how the hours of usage are declining at home, although the hours of usage at work may be increasing. This trend will continue as good information becomes even more difficult to locate, and the average user loses interest. The result will be that the Internet will become a utility of sorts for users to gather knowledge on specific technologies, read their email, get updates on their real-time news delivery sites, or purchase a product at one of a handful of shopping sites. The total volume of users will continue to increase as access is granted to more people throughout the world. The thing that will stop this trend towards decreasing repeat usage, and present a number of opportunities, is the creation of communities of value that save the average user time in their already hectic lives.

Making Sticky Sites

The key e-commerce question is how do you make seasoned Internet users visit your site repeatedly, given this information? The answer is that you make a conscientious decision to act like a utility. That means your users will generally return to your site to make their surf quick and efficient. There are other things that users value in a utility, such as the convenience of use and reliability of service. These same principles should be the underlying foundation of your online web presence. Providing a reliable source of knowledge, an application, or a community will start the process of getting regular users to return to your site. People will tend to take the easiest and most certain route since it is an inherent trait in human nature to make things easy. That's why TV is so popular. It has to be one of the easiest forms of entertainment – point and click. Before the Internet will seriously start to dent TV viewership, it will have to capture the ease of use that TV enjoys, or provide significantly more value. Quite a large number of people tend to be, essentially, couch potatoes.

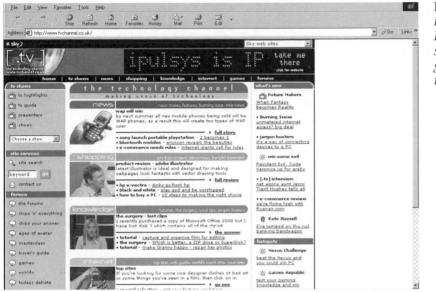

Figure 22.1 *dot tv is one of the first European TV stations to bridge the gap between TV and the internet*

If you were to take a quick poll of your Internet using friends you would probably find that the number one use of the Internet, for hit generation (for example, what causes you to surf to a new site), is information gathering. The searches would be performed because Aunt Ethel has a pain in her side and needs information, or your goldfish has turned blue and you are uncertain why, or you don't trust the work your dentist wants to do on your teeth or your mechanic wants to do to your car. The second biggest use will probably be entertainment, such as games or music or reading news. Then you might find shopping or downloading music or software in third place.

Repetitive Value

e-Commerce is not about building a great app and then watching users beat a traffic path to your website. It's all about trying to get customers to consider your site as something of value that they should return to again and again. This means that it must provide 'repetitive value'. Without repetitive value, your customers will not return, and you will be forever spending money and resources on promotion and advertising to get new customers to visit your site. It's far more efficient to build repetitive value and promote less and less as your critical mass continues to grow. However, since more and more websites will be gunning for your customers, you will have to continue to work at keeping your customers loyal. Now loyalty building becomes a part of the mix.

Lawyers – Alive And Well On The Net

Affiliate partnerships, links, click-through payments, commissions, content agreements, trademarking, cyber squatting, and intellectual property. You can almost

Figure 22.2 *Reward programmes are designed to keep visitors coming back for more*

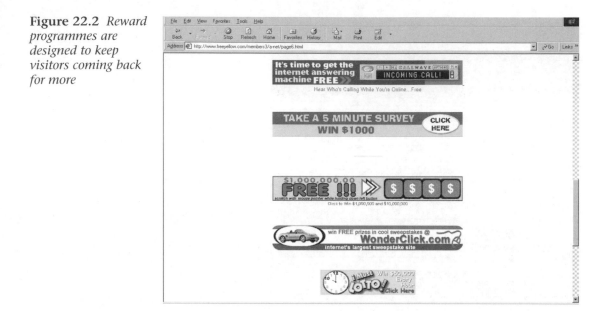

hear the battle cry from the hordes of lawyers making Internet law their speciality. Many law firms have individuals dedicated to studying the Internet and its legal ramifications. There are, in fact, a wide variety of online law resources and online law firms dedicated to Internet law.

Figure 22.3 *ABC is an established and respected law firm which has grasped the opportunities of the internet*

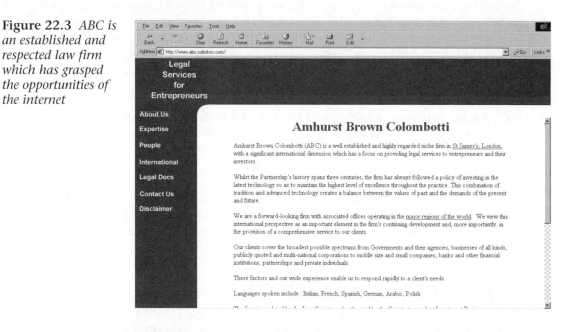

The Growth Of Internet Law

The Internet is drawing lawyers like moths to a flame, and it is becoming increasingly difficult for commerce to occur on the net without a lawyer lurking somewhere nearby. Part of this is a simple function of protecting the rights and responsibilities of e-commerce organisations and their customers. The other part is pure opportunistic malice. The Internet has been called the equivalent of the business 'wild west'. All the traditional rules have been set aside in favour of a flexible and rapidly changing environment, and lawyers have had some difficulty adapting to this constantly changing target. More than one major technical partnership has been scuttled by delays in the agreement phase of the partnering programme.

Lawyers have learned to adapt to this world of 'easy-to-understand' short agreements and semi-handshake partnering deals by drawing up agreements that avoid extensive legalese and by fast tracking on-the-fly business partnerships. They have done this unwillingly because they understand the risks and consequences of taking short cuts in documentation. e-Commerce businesses and in particular e-businesses have forced the issue with a blistering pace of development and stratospheric growth rates. The ability of traditional law firms to keep pace was just not there. However, organisations that require partnerships are now drafting fast, simple agreements that provide the opportunity to close partnering deals quickly, or they are using standard agreements that are provided by one of the partners.

The Rise Of The e-Lawyer

There is a vast amount of legal territory to cover for the average law firm trying to get a handle on the Internet. Content providers are seeking protection for their copyrights so that their work cannot be freely distributed on the Internet. This includes authors, musicians, artists, and the big content providers such as Time Warner or Disney. Another task of Internet law is the protection of partners to ensure they receive click-through and commission payments and, more importantly, to define what constitutes a payable transaction and how these transactions are measured. The principle here is to protect the smaller sites and individuals to ensure they are paid for their traffic.

Problems related to site content are also becoming an issue, not just for copyright infringement but for illegal use of trademarks in domains. This ties in with the act of cyber squatting or stealing customers from legitimate sites by trying to mimic those sites. Obviously, if you set up an Amazon duplicate, there are grounds for legal action. But what if you own the domain to a traditional company and are using it to direct URL calls to your own site? Is that considered cyber squatting?

There are a wide variety of other legal issues on the Internet that are drawing the interest of lawyers and lawmakers. The distribution of pornography and hate literature, the always sensitive area of defamation, and the growing work in fraud and hacking. It has created so many new areas of law that combining it into one area called Internet law or e-commerce law is definitely a step in the right direction. This will allow lawyers to focus on some of the unique aspects of the Internet and how to manage the legal aspects while still freeing clients to move quickly with new developments and partnerships. The question is whether the law profession can itself change to meet the challenges of e-commerce without being driven to it by its clients.

The Legal Impact On e-Commerce

The whole issue of e-commerce and the legal questions surrounding it are going to be one of the most significant hurdles to the growth of commerce on the net. If simple partnering arrangements turn into long, formal legal agreements, the creation of barriers to business on the Internet will have started. Hiring a lawyer is a significant disadvantage for smaller businesses trying to formalise a partnering agreement, and it is especially hard on low- or no-resource virtual corporations.

Creating barriers to the free flow of small business commerce is one of the best ways to take control of the Internet. We need to lobby to have laws passed that regulate the Internet through the use of formal registration processes, set up rigorous certification programmes, force a strict adherence to a set of standards or attempt otherwise to control the free flow of ideas, partnerships, and innovation. Obviously, there are limits as to what a democratic society can or should allow and luckily that's up to the politicians and not the authors of this book.

The problem is that if I am a small e-business that wants to offer an application that could terminate the existence of a large technology company, should it have any right to stop me? For the Internet to flow smoothly, the answer should be 'no', but the legal land mine lurking in the distance is that the large company can now legally strangle my ability to partner through the use of exclusionary practices. There are a variety of these exclusionary practices starting to happen on the Internet, such as charging fees for search engine placement or locked-in distribution of software with new computers. As more of these exclusionary tactics occur, you will start to see more private actions arise that will provide e-law firms with a significant amount of work.

Overvaluation Of Internet Stocks

There's nothing quite like an overheated stock market. In the good old days of share trading, the market suffered significantly in October 1987, losing more than 20% of its value. It fell in spite of the fact that assets of the vast majority of the largest companies were hard assets or assets that had a marketable value, such as lorries or equipment. Imagine what would have happened if those companies hadn't had hard assets?

The problem with the stock market today is that shares are trading on historically unheard of price/earnings ratios. There is no single individual who can clearly explain whether these inflated values are justifiable or not simply because no one has ever lived during such a period of technological change. Is technology powering the growth of our economies to new heights, or is the hype just hype? Was it Lastminute.com or Boo.com that started the bubble bursting, or has it only just begun to grow given the potential of today's global economy? There are so many dynamics at play, such as the globalisation of the world economy, the rapid advances in technology at the end of the 1990s, and the low-cost, instantaneous worldwide communications capability of the Internet. With all these variables, it is little wonder that no one has a clue where the existing market is going over the next two years.

They do, however, have a clear view of where solid e-commerce IPOs are going. The direction, purely and simply, is up. Are the IPO values justified? We can look at some simple statistics to do the maths. If you sell a book and make 30 pence gross margin, then selling two million books will net £600 000 in gross margin before operating expenses. If you have to pay for the retail overheads required to sell two million books or 50 stores, you would have £12 000 per location or £1000 per month for rent, utilities, overheads, etc. You can see that at 30 pence gross margin, it's going to be pretty tough to make a living. Now, let's say you raised £30 million and built a state-of-the-art online e-business and warehouse. Your current attainable market is now 100 million people. At 30 pence a book profit, how many customers do you need to provide a return to the people who invested the £30 million?

Two per cent of the market returns 2%, and 10% returns 10% before operating expenses for warehouse and office space. Increasing the mark-up per book to net 60 pence drives the return from 10% to 20%. The average retail mark-up on books is significantly higher than 60 pence.

Potential Growth And Profit

Let's say that Amazon never got another customer and each of its existing customers purchased one book next year with an average mark-up per book of £1. The gross margin on the sales of these books would be £12 million. Assuming an investment in systems of £40 million, the return is 30%. Now factor in the growth in new online areas such as electronics and auctions, or the growth of the sales base given the lack of comparable competitors. What you will quickly realise is that the potential profitability of this concept is phenomenal, regardless of whether there are enough hard assets to protect your investment. Also, let's not forget about some of our e-commerce principles, such as critical mass, first to market, or the killer app rules. All of this makes a company like Amazon.com an extremely valuable property for investors.

Can The Market Keep The Value Up?

Although there is some merit to the high value of on-net organisations, the next big question has to be, can the market sustain these values? The answer is, it's anybody's guess. However, the impact of a sell-off of Internet stocks would have significant implications for e-businesses that were positioned incorrectly. Since most of these organisations do not have any substantial hard assets to support their valuation, anything that might slow the growth of the Internet, such as a recession, would seriously affect these inflated valuations. Already some companies are having trouble successfully executing an IPO to 'spin off' new Internet offerings backed by traditional businesses. In this case, a traditional retailer who decides to enter the e-commerce field might find the competition daunting and numerous. If the company is considered by the market to be lacking the sophistication necessary to compete in the new online world, it will have difficulty raising the capital it needs through an IPO.

Providing Real Value

Although the potential of the Internet probably more than justifies the stratospheric prices of online companies, a hiccup in these valuations could make it difficult for your organisation to raise capital. So there are two pieces of advice. Hurry and try to provide real value. Providing real value is giving the investor a reason to hold or want your stock. It won't protect you if the market decides to crash, but it will cushion the fall. When you do go to market, providing real value should help to ensure the success of your offering, although this is not always the case. IPO investors can be finicky and sometime a company with little in the way of value but with a great story will capture the hearts of the investment community ahead of one that provides real value.

Providing value, however, is a long-term growth model. It can be done by owning proprietary technology that gives your website something unique, or it can be through an investment in infrastructure such as a distribution chain. Real value can also be provided through the ownership of the content of your site (but not hoarding). This value can be intellectual or entertainment property, and an application or an online service that is difficult or impossible to duplicate. Real value can also be the strength of the online community that you create.

Recessions happen, and no one can predict when they will occur or how deep they will be. In fact, we may be only at the very start of the longest period of economic growth ever. Or maybe we are at the end. The best thing you can do is to go to market before anything else causes Internet funding to falter. You don't have to go mad for the tripling of your share price; just try to raise the funds you will need to grow your business over the next few years. Your aim should be slow, steady growth if your goal is longevity, but if your goal is short-term gain, then give it all you have, hype it to the roof, cross your fingers and hope that it holds until you can get out. Of course, companies with a short game plan often fall short in the IPO world and wind up pulling the offering at a high cost.

Commercialism

The rush of e-businesses is going to be immense in the coming years as the concepts contained in this and other e-commerce books start to filter into the offices and boardrooms of the millions of businesses that have not started the migration to the net.

This mass commercialisation of the Internet is going to once again change everything. As each new business sets out a virtual store, the volume of clutter in the guise of advertising will grow on the Internet. Let's say you hopped into your car and went over to the local electrical retailer to purchase some electronics but instead of seeing one or two electronics stores, you were faced with 3000. Which one would you go to?

They will all claim to have the lowest price, and they will all claim to offer the best service. Some will provide information and help on how to use the products, some will let you try the product first, and some will provide financing or someone to install it. But 3000 choices – who has the time? You will be likely to choose one or two retailers that you feel most comfortable with or that were recommended and forget the others. If enough people do this, you will see something called a shakeout.

How To Survive A Shakeout

There is no real solution to a shakeout because it's almost like a 'catch-22'. If you don't grow fast enough or take on more risk, you will eventually be taken out of the market by those organisations that grow substantially, thanks to the dynamics of the shakeout. However, your best protection in a shakeout is not to over-extend your organisation by taking on the added risk of large expansion, unless of course you are headed for the top. There are a number of survival options, such as 'niching' a market.

The massive growth in the volume of commercial websites that is looming is certain to create an environment for a shakeout, as some online companies that are competing in an increasingly crowded market find partnering doors closed and promotion expensive. Some other pitfalls might include declining surfing habits of users as valuable information becomes more difficult to locate. Another land mine could be a company the size of Microsoft obtaining a technology or standard that provides it with control of the market. For example, the hypothetical amalgamation of Sun and Microsoft would position a super-organisation to control many of the standards that are the basis for the Internet.

The Shakeout

A shakeout is where too many companies are all trying to compete for business in the same market and eventually start to fail. They fail because the customers will cluster around a few companies with the right image or product offering. These firms will use the windfall of proceeds to buy up smaller firms in the market or promote and compete hard against the existing companies. Eventually, only one or two companies will remain in the market.

A concentration of ownership of the key software and websites that control the Internet would create a significant threat and add potential barriers to entry. However, legislation, the speed of technological change, and some of the new applications and business models under construction promise fundamentally to change the structure of e-commerce, significantly mitigating this type of threat.

Privatisation

Imagine if you had billions of pounds and you were able to privatise the net.
Not likely to happen, you say? How about if we tell you that to exercise control on the
Internet you don't have to own control of everything, just some of the key pieces.
In fact, most of the key pieces that make the Internet work are already owned by a
handful of companies. Luckily, it is in their best interests and in the best interest of
their shareholders to capitalise on their ownership as soon as possible. Very few
investors are farsighted enough to sacrifice today's gains for long-term control. If a
maniacal CEO wanted to control the Internet, he would always be up against a
boardroom that wanted immediate and maximum returns today.

The privatisation of the Internet is a real concern for the e-business of tomorrow
simply because privatisation can close access or make it costly to operate.
Search engines that charge for listings, presentation of controlled information, high
fees for the use of critical applications or standards, and charges for access to
information are all land mines on the Internet that can increase the barriers to entry or
limit a new company's ability to access the market.

As companies become more sophisticated about the Internet, some will attempt to
capitalise on their position in the market. Sun may distribute Java free to the Internet
community for now, but eventually some sort of corresponding return may be
required. It will probably come in the form of compatible products such as web server
software, publications and training, or other products. However, there is nothing to
stop Sun from charging a fee for future releases of Java, although it would probably do
this at its peril. The good news about privatisation at this point is that most of the
large companies are not only driven by their shareholders to perform in the near term,

Figure 22.4
goto.com is one of a new breed of American websites that charges for listing a site – and where America goes, Europe tends to follow

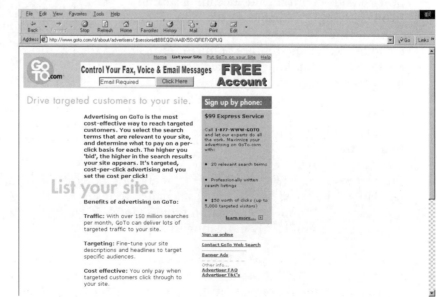

they are also deathly afraid of the next whiz kid and his annoying little system. Imagine the person who creates the ability for all households and businesses to communicate without an ISP, telephone company, or operating software.

The best protection available to the new e-commerce company is to avoid dependence on a single supplier of technology. You can always run one technology as your main 'in-house' standard, but experiment and be ready with other technologies or do what Microsoft is doing and diversify your investment so that you are a partner in the new technology of tomorrow. Also, ensure that you partner with those cutting-edge corporations that may be creating the next standard for the industry, such as Linux.

Divergent Standards

Nothing would do more harm than a movement away from standards and towards divergence. However, this scenario is not impossible. Software companies that become the standard may abandon other industry standards or attempt to scuttle emerging standards. The goal is that by creating divergence in the market, no clear standard will emerge. This was the concern that Sun raised when Microsoft attempted to alter its release of the Java software. If Microsoft had been successful, the Internet would have had to deal with two versions of Java that might not have been compatible.

A more likely scenario is the divergence of standards for proprietary gain.
Some companies believe that if they produce a product that has wide acceptance, the standard should be what they dictate. For example, there are currently two main browsers, Netscape and Explorer. Netscape used to command the vast majority of the browser market but has since fallen behind Explorer, thanks to the free distribution of Explorer with new computers. The two technologies predominantly use the current standards of the Internet so they both operate effectively and efficiently. However, if a gaming company wants to create some sort of new browser plug-in, it may have to work with two different standards. If one browser becomes the single standard of the net, it may have the clout to change the underlying standards of the Internet or force companies to meet whatever standard it builds into its product. This could result in the gaming company having to pay a fee for the privilege of interfacing with the dominant browser.

There is very little an e-commerce company can do to avoid this scenario, but there are a couple of bright spots. The first is that technology is changing rapidly so that standards of today may eventually be wiped out by the developments of tomorrow. Second, the young techno generation is very keen to ensure their place in the future. The Internet was not given its massive push from obscurity by the established corporations; it was pushed by a small subculture of people who built bulletin board systems and eventually grew into the local ISPs of today. The attitude that led to the creation of Linux is the same attitude that is likely to keep a limit on the privatisation of the Internet.

So there are a lot of risks and land mines out there, and there are a lot of options and opportunities. Where you position your e-commerce organisation is critical to its survival. Knowing which options to select or which paths to follow is the million-dollar question. Keeping in tune with the world of technology, whether by hiring techno-savvy staff or learning it yourself, is a critical component of divining the future direction of the business world. Avoiding the above land mines or the ones that are certain to crop up will be a regular task of managing and building an e-commerce organisation and also critical to its long-term survival.

The Least You Need To Know

➤ How to manage diminishing hits.

➤ What the impact of lawyers on the net will be.

➤ How market overvaluation can impact your IPO.

➤ What are some commercialism problems and opportunities.

➤ How to avoid the privatisation land mine.

➤ What divergent standards mean to your e-business.

Part 5

Pulling It All Together

It doesn't do you any good to just get bits and pieces of sporadic information, so in this section we will bring it all together in the definitive e-commerce model. We will cover what you have to do from start to finish to build an e-commerce empire.

This model is applicable to small and large businesses, as well as traditional businesses that are going to update their operations for the new era of technology.

Pulling it all together completes the process of moving you from an e-commerce idiot to an e-commerce professional. At the end of this section, you will know more about e-commerce than most e-commerce 'experts'. But that can be our little secret.

Chapter 23

The Definitive e-Commerce Model

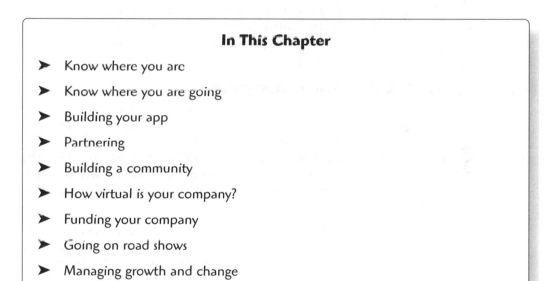

In This Chapter

➤ Know where you are

➤ Know where you are going

➤ Building your app

➤ Partnering

➤ Building a community

➤ How virtual is your company?

➤ Funding your company

➤ Going on road shows

➤ Managing growth and change

Knowing Where You Are Is Important

In order to implement any business model, you first have to understand and appreciate where you are. Imagine trying to travel somewhere, but you're lost. How would you know which way to go? You couldn't choose a location to head towards or a path to get there or even decide how much you would need in supplies. Like any strategy, the starting point is to find out where you are. Then you will know how far you have to go and in which direction to head.

Information technology is the foundation upon which the e-business model is built. The fancy doors and windows of the company are important to the outside world, but the foundation has to be rock solid. Therefore, one of the first things any company, individual, or organisation should do is an IT inventory. This isn't about counting the number of computers that you have or the bandwidth of your fibre pipe. It is vital to know both of these statistics, along with the following information:

➤ The depth of your technical knowledge resources.

➤ Your current technology standards.

➤ What your infrastructure is composed of.

➤ What technology needs to be upgraded.

➤ What technology must stay.

➤ What your technological philosophy is (Internet based, in-house systems, outsourced technology, direction of technological change, etc.).

The goal is to create an itemised list of your technological resources along with your future technological direction. This will at least indicate where you are now and the direction in which you are headed from a technological perspective.

Taking Stock Of Your Company

Just as you would analyse where you are from a technology perspective, you also have to analyse where you are from a company perspective. This includes identifying your corporate knowledge assets, as well as your proprietary strengths and weaknesses. You should evaluate the strength of your corporate culture by trying to define what the culture is and how it should change. Obviously, you should also identify your real assets, including capital and hard resources such as stock, as well as any and all risks that the current business faces.

You should also look at what changes you need to make to the existing corporate resources in order for the company to change its operations. These can include the addition of transitional staff, a research and development lab, or more investment in a subsidiary. For example, if you have a traditional warehouse operation, you may need more warehouse space, a new configuration for the existing warehouse space, changes to shipping and receiving methodologies, etc.

The objectives for taking stock of your company, like that of the IT, should be to identify where exactly the business is in its world so that you can understand your starting point. For example, if you are a medical test lab that is going to use international despatch and shipping but you only have accounts with local and national couriers, you will have to plan on establishing international courier accounts and dedicate resources to understanding how to change your shipping procedures.

Taking Stock Of The Competition

It is pretty difficult to fight a battle if you don't know anything about your competition. You need to identify who your competition is, including indirect competitors, such as companies that supply a product that can impact your sales. For example, the car was actually indirect competition to the hay feed distributor (and, in fact, for many years London cabbies were obliged, by law, to carry a bale of hay in the boot of their cab, even though the only horse power they used was diesel!). Knowing the size and potential impact on your operations as a result of your competition is also important. If they are further ahead in the development of an identical application to yours, they stand a higher chance of becoming the standard before you can reach them.

It's important to understand where the competition is relative to your own organisation. If they have comparable resources and size to your company, including their knowledge assets, they will be a formidable threat. If they are significantly smaller, and in some cases larger, they might not be a threat at all. You should also try to identify which markets they operate in and any proprietary advantage they may have.

Taking Stock Of Your Industry

You need to take account of where your company stands in relation to the rest of your industry. Is it far down the technology learning curve or back at the start? In some cases, an industry in the early stages of an e-commerce evaluation presents numerous opportunities, but in other cases if you exceed the technological capability of your suppliers, they may not be able to meet your goals for an automated supply chain. This may require you to take a leadership role in moving your industry forward, or it may require you to take a more supportive role and search for other opportunities.

All of these stock takes are nothing more than a simple session of information gathering and documentation to identify the strengths, weaknesses, opportunities and threats for the organisation. In other words, the traditional SWOT analysis. These tasks should not take a great deal of time or resources, but should take enough time to produce some documentation for the business plan that will be included in publications such as a prospectus. Your goal should be to produce a few written sections, such as:

➤ Who is the company?

➤ What are the company's strengths?

➤ Who is the competition?

➤ What is the state of the industry?

➤ What are the opportunities ... and the threats?

Know Where You Are Going

Once you have decided on where you are, you can decide where you want to be. This is essentially giving your organisation a target to head towards. Often, these targets

Figure 23.1
Amazon has already started to offer services using wireless application protocol which, at the time of writing, is still in its infancy

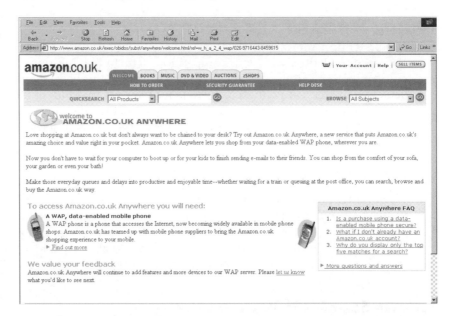

are spelled out in annual goals, five-year plans, business strategies, or mission statements. The point is that it is very difficult to move an organisation if you don't have a clear idea of where you are going. You may change the target as you go, but at least have something to head towards initially.

The Business Plan

You have already started formulating a business plan in the last section. In fact, you should have been able to formalise and create the first few pages of a draft business plan. The next step is to expand on the opportunities section by choosing one or two targets and creating a long-term corporate goal. We say goal as opposed to mission because mission statements are far more general and philosophical than goals. For example, you may choose to fight a war to protect the principles of democracy, but your actual goal may be to eliminate your opponent's weapons and infrastructure in the first few weeks.

Now you know where you are and where you are going. The next step in the process is to define all the smaller goals that have to be accomplished to get you to the main goal. These goals can include changing your infrastructure, updating your servers, installing an ADSL or satellite connection, purchasing software and hiring consultants. Each of these goals should be clear and concise. There should be no ambiguity, and you should always be able to identify a clear path to the main goal that indicates how far you have yet to go. For example, you can state that your main goal is to supply 'how to' information free of charge on the Internet. Your sub-goals could include something like get four major sponsors or partners by October or have a functional website online by August. They should not be fuzzy or soft goals.

Now that you have defined where you are, where you are going, and all the milestones in between, define a schedule of when these goals will be accomplished. Again the date should be clear and not soft. These dates are essential because they indicate the progress of the organisation and should result in a graduated level of rewards.

This route map is usually not published in a widely distributed business plan. Instead, a page or two outlining how your company plans to capitalise on the opportunities noted in the industry section of the business plan should be enough.

Staffing Up

The next step in the process is to start defining the structure of your organisation and the executive staff who will be required to run it. You will then need to find those staff members, and the best way to do this is to steal them from other organisations, although we recommend that you always mix in some of the best young talent from the schools. Your most senior staff should bring either an extremely high level of talent or some other significant benefit, such as contacts, salesmanship, reputation, etc. These individual talents should be documented in an executive's list and included in the business plan.

It is vital that if you hire your friends for moral support their role is backed by others with talent or reputation. Some of the most successful companies that we are familiar with were the product of two or more partners. Defining the founding partner roles and responsibilities and ensuring a very selective hiring policy from that point on is essential to ensuring that you get the right individuals on your corporate team.

The Technology Strategy

Just as you set goals for the organisation, you should prepare a sub-map just for technology. This is critical because of the nature of our new businesses. Technology is so vital to any business plan today that a separate set of goals should be established to define such things as which standards are going to be used over the short term, what technological partnerships will be developed, what proprietary technology you will develop, and what technologies you will have tested for future applications. This particular map can still use the corporate goal as the main technological target, but the sub-goals should all be clear, concise, and related to technology. Installing a new server is a good goal, but defining corporate direction as it relates to emergent structures is not. It is important to note that in some cases the technology may not yet be in existence and may require development. This fact also can be noted in the strategy.

Once again the technology strategy and its strategy map should include hard target dates for measuring the performance of the company and for giving rewards. A single-page technology section should be added to the business plan that identifies both the existing technology and the new strategy. Both the main strategic map and the technology map may have to be altered at a later date if the resources are not available to meet the goals.

319

Resource Map

The resource map is the same as any other strategic map except that it deals with the amount of resources that will be needed to achieve your goal. It should first of all identify what resources the organisation actually has to play with. This includes financial, knowledge and technical resources, as well as hard assets. The next step is to identify what new resources you will require and how much they are going to cost.

Once again you will have to establish milestones as to how you are going to achieve your resource goals. These should include such items as the amounts that you will require from the different levels of funding along with some pro forma financial statements. If you follow professional accounting guidelines in the production of those statements, you will be able to move easily to audited statements at a later date. These statements, along with financial notes and a comprehensive statement of the risks facing your firm, should also be added to the business plan.

At this point, you should essentially have 95% of a comprehensive business plan drafted. It will change as the organisation moves ahead, but for now you have performed the most difficult task, the rough draft. The business plan that you have drafted is your story, and the story is what you sell to the world.

Building Your Killer App

Business Plans

Surf to just about any company and look at a prospectus. You will see a standard business plan. Look at a lot of them, and you will see a pattern emerging. Better still, surf to www.e-biz-pro.com and you'll be able to download a business plan template.

Now you have spent enough time on the planning and those off-the-wall brainstorming sessions. It is time to get to work. You can do one of two things: prototype your concept on a shoestring, or you can go directly to your seed corn investors with your business plan. Either way, once the money is in the bank, the real work begins. You will have to locate the resources that you will need to complete your app. This could be systems, software, people, or partnerships, and obtaining these resources may include travel and promotion. You should take the time to practise presenting the story that you have just drafted so that you are fully prepared. Remember that rejection is simply a part of the game.

You must clearly understand why and how your application will become a killer app. Of course, you can still be profitable if your application is not a killer app, but it probably means that someone else is becoming the standard, and they will eventually wipe you out. There is no sense in picking a head-on fight with the leading app unless you have a reasonable expectation that you will eventually come out on top. Part of this is that you must understand what makes your application different from your competition's application.

You must also understand how your application will earn revenue and establish your goals so that eventually your organisation will be profitable. This is a growing concern because some of the high-tech stocks are under careful scrutiny for expected profitability. Their revenue is not in question, but their profitability is. Therefore, you should anticipate some hard questions from your investors about when your company will become profitable. You must not just understand how the company will be profitable and set your budgets accordingly; you must also set financial performance goals so that you know how you are doing. These goals will also indicate whether you can afford all the resources you require, or whether you will need more funding. A schedule for the proposed receipt of funding tranches will also be necessary.

Partnering

You must first identify a target list of partners who are essential to the operation of your business. These partners must be located, identified, contacted, and then visited. Agreements must be negotiated and signed, and the technical requirements for linking the two organisations must be completed. You should be expecting from your partners the same level of enthusiasm for your application that you have. If they reject your idea wholesale, you may have to re-evaluate the potential of your application.

Rejection

Investors and partners have rejected almost all successful online organisations at one time. Some of these companies have gone on to become some of the largest technology companies in the world. Just imagine what would have happened if you had jumped on board financially with Microsoft or Amazon very early in their corporate lives. They received rejections along the way just like everyone else, but their perseverance is what eventually won the day. Just remember that someone rejected Bill's little DOS idea as having no value. Ouch.

The next step is to identify the secondary partners. These partners are not critical to your business, but they are just as important because they will supply you with traffic, content, mutual promotion or advertising, etc. They should also be identified, located, and visited if their contribution is significant enough to warrant the cost. Don't forget that they may also provide industry buzz depending on who they are.

Finally, you may want to establish share and share option agreements for the general partners with whom you exchange a mutual benefit, such as linking sites. Depending on the size of the site, it may justify travelling to visit these partners or inviting them to visit you.

Building A Community

Now that you have started building the application, you have to start building your community of value. The first step in this process is to define your base target customers. Then you will start defining any sub-classifications of this group, such as a niche. The result will be an identifiable group, although it may not be identified by pure demographics, but may instead be defined by attitudes. Be aware that these groups may change as you develop your application.

The next step is to define the image that you will portray to the world and in particular to your customers. This is a bit of a chicken and egg argument since some will argue that you can't define an image without knowing the market. Others will argue that you can't define a psychographic niche without knowing the overall image. In general, just pick the market, define the niche, and choose the image; then reiterate the process until you find the right mix. You can always choose the image first and try to define the market later.

Identify what repetitive value you will provide to your customers and how you will keep the value repeating. This may mean that you will require an editor who will update the content on your site, or it may mean that you will link with a site that provides updated information on a regular basis, such as a news service. You may also require development staff to change your application, or an onsite e-commerce specialist to keep your product offering changing constantly.

You will have to decide what type of advertising you will need to reach your customers. This will include the type of medium that will be used to deliver the image as well as the media mix that will be used. You must choose the targeting for the ads by carefully selecting sites and develop a schedule for distribution to ensure the correct timing of the delivery. How much of the task you will outsource is also a consideration at this point.

At the same time, you will have to decide what type of promotions you will require. This will include the delivery method of the promotion, whether it is face-to-face meetings, a road show, news event, or bulletin. You will need to identify media contacts and choose the best method for delivering your message to them. Scheduling and outsourcing are two critical pieces of the promotion strategy that will have to be decided at this point.

Finally, you will need to choose the marketing model that is most appropriate for your company and your customers, as noted in Chapter 16. The most important step in the marketing process is execution, and you will have to start that process as soon as possible.

How Virtual Is Your Company?

Another step is to start defining the structure of your organisation in more detail. Identify which functions you will partner out and which you will keep in the company. For those that are partnered out, identify the companies that will perform the function and ensure that adequate agreements are in place if the function is deemed critical to your business. For functions that are staying in-house, map the tasks that are to be performed, identify systems that are to automate the task, and try to define staffing requirements. Implement and test the structure of the organisation prior to opening.

For those tasks that are to be outsourced, carefully choose the organisation that you will work with and test its references. Define how the two organisations will connect technology and identify such factors as pricing, security, disaster recovery, etc. Ensure that there is adequate testing and negotiated agreements prior to the commencement of online business.

You will have to define those employee functions that will be outsourced, those that will be made virtual, and those that will be essential and left onsite. You will also have to define the company's policy regarding offsite employees. Choosing the location of the company and building the environment to handle the mix of employees will also be necessary, whether it's a traditional environment or a virtual-style environment. You should clearly map out any existing back-office process and any existing systems. Then you should identify how the back office will change according to the corporate and technological strategy maps. The systems will have to be purchased and implemented, and the new policies and procedures will have to be defined. Don't forget, employees will have to be trained on the new systems.

Funding

Funding will be the single most essential piece of your start-up costs. You will have to map out a quick strategy as to how you are going to gather capital. This should include a list of individuals who are likely to support the project in the seed stages without requiring control of the organisation. It should also establish some form of tracking and keeping in contact with these investors. Regulatory requirements should be noted, and legal agreements should be drawn up to ensure all parties are protected.

You should be using your pro forma statements as an indicator of how much funding will be required and on what dates. You will have to map a strategy to start creating investment buzz by visiting investors and their representatives to present the story of your company. The good news is that you will have already completed most of a prospectus that can be used as a brochure. You will need assistance in this funding process, and that will require you to contact the start-up funding specialists at the brokerages. This will mean scheduling and travel. Once again, you will use the goals of the corporate plan to indicate how much funding will be required and by what date.

Finally, you will have to start the process of preparing for the IPO. Review the business plan, fill in any of the missing gaps, and verify that the information is still accurate. Identify those individuals in the brokerages and banks who can assist in taking you through the IPO and allow them to do their work. While this is going on, you can continue work on developing the application and growing the organisation.

Road Shows – Presentations

You will have already performed some road shows during the start-up phase, but now they will change. The first question you will have to answer is, do you have the resources to carry out public relations effectively? A good PR firm with a track record for your type of organisation can easily get you through the doors of the media firms that will spread the word about your organisation. Usually, these funds are well spent, since your initial media public relations can make or break your firm. Choosing the correct PR partner is essential.

You should start creating buzz in the market through the use of road shows with your industry and your partners. These do not necessarily have to be planned by your PR firm. Instead, they can be managed very early in the process by identifying which industry partners are most likely to be receptive to your application or product and visiting them to obtain their sign-on. Some very small organisations have had a great deal of success thanks to relationships established with larger partners.

Choosing the investor for your road show is usually best left to the start-up pros in the banks, brokerages, investment firms, venture capital funds, etc. Although a PR firm can provide some assistance in fine-tuning your presentation, the best resource to present the company is you. They can, however, provide support in the investor relations area by assisting in managing the entire investor relations programme if needed.

Where your PR firm will have its greatest impact is in your dealings with the media. They will choose the media best suited for your company, establish contacts, set up interviews, create and manage press releases, choose the type of media, schedule the presentations, create newsworthy events, and execute those events. They will manage the verbal presentation of your image, and can usually go one step further by designing your entire corporate image.

Managing Growth And Change

Finally, your little concept has started to grow into an e-commerce success story, and the next task is certainly not covered in this book. It's the process of managing the growth and change of your company. All we can say is hang on because the ride is very fast and very bumpy.

Enjoy your e-commerce success!

The Least You Need To Know

➤ How to implement the definitive e-commerce model for your company.

Glossary

24 × 7 A reference to something that is open 24 hours a day, 7 days a week.

Affiliate An organisation or individual with whom you have established a formal or informal agreement to either sell or receive products, services, content, traffic, etc.

Animated Gif A graphical interchange format (image) that appears to move or change as a result of multiple layered images.

Applet A small piece of Java code that can perform functions such as moving images or providing a lookup list. This software is sent to and works inside browsers.

Backbone The term used to describe all the wiring and routers that make up the Internet.

Back office All of the functions in a company that occur behind the scenes away from the public such as accounting, service work, warehousing, and management.

Bandwidth The capacity of an electronic transmission medium, such as a cable, to carry electronic signals.

Banner ad The long thin ads usually located at the top and bottom of web pages.

Browser A software package that displays HTML (hyper text markup language) documents primarily from the Internet.

Buzz A term used to describe conversations and general discussions about a particular company or technology.

Certificates Electronic security forms or documents that verify the authenticity of a website.

Chat room An online place for people to post and read electronic messages.

Click-through The term that describes when a visitor to a website uses a link to access another website.

Client An application used to access the Internet, which is resident on a user's machine. For example, a browser is a web client.

Community of value A concept where the visitors to a website believe they belong to a community of people who share the same interests and that membership in the online community has a value to these visitors.

Content Anything contained on a website, such as files, software, information, graphics, etc.

Convergence The movement of various types of software towards common standards.

Critical mass The gathering of enough users of an application to make the application viable and necessary.

Cross-niching Finding commonality between two or more sub-divisions of the customers in a market after they have been divided into niches.

Cybersquatting The act of trying to divert customers from a website by using a similar name and identical look to that of another site or the act of obtaining and holding domain names for resale.

Data mining Locating, reviewing, and analysing stored operational information to assist in decision making.

Data warehouse A large electronic storage area that is structured so that the data stored in divergent formats is converted to consistent output, such as the same type of database.

Distributed computing The technical architecture where the network clients, as opposed to central processing and storage areas, perform some or all application processing or information storage.

Domain name A plain-language name for a website. This is translated into an Internet protocol number that is used to locate and access the site on the Internet.

e-Bank An online bank that provides regular banking services over the Internet.

e-Commerce Business conducted exclusively through an electronic format.

EDI (electronic data interchange) The transmission of electronic data in a specific EDI format or series of EDI standards.

EFT (electronic funds transfer) An electronic transfer of information that equates to moving funds from one financial institution to another.

Electronic cheque A type of electronic funds transfer that can be given to an online company for deposit at an online financial institution.

Encryption The scrambling of digital messages in such a way that only the sender and receiver can read the message.

ERP (enterprise resource planning) A model for building software in which all the operation processes that impact resource management use integrated software.

e-Zine An online magazine.

FAQ (frequently asked questions) A listing of questions that have already been asked along with the answers to those questions.

Firewall A piece of software that regulates who can access a network from outside the network via a modem or router.

FTP (file transfer protocol) A standard used to transfer large files or large amounts of data over the Internet.

GIF (graphical interchange format) A file format for electronic images and pictures used on web pages.

GPS (global positioning system) A series of low-level satellites that transmit a signal used by devices on the ground to indicate the longitude and latitude of the device.

Hit A visit to a website by a web surfer.

HTML (hyper text markup language) A standard markup language created by a worldwide consortium and used to format web documents.

Integrated systems The concept of having software that communicates and operates as one seamless unit.

Internetwork A connection of networks usually connected through routers.

IP (Internet protocol) address The numeric address used to locate physical or virtual computers or sites on the Internet.

IPO (initial public offering) The first public offering of a stock.

IRQ (interrupt request) Hardware channels over which devices can send interrupt signals to the microprocessor. When you add a new device to a PC, you sometimes need to set its IRQ number by setting a DIP switch. This specifies which interrupt line the device may use.

ISP (Internet service provider) A company that has a connection to the Internet and charges the public a fee to use part of that connection.

Java An object-oriented programming language created and distributed for free by Sun Microsystems.

Keys Alphanumeric codes that are used in encryption to ensure that other computers on the network cannot read encrypted information without the keys.

LAN (local area network) A network that is confined to a specific, single physical area (i.e. not connected directly to any other network via a router).

Link Also known as a hyperlink, a link is an address embedded in a web document. The browser transfers to that address when the link is clicked.

Linux A free, UNIX-like operating system created by Linus Torvalds.

Logistics Shipping and distribution functions in an organisation. Sometimes used to define a role that manages all the company's resources.

Metcalf's Law Utility = (number of users)^2 where 2 denotes the square.

Micropayment A very small payment that is accumulated and paid once a specified threshold is attained. Usually used for traffic or click-throughs.

Moore's Law In the 1960s, Gordon Moore, Intel's founder, predicted that every 18 months, chip processing power (as established by chip transistor density) would double while the costs would stay the same.

MP3 A digital file standard for recording sound. The files can be sent and played on the Internet.

Network A series of computers connected in some way to allow for the sending of electronic information.

Neural network The storage and retrieval of data by systems that have the capability of making changes to their methodologies through the use of statistical and mathematical algorithms.

Niche A small sub-division of a large market demographic.

Outsourcing The contracting of work to another company.

Packet A small piece of data that has addresses appended to it to allow it to be sent from one computer to another.

PC Abbreviation for a personal computer.

Plug-in A piece of software that is 'plugged in' to a browser for running special objects or content over the Internet.

Point of presence (POP) An Internet service provider's point of connection to the Internet in a specific city or community.

Pop-up windows Windows, other than the main browser window, that open when you open a website.

Private placement Raising money through invitation to a select few individuals or organisations.

Prospectus An information document provided to investors that identifies information about the company. Usually provided to raise money through the sale of stock.

Protocol A standardised way to transfer data so that computers on a network can communicate with one another.

Psychographic A way in which members of a population are differentiated by action, moods, identity, etc.

Public key infrastructure The provision of public electronic security keys for use by companies and individuals who want to send encrypted messages.

Push technology The delivery of content to users periodically as opposed to when the user requests it. Primarily used to deliver time-sensitive information such as stock market quotes, news, or sports scores.

Real-time systems Information systems that instantaneously process a transaction and all associated information about the transaction.

Relational database A structured table of data, where data in records are keyed or related to data records in another table or tables.

Rich media Online advertising that has some form of functionality that allows the user to obtain objects, such as video or sound, or interact with the ad by providing information, choosing information, etc.

Road show A series of presentations used to gather interest in a company or an application.

Router An Internetworking device that determines the route a data packet will travel between nodes on the Internet.

SAN (storage area network) The storage of data in various storage servers on the same network.

Search engine A website that allows a visitor to enter a search phrase and get the engine to search all the shared files on a network.

Second-level financing Private funding for an organisation that bridges the gap between the seed capital and the IPO.

Seed capital The initial funding of the organisation.

Server A computer that acts as a central control point for a network to manage applications.

Spam Unsolicited email usually sent to try to sell or market a product or service.

Spoofing Deceptive identification of an address or point of origin on the Internet.

SSL (secure sockets layer) A security measure in which encryption is used to make a secure connection between a web server and a client so that others cannot see the transfer of information.

Streaming The sending of a repeated stream of packets from a server to another computer connected to the same network or intranet. Usually used for sound or video broadcasts.

Supply chain The entire process of accepting a customer order through to the delivery of the product to the customer inclusive of supply procurement and production of the product.

Surfing Using a browser to visit sites on the Internet

Technology template A series of standards that the corporation has decided will be the long-term technological environment of the organisation.

Telecommuting Working away from an office and using a PC to communicate with the organisation.

Thin client A client computer on a network that has limited peripheral devices and storage.

Traffic Visits to a website.

Uniform resource locator (URL) The full address of an Internet service, including the protocol and domain.

Virtual employees Employees who work offsite or away from their organisation.

WAN (wide area network) A network over a wide physical area and usually connected through high-speed phone lines or wireless devices.

WAP (wireless application protocol) A standard markup language created by a worldwide consortium and used to format documents intended for the new generation of mobile phones.

Webcast The streaming of electronic data between a server and a client computer.

Web page A series of HTML or XML files that can be viewed by using a browser.

WML (wireless (application) markup language) A standard markup language for WAP-enabled phones.

XML (extensible markup language) The next generation of standard Internet presentation language created by a worldwide consortium.

Index

D

E